CHANNEL ISLANDS
AT WAR
A German Perspective

CHANNEL ISLANDS
AT WAR

A German Perspective

GEORGE FORTY

Ian Allan
PUBLISHING

Page 1: '*Wir denn fahren gegen England!*' The high morale of exuberant young veterans such as these photographed whilst marching through conquered France, confident in their leaders, their equipment and their fighting prowess, appeared irresistible. *Author's collection*

Previous page: After the initial air trooping, most reinforcements came by sea, like this shipload of coastal artillerymen arriving at St Helier. *Société Jersiaise*

This page: A column of German Troops marching past St Peter Port Parish Church, Guernsey. *IWM — HU25958*

Opposite page: One of the finest dual-purpose machine guns in the world was the MG34, seen here on its tripod mounting as a heavy machine gun, but it could also be used on a bipod as an LMG. The tripod could also be adjusted for use in the AA role. *IWM — HU 29007*

Map of Jersey: The map which appears on pages 44-5 is entitled 'The German Occupation of Jersey, 1940-45' and appears courtesy of Mr Howard B. Baker. Anyone wanting information on how to obtain a copy of the map should contact Mr Baker at 'Lindisfarne', St John's Road, St Helier, Jersey. Tel: 01534 34495.

First published 1999

ISBN 0 7110 2678 5

© George Forty 1999

Published by Ian Allan Publishing

an imprint of Ian Allan Publishing Ltd,
Terminal House, Shepperton, Surrey TW17 8AS.
Printed by Ian Allan Printing Ltd,
Riverdene Business Park, Hersham, Surrey KT12 4RG.

Code: 9911/B2

Contents

Preface 6

Acknowledgements 7

Chronology of Major Events 8

Glossary 10

Festung Jersey und Festung Guernsey 13

Introduction 17

1 Arrival 27

2 Military Organisation: Higher Organisations 38

3 Military Organisation: The Years of Occupation 42

4 The Soldier 63

5 The Sailor 92

6 The Airman 109

7 German Civil Organisations 123

8 Daily Life on the Islands .136

9 Fortifications 157

10 British Operations against the Islands 182

11 Surrender 198

Postscript: What is left to see? 211

Appendices 243

Notes to the text 245

Bibliography 249

Index 250

Preface

There have been many books written about the German occupation of the Channel Islands. Some, such as Charles Cruickshank's *The German Occupation of the Channel Islands* and Peter King's *The Channel Islands War 1940-1945*, have been definitive histories; others have been written by sensation-seekers who have tried to ferret out all that went wrong during the Occupation, to quote from lurid tales of collaboration or of thousands of bodies buried in the foundations of the fortresses, despite the lack of hard evidence. This does no one any good; neither the poor, unfortunate slave workers who were beaten to death by the SS in their Sylt Camp on Alderney, nor the run-of-the-mill German serviceman, who did his job to the best of his ability, and also did his best to get on with the local, mainly hostile, population. What all these books have in common is that they deal with the Islanders' experiences and have been written from their point of view. Few have chosen to tell the story from the other side of the fence, to explain what it was like to be a German sailor, soldier or airman, serving in the Channel Islands.

Ian Allan's 'At War' series seeks to tell the story of a particular unit or formation using eyewitness reporting, backed up with photographs — many taken by the men themselves — which help to evoke the environment and conditions in which they found themselves. So, for example, in addition to a soldier telling about his experiences manning a coastal artillery position, there are photographs of his gun position, weaponry, living conditions and off-duty experiences. I have written books in this series about American, British and German formations such as Winston Churchill's 'Dear Desert Rats', Erwin Rommel's Afrika Korps and George Patton's US Third Army, invariably using this formula to tell their story and, I hope, bring their experiences to life in a way that more detailed, factual histories cannot.

In *Channel Islands at War*, I have tried to do the same for the German serviceman in the Channel Islands. After an historical introduction to explain how and why the Channel Islands found themselves being invaded, I have dealt with the 'model occupation', how it came about, and how the German forces were organised within the Islands. Then there are chapters on the three services — land, sea and air — followed by the quasi-military organisations such as the Organization Todt and the infamous SS. Subjects such as the building of fortifications and tunnels, combat operations undertaken by the British commandos against the Islands, the final surrender and, of course, the delicate subject of off-duty activities and living with the locals, are all explored. The text is backed up by a mass of photographs, many from private collections and many which have not been published before. Finally, to bring things up to date, there is a section that covers what remains to be seen today both for the casual visitor and for the dedicated World War 2 historian.

I hope this provides something for everyone and that my book will help people to understand a little better this vitally important part of life in what were five of the most momentous years of the 20th century.

It has given me considerable personal pleasure to be asked to write this book, because in doing so I have met and corresponded with a large number of extremely interesting and helpful people, especially during my all too brief visit to Guernsey in December 1998. Sadly, illness prevented me from making a similar visit to Jersey. I can also announce, with a great deal of family pride, that there are Fortys alive and well and living on Guernsey, and, as the name is a fairly uncommon one, we must be related! Throughout the German occupation, Lt-Col (Retd) C. Heber Forty lived at Cambridge Park, Guernsey and, as far as I can tell, made a thorough nuisance of himself to the German authorities. Initially they wanted to turn his house into a barracks, but he managed to persuade the contractors to report against the project and was allowed to keep his home. He next avoided being deported by 'obtaining' some sheets of a doctor's writing paper and, having some knowledge of medicine, concocted a medical certificate and forged the doctor's signature. In company with many others he was then examined by three doctors, who, on reading the certificate, came to the conclusion that he was unfit to travel!

He had seen service in Siam and HM King Rama had presented him with a smooth bore sporting gun, which he had to hand in with his other weapons (a rifle, two revolvers, an air pistol and two other sporting guns!). He wrote to the German commandant, asking for his presentation weapon back — the German commandant agreed, making Col Heber the only armed Englishman on the island! In addition, he was a crack shot with a catapult which provided him with plenty of birds for the pot! Later he wrote of the Occupation:

'Five years of hell for the Guernsey people who were reduced to walking scarecrows — nearly starved to death. My days were spent in foraging for food — the produce of my garden helped a lot. I had my bicycle which enabled me to get a special permit to go on the beaches which were mined, but in spite of that I managed to get some shellfish. I also ate snails, boiled with cabbage, got blood from the slaughterhouse and baked in the oven big pies of blood, vegetables and flour if available, or any kind of bean of which I grew many. In this way I managed to keep alive, though I lost weight, but kept active throughout . . . The hungry German soldiers broke into many homes in search of food. I barricaded my house and garden with barbed wire and slept in my lower room with my loaded gun by my side.'

What a pity I never met him.

Acknowledgements

As always I have a large number of organisations and individuals to thank for their kind assistance with the preparation of this book:

Organisations

The Channel Islands Occupation Society (Guernsey) and the Channel Islands Occupation Society (Jersey), both of whom have provided invaluable assistance in all aspects of the preparation of this book, including allowing me to quote from a number of their *Reviews* and use some of their photographs. In all cases I have also endeavoured to obtain permission from the writer of the article (mainly German ex-servicemen), but of course some of them are now deceased. The Guernsey Museum Service (Mr Brian Owen) and Fortress Guernsey (Maj Evan Ozanne) whose help with the provision of photographs and information has been exceptional. Tomahawk Films (Mr Brian Matthews) whose individual kindness during my all too brief visit to Guernsey was especially appreciated. The Jersey Museum Service (Mr Christopher Journeaux), Jersey Tourism (Ms Kate Lewis), Direct Input and the German Underground Hospital (Mr Peter Tabb) who have all provided up-to-date information on tourist attractions, etc. The Société Jersiaise Photographic Archive, Jersey (Miss Julia Coutanche) by whose courtesy all those photographs marked Société Jersiaise appear. The Alderney Society (Mrs C. Grabham, Administrator) for her help especially with provision of photographs via Mrs Pantcheff. The Imperial War Museum, Department of Photographs (Mr Ian Carter) from whose collection come many of the photographs in this book. The Imperial War Museum, Sound Archive (Ms Margaret Brooks and Mrs Rosemary Tudge) who have allowed me to quote from some of their amazing collection of oral history recordings. The MOD Whitehall Library, the RAF Museum, *Air-Britain Digest* (Mr R. W. Simpson), the Tank Museum (Mr David Fletcher), La Valette Museum (Mr Paul Balshaw and Mr Peter Balshaw), St Peter's Bunker Museum, the CI Military Museum (Mr Damien Horn) and last but by no means least of the museums in the Islands, the German Occupation Museum (Mr Richard Heaume).

In Germany, as well as many named individuals I must thank the *Traditionsverband der ehem. NDS. Inf Div 216/272* (Herr Hans-Gerhard Sandmann) and the *Traditionsverband der 83. Inf Div* (Herr Karl Pfeifer) for their invaluable assistance.

I must also include my sincere thanks to Maj Phil Ventham, who, like me, lives in Bryantspuddle and some ten years ago ran a very successful exhibition at nearby Anderson Manor on the Small Scale Raiding Force which was stationed there. Thanks to him I have been able to read many of the wartime Combined Operations reports and also to include some of the photographs which appeared in his exhibition.

As far as publishers are concerned I must thank all the publishers from whose work I have quoted, in particular Phillimore & Co Ltd for allowing me to quote from *Alderney, Fortress Island* and from *The Von Aufsess Occupation Diary*, and use the sketch-map of the Sylt Concentration Camp that appears in Maj Pantcheff's book; *The Guernsey Evening Press* (Mr Nick Machon) and *Jersey Evening Post* (Mr Chris Bright) for not only allowing me to use extracts from their newspapers but also for publishing my appeal for material; and the Brelade's Bay Hotel (Mr Robert Colley) for allowing me to copy pages of its fascinating guest book from when the hotel was a German *Soldatenheim*.

Finally, I must thank Fortress Guernsey for allowing me to use its map of wartime Guernsey, Colin Partridge for his map of wartime Alderney and Mr Howard Butlin Baker for his remarkably detailed map of wartime Jersey.

Individuals

My sincere thanks go to:
Mr Chris Ashworth, Herr Karl Baser, Mr Lawrence Brooksby, Mrs M. Cruickshank, Mr Alec Forty, Herr Josef Gerhaher, Mr Gilbert van Grieken, Herr Erwin Grubba, Herr Dieter Hankel, Herr Dr Hardy Hoogh, Herr Theo Krausen, Mr Hans Lucke, Mr Owen Maindonald, Lt-Col C. R. Messenger, Ms June Money, Mrs Patricia Pantcheff, Mr Michael Payne, Mr Martin Pocock, Mr Winston G. Ramsey, Mr T. W. Rang, BEM, Mr Pierre Renier, Mr Bruce Robertson, Herr Hans Schiffers, Oberstlt Dr Ernst Schmidt, Mr Jak P. Mallmann Showell, Herr Werner Wagenknecht and Capt John Wallbridge.

All these organisations and individuals have helped me in one way or another with text and photographs, as will be seen within the book. I apologise to anyone whose name I have missed, but it was not intentional.

Finally, and most importantly, I must thank Mr Michael Ginns MBE, who has generously given me very considerable assistance with the book over the past year. He has allowed me to quote from some of his excellent articles which have appeared in *CIOS Reviews* from time to time, and also to use some of his own picture collection. In addition, he has been my 'guide, philosopher and friend', ensuring that I haven't made too many bloomers in the book. It is an extremely complicated subject and one on which he is an acknowledged expert, so his help has been invaluable.

I hope that all who have helped me will consider the finished result worthwhile and that it will help to promote better understanding between the erstwhile combatants of World War 2.

George Forty
Bryantspuddle, Dorset
February 1999

Chronology of Major Events

Included here for the sake of brevity are primarily military events and not many important civilian ones — such as the introduction of laws, detailed food rationing, escapes, deaths, imprisonments, deportations, etc. These can be found — well covered and in full detail — in the books of Charles Cruickshank and Peter King (see Bibliography).

1940

15 June	Decision made to demilitarise the Channel Islands.
16–20 June	Military evacuation.
17–19 June	Small boats from Jersey help with British evacuation from St Malo.
21–23 June	Some civilian evacuation takes place (third of population go).
23 June	Alderney depopulated; all but 20 leave (1,442 go).
28 June	German air raids on St Peter Port and St Helier kill 44 civilians.
30 June	German high-level conference in Paris decides to invade — Operation 'Grüne Pfeil' ('Green Arrow'), but Luftwaffe landing on Guernsey forestalls need for any aggressive military operation and instead a small German force arrives peacefully at Guernsey by air.
1 July	Jersey also occupied by a token German force.
2 July	Alderney occupied by a token German force.
3 July	Sark occupied by a token German force.
9–28 July	Operation 'Ambassador' — commando raid on Guernsey — it is a failure.
9 August	FK515 established in Jersey under Oberst Schumacher.
16 August	Civilian purchasing mission (for foodstuffs mainly) established with French at Granville.
27 September	Arrival of the first Channel Islands military commander — Oberst Graf Rudolf von Schmettow. First anti-Jewish laws passed.

1941

24 March	Bread rationing starts.
30 March	Arrival of 319. ID.
15 June	Hitler orders the fortification of the Channel Islands.
8 July	Maj Carl Hoffman becomes commander of Alderney.

August	Milk rationing starts.
18 October	Maj Friedrich Knackfuss replaces Schumacher in charge of FK515.
20 October	Hitler's Fortification Directive published.
	GenMaj Erich Müller becomes military commander.
November	Visit by Dr Fritz Todt, head of OT, followed by the arrival of some 16,000 OT workers.
December	Fuel rationing starts.

1942

January	RAF raids on St Peter Port.
	Baron von Aufsess becomes Chief of Administration in Jersey vice Dr Casper.
	Four workers' camps built on Alderney.
February	First of three German brothels opens.
	Oberstlt Zuske appointed Commandant of Alderney.
6 April	Start of teaching German in primary schools.
May	Guernsey Underground News service begins with a circulation of about 300.
26 June	All civilian wireless sets have to be surrendered.
7 July	New rail line extensions to quarries opened on Jersey Railway.
15 July	GenOb Dollmann, CG Seventh Army, visits Jersey.
8 August	Casquets Lighthouse raided and seven Germans captured.
15 September	Deportation orders issued in retaliation for handover of Germans in Persia.
16–29 September	Over 2,000 Islanders who were born in UK and not on the Islands are deported.
October	Non-fraternisation order issued to all German troops.
3–4 October	Commando raid (Operation 'Basalt') on Sark.
November	Lancaster bomber crashes on Sark.

1943

January	Coaster *Xaver Dorch* runs aground at Braye and *Shockland* sunk off Jersey.
12 February	Second deportation order — 201 more deported.
March	Sylt becomes a concentration camp on Alderney, with List as its commandant.
	Conscription of labour begins.
2 August	Ban on fishing promulgated.
September	Von Schmettow resumes command on departure of Müller (he also assumes command of 319. ID).
	Oberstlt Siegfried Heine becomes island Commander Jersey.
	Convoy battle off west of Islands. HMS *Charybdis* and HMS *Limbourne* sunk, with over 500 killed/drowned.
November	Oberstlt Schwalm becomes island commander Alderney.
17 November	*Charybdis* Day, 41 British naval dead buried in public ceremony.
27–28 December	Commando raid on Jersey fails.

1944

3 March	The Channel Islands are given 'Fortress' status.
	Knackfuss replaced at FK515 by Heider.
1 April	Von Schmettow promoted Generalleutnant.
19 May	FK515 becomes PKI with reduced status.
May–August	Increased air activity because of D-Day operations, Islands' fortifications attacked, port facilities bombed and also shipping (approx 25 ships sunk/damaged). All this action begins to isolate the Islands from their French supply ports.
17 June	Hitler declares that the Islands, plus various French ports, will be defended to the last man.
June onwards	Capture by the Allies of French ports such as Cherbourg (27 June), Granville (30 July) and St Malo (17 August) further isolates the Islands.
7 July	Sinking of the *Minotaure* by the British, with the loss of 250 lives (including forced labourers).
27 July	Lancaster bomber shot down off Alderney, German harbour commander refuses to allow a rescue ship to go out.
July onwards	Arrival of German casualties for treatment in the underground hospitals on Jersey and Guernsey.

8 August	HMS *Rodney* shells gun positions on Alderney killing two German crew of *Blücher* battery.
25 August	First civilian casualties from members of the German garrison trying to steal food.
September	Hüffmeier replaces von Helldorf as von Schmettow's chief of staff this month.
1 September	Death penalty imposed for violation of food regulations.
9 September	No more gas supplies available on Jersey.
18 September	OKW directive signed to stop all rations to civilian population of the Islands, if and when necessary.
19 September	Germany tells the Swiss (Red Cross) that the civilian rations are exhausted.
22 September	Attempts made to get GenLt von Schmettow to surrender.
5 November	Germans agree to allow the Islands to ask the Red Cross for relief.
7 November	London agrees to Red Cross relief being sent in, provided Germans will maintain basic rations.
23 November	Germans agree to maintain basic rations.
27–30 December	First visit of Red Cross ship *Vega* bringing 750 tons of food and medical supplies.

1945

28 January	Adm Hüffmeier replaces von Schmettow. Kapts zur See Kleve and Reich put in charge of Jersey and Guernsey.
	GenMaj Wulf becomes commander of 319. ID.
7–11 February	Second visit of *Vega*.
6–9 March	Third visit of *Vega*.
7 March	Explosion at Palace Hotel, Bagatele, kills nine Germans.
8–9 March	German raid on Granville from Channel Islands
18 March	Attempt to kill Wulf fails.
25 March	Hüffmeier makes 'never surrender' speech.
3–7 May	Fourth visit of *Vega*.
8 May	Operation 'Nestegg' convoy arrives off Islands.
9 May	German surrender, 27,000 captured. Jersey, Guernsey and Sark liberated. British military government established under Brig Snow.
13 May	German POWs start to leave.
16 May	Alderney liberated.
7 June	Visit of King George VI and Queen Elizabeth.
August	Deportees return.
25 August	Islands' governments restored, new Lieutenant-Governors arrive.

Glossary

General Notes:

1. To keep italics to a minimum, following this section where most of the German words used in the book will be explained, ranks, frequently used German words (Luftwaffe, Bataillon, unit designations, etc) will not be italicised.

2. For convenience, in this book the Occupation (capital O) is used as shorthand for the German Occupation and the Island(er)s (capital I) is used to mean the Channel Islands (and their inhabitants) as a whole.

ABBREVIATIONS

AA	Anti-aircraft
BdbK	*Befehlshaber der britische Kanalinseln* (Commander of the Channel Islands)
Bn	Battalion
Btl	*Bataillon* (Battalion). German *Bataillonen* were shown with Roman numerals thus: II./IR 396 (2nd Battalion *Infanterie Regiment* 396)
CG	Commanding general
C-in-C	Commander-in-Chief
CGS (CIGS)	Chief of the General Staff (Chief of the Imperial General Staff = British)
CIOS	Channel Islands Occupation Society
CO	Commanding officer
Coy	Company (GER: 1. *Kompanie*. 1./IR 396 = No 1 Company Inf Regt 396)
FK	*Feldkommandant* = Field Commander
FK515	*Feldkommandantur 515*. This was the German Channel Islands' administrative unit.
GOC-in-C	General officer commander-in-chief
'Gotenhafen'	*Kriegsmarine* Assault Detachment 'Gotenhafen'
GUNS	Guernsey Underground News Service
HNorMS	His Norwegian Majesty's Ship; ie a ship of the Royal Norwegian Navy
Hptm	*Hauptmann* (Captain)
HSF	*Hafenschutzflotillen* — Harbour Defence Flotillas
219 ID	*Infanterie Division* (Infantry Division). In German 219th is rendered 219. (full stop), so 219.ID is the 219th *Infanterie Division*
IR 396	*Infanterie Regiment* (Infantry Regiment). In German the regimental number comes afterwards, so IR 396 is *Infanterie Regiment* 396

JG	*Jagdgeschwader* (Fighter Group)
LCA	Landing Craft Assault
LCI(L)	Landing Craft Infantry (Logistic)
LCM	Landing Craft Mechanised
LS	Landing Ship
LST	Landing Ship Tank
MGB	Motor gunboat
MG Btl	*Maschinengewehr Bataillon* (Machine Gun Battalion)
M/S	Minesweeping
MTB	Motor torpedo boat
OB	*Oberbefelshaber* (Senior command)
Oberstlt	*Oberstleutnant* (lieutenant-colonel)
OC	Officer commanding
OT	*Organization Todt*
PzJgAbt	*Panzerjägerabteilung* (Anti-Tank Battalion)
RAF	Royal Air Force
RAMC	Royal Army Medical Corps
RASC	Royal Army Service Corps
RCAF	Royal Canadian Air Force
RE	Royal Engineers
Regt	Regiment
RAD	*Reichsarbeitsdienst* (State Labour Service)
QMG	Quartermaster general
SHAEF	Supreme Headquarters Allied Expeditionary Force
SOE	Special Operations Executive
SSRF	Small Scale Raiding Force
Wkr	*Wehrkreis*
ZG	*Zerstörergeschwader* (Fighter-bomber Wing)

GLOSSARY

Air Corps	*Fliegerkorps*
Air Division	*Fliegerdivision*
Air Fleet	*Luftflotte*
Air Force	*Luftwaffe* (L)
Air Force (High Command)	*Oberkommando der Luftwaffe* (OKL)
Ammunition store	*Munitionsraum* (Muni-R)
Ammunition dump	*Munitionslager*
Anti-aircraft position	*Flakstand*
Anti-tank position	*Pakstand*
Armed Forces (High Command)	*Oberkommando der Wehrmacht* (OKW)
Armoured gunshield	*Panzerplatte*
Armoured observation turret	*Panzerbeobachtungsturm*
Army	*Heer* (H)
Army [formation]	*Armee* (A)
Army Group	*Armeegruppe* (AGr)
Army (high command)	*Oberkommando des Heeres* (OKH)
Artillery	*Artillerie* (Artl)
Artillery (naval command)	*Marineartillerie* (MA)
Artillery commander	*Artilleriekommandeur* (ARKO)
Artillery carrier	*Artillerieträger*
Battalion (Bn)	*Bataillon* (Btl) or *Abteilung* (Abt) although the latter could also mean a unit, a section, a detachment or a department
Battery	*Batterie* (Batt)
Battery (naval)	*Marinebatterie* (MB)
Battery command post	*Batterie-Offizierstand*
Battle position	*Kampfstand*
Bomb-proof	*Bombensicher*
Bunker	*Unterstand* (USt)
Camouflage	*Tarnun*
Channel Islands	*Kanalinseln* (KI)
Coastal	*Kusten*
Coastal Defence	*Kustenverteidigung* (KV)
Commander	*Befehlsshaber* (Bfh)
Command Post	*Befehlsstand*
Corps	*Armeekorps* (AK)
Crew room	*Mannschaftsraum*
Direction-finder (naval)	*Marine Peilstelle* (MP)
Division	*Division* (Div)
Emergency exit	*Notausgang*
Engineer	*Pionier* (Pi)
Equipment room	*Geräteraum*
Fire control	*Feuerleitung*
First aid post	*Verbandplatz*
Flanking fire	*Flankenfeuer*
Fortress	*Festung* (Fest)
Fuel dump	*Betriebsstofflager*
Group (of aircraft RAF Wing)	*Gruppe*
Gun	*Geschutz* (Gesch)
Gun (artillery)	*Kanone* (Kan)
Headquarters	*Stabsquartier* (St.Qu)
Heavy	*Schwere* (schw)
Hospital	*Lazarett*
Light	*Leichte* (leich)
Map room	*Planraum*
Machine gun position	*Blockhaus*
Medical bunker	*Sanitätsunterstand*
Medium	*Mittlere* (mittl)
Minesweeper	*Minenesuchboot* (MB)
Minesweeper (motorised)	*Minenraumboot* (R-boot)
Naval Defence Commander	*Kommandeur der Seeverteidigung* (SEEKO)
Naval Artillery Commander	*Marineartilleriekommandeur* (MARKO)
Navy	*Kriegsmarine* (K)
Navy (high command)	*Oberkommando der Kriegsmarine* (OKM)
Objective	*Zielpunkt* (ZP)
Observation slit	*Sehschlitze*
Officer of the watch	*Wachoffizier*
Operations room	*Betriebsraum*
Order of battle	*Kriegsgliederung*
Ordnance Department	*Waffenamt* (Wa)
Position	*Anlage* (Anl)
Rangefinder	*Entfernungsmesser* (EM)
Rations dump	*Verpflegungslage*
Rear	*Rückwärts* (ruckw)
Reconnaissance	*Aufklärung* (Aufkl)
Reservoir	*Wasserbehalter*
Searchlight	*Scheinwerfer* (Schwf)
Section (of aircraft)	*Kette* (called *Schwarm* in fighter units)
Sentry post	*Postenstand*
Speed boat	*Schnellboot* (S-boot)
Signals	*Nachrichten* (Nahk)
Signals post	*Nachrichtenstand* (N)
Soldiers' homes	*Soldatenheime*
Squadron (of aircraft)	*Staffel*
Staff	*Stab* (St)
Strengthened	*Verstärkt* (verst)
Strongpoint	*Stutzpunkt* (Stp)
Supply	*Verpflegung* (Vpl)
Tank	*Panzerkampfwagen* (PzKpfw) *Panzer* (Pz)
Telephone	*Fernsprecher* (Fsp)
Toilet	*Notabort*
Torpedo boat (motor)	*Torpedoboot* (T-Boot or E-Boot)
Trench	*Laufgraben*
War Diary	*Kriegstagebuch* (KTB)
Wireless	*Funken* (Fk or Funk)
Wireless room	*Funkraum*

COMPARISON OF RANKS

English	German
Army	*Heer*
Field Marshal	*Generalfeldmarschall*
General (Gen)	*Generaloberst (GenOb)*
General	*General der Infanterie/Artillerie/Panzertruppe*, etc
Lieutenant-General (Lt-Gen)	*Generalleutnant (GenLt)*
Major-General (Maj-Gen)	*Generalmajor (GenMaj)*
Brigadier (Brig)	no equivalent
Colonel (Col)	*Oberst (Ob)*
Lieutenant-Colonel (Lt-Col)	*Oberstleutnant (Oberstlt)*
Major (Maj)	*Major (Maj)*
Captain (Capt)	*Hauptmann (Hptm)*
Lieutenant (Lt)	*Oberleutnant (Oblt)*
2nd Lieutenant (2-Lt)	*Leutnant (Lt)*
Regimental Sergeant Major (RSM)	*Hauptfeldwebel*
Sergeant-Major	*Oberfeldwebel*
Company Sergeant-Major (CSM)	*Feldwebel (FW)*
Sergeant (Sgt)	*Unterfeldwebel*
Corporal (Cpl)	*Obergefreiter*
Lance Corporal (L Cpl)	*Gefreiter*
Private (Pte)	*Schutze* (or *Oberschutze* for a senior private)

Royal Navy	*Kriegsmarine*
Admiral of the Fleet	*Grossadmiral*
No equivalent	*Generaladmiral*
Admiral	*Admiral*
Vice-Admiral	*Vizeadmiral*
Rear-Admiral	*Konteradmiral*
Commodore (Cdre)	*Kommodore*
Captain (Capt)	*Kapitän zur See*
Captain (junior)	*Fregattenkapitän*
Commander (Cdr)	*Korvettenkapitän*

Lieutenant Commander (Lt-Cdr)	*Kapitänleutnant*
Senior Lieutenant	*Oberleutnant zur See*
Junior Lieutenant	*Leutnant zur See*
Sub-Lieutenant (Sub-Lt)	*Oberfähnrich zur See*
Midshipman/cadet	*Fähnrich zur See*
Chief Boatswain	*Oberbootsmann*
Boatswain	*Bootsmann*
Chief Petty Officer (CPO)	*Obermaat*
Petty Officer (PO)	*Maat*
Leading Seaman (4.5yrs svc)	*Matrosen-Hauptgefreiter*
Leading Seaman	*Matrosen-Obergefreiter*
Able Seaman (AB)	*Matrosen-Gefreiter*
Ordinary Seaman	*Matrose*

Royal Air Force	*Luftwaffe*
Marshal of the RAF	*Reichsmarschall*
Air Chief Marshal (ACM)	*Generalfeldmarschall*, also *Generaloberst*
Air Marshal	*General der Fliegers*, etc
Air Vice-Marshal (AVM)	*Generalleutnant*
Air Commodore (Air Cdre)	*Generalmajor*
Group Captain (Gp Capt)	*Oberst*
Wing Commander (Wg Cdr)	*Oberstleutnant*
Squadron Leader (Sqn Ldr)	*Major*
Flight Lieutenant (Flt Lt)	*Hauptmann*
Flying Officer (Flg Off)	*Oberleutnant*
Pilot Officer (Plt Off)	*Leutnant*
Warrant Officer (WO)	*Stabsfeldwebel*
Flight Sergeant (Flt Sgt)	*Oberfeldwebel*
Sergeant (Sgt)	*Feldwebel*
No Equivalent	*Unterfeldwebel*
Corporal (Cpl)	*Unteroffizier*
No Equivalent	*Hauptgefreiter*
Leading Aircraftsman	*Obergefreiter*
Aircraftsman 1st Class	*Gefreiter*
Aircraftsman 2nd Class	*Flieger*

Ranks of the Organization Todt and their approximate military equivalent

ENGLISH	GERMAN	FUNCTION
Major	*Bauleiter*	Construction Superintendent
Captain/Lieutenant	*Frontführer*	Senior Administrator
Warrant Officer	*Obertruppführer* *Haupttruppführer*	Camp Commander (also *Lagerführer* or *Lagerleiter*)
Sergeant	*Truppführer*	Overseer of part of workforce
Corporal	*Meister*	Overseer
Lance Corporal	*Vorarbeiter*	Overseer

Festung Jersey und Festung Guernsey

'One evening the General took me upstairs to his private study and showed me a magnificent work which had been produced under his auspices: Fortress Jersey and Guernsey. The best artists and photographers have been commissioned as contributors to this highly artistic multi-volume book. He insisted that I sit at his desk and brought me all sorts of interesting items to look at.' [1]

Below: The Tramsheds Bunker by moonlight — one of the remarkable drawings from *Festung Guernsey*, the German fortress manual. The bunker housed a 4.7cm Skoda anti-tank gun. *CIOS (Guernsey)*

That is how Baron von Aufsess, Head of Civil Affairs in the German Field Command, tells of his first glimpse at a remarkable, lavishly illustrated record of the German defences on the Channel Islands. The date of this viewing was 15 December 1944 and the location 'La Corbinérie', the country house which was occupied by GenLt Graf von Schmettow, the divisional commander of 319. ID and the German C-in-C of the Channel Islands at that time. This time-consuming study had been undertaken by members of GenLt Schmettow's staff, at his personal behest, employing the best artists and the most skilled photographers available. They were drawn from the *Divisionskartestelle* (Divisional Cartographic Section) and the team was clearly highly skilled at drawing, photography and calligraphy. The Guernsey set of this remarkable record runs into four volumes and Mr Pierre Renier of CIOS (Guernsey) carried out a detailed study some years ago, using the two existing copies which are located in the Priaulx and Royal Court Libraries of Guernsey. Thus there is still in existence an amazingly detailed record of the defences of the Islands, something Allied Intelligence would dearly have loved to have possessed in 1944!

Nevertheless, despite not having access to von Schmettow's 'work of art', Allied intelligence had managed to build up a reasonably accurate picture of the German defences on the Islands — which, to quote Rommel's Chief of Staff, GenLt Hans Speidel, contained far more than their fair share of fortifications:

> *'The Channel Islands, a small group on this vast front, received eleven heavy batteries with 38 guns early in February 1944, but the whole coast of the mainland between Dieppe and St Nazaire, a distance of 600 miles, had no more than the equivalent number of batteries with 37 guns in all.'* [2]

He goes on to delineate the massive infantry division, strengthened with armoured vehicles and AA guns, whilst he bemoans the fact that no airfields were built to make the Islands into 'aircraft carriers'. Rommel's opposition to the strengthening of Channel Islands defences is well known, but even he was unable to get the Führer to change his mind. Thus the magnificent defences, so proudly documented by GenLt von Schmettow, were never properly tested. Many were subsequently destroyed after the war, but fortunately the detailed and complete record — *Festung Jersey und Festung Guernsey* — still remains for us to study.

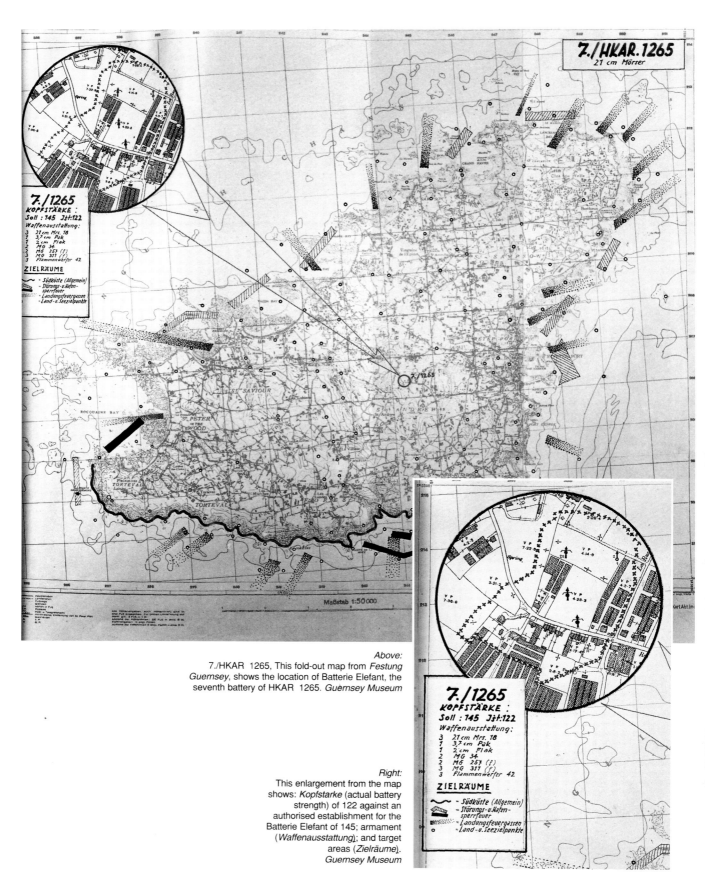

7./1265
KOPFSTÄRKE:
Soll : 145   Jst:122
Waffenausstattung:
3   21 cm Mrs. 16
1   3,7 cm Pak
1   2 cm Flak
2   MG 34
2   MG 257 (f)
3   MG 311 (f)
3   Flammenwerfer 42
ZIELRÄUME

~ Südküste (Allgemein)
~ Störungs-u.Hafen-
    sperrfeuer
= Landungsfeuergassen
= Land-u.Seezielpunkte

Maßstab 1:50 000

Above:
7./HKAR 1265, This fold-out map from *Festung Guernsey*, shows the location of Batterie Elefant, the seventh battery of HKAR 1265. *Guernsey Museum*

Right:
This enlargement from the map shows: *Kopfstärke* (actual battery strength) of 122 against an authorised establishment for the Batterie Elefant of 145; armament (*Waffenausstattung*); and target areas (*Zielräume*). *Guernsey Museum*

7./1265
KOPFSTÄRKE:
Soll : 145   Jst:122
Waffenausstattung:
3   21 cm Mrs. 16
1   3,7 cm Pak
1   2 cm Flak
2   MG 34
2   MG 257 (f)
3   MG 311 (f)
3   Flammenwerfer 42
ZIELRÄUME

~ Südküste (Allgemein)
~ Störungs-u.Hafen-
    sperrfeuer
= Landungsfeuergassen
= Land-u.Seezielpunkte

Einsatz der Artillerie — artillery
in action, frontispiece of the artillery
section in *Festung Guernsey*.
It shows one of the nine 21cm
Mörser 18 gun-howitzers stationed
in Guernsey, which made up the
three batteries each of three guns
in HKAR 1265. *Guernsey Museum*

Below:
A good action shot of one of the battery's 21cm M18s having just fired — note
the cylinder rod of the upper recuperator assembly drawn to the rear by the
recoil of the gun. See also pages 86–91. *Guernsey Museum*

21cm MÖRSER 18   7./H.K.A.R. 1265

Introduction

HISTORY

Before the Norman invasion of England in 1066, the islands known as *Les Îles Normandes* formed part of the Duchy of Normandy; so, when William, Duke of Normandy, became King William I of England, they automatically became linked to the English crown. Even when Normandy became part of France at the beginning of the 13th century, the Islands remained loyal to the Crown of England. In 1461, Pierre de Breze, Grand Seneschal of Normandy, sent an expeditionary force to capture Jersey, under the command of one Jean de Carbonnel. He captured Mont Orgueil Castle and for the next seven years Jersey was under French rule.

It was retaken by the English in 1468, after a five-month siege, and since that date the Islands had, until 1 July 1940, remained as dependencies under the British Crown. However, they were never strictly part of the United Kingdom: their laws and institutions, being derived from Normandy, were and still are different from those of the United Kingdom — and, it must also be said, different from one another. However, both had Lieutenant-Governors — normally senior British officers and Bailiffs (Chief Justices) — appointed by the Crown. The latter are the link between the Lieutenant-Governors and the Islands' various administrative bodies. At the start of the war the Lieutenant-Governors and Bailiffs were: Jersey, Maj-Gen J. M. R. Harrison and Alexander Coutanche; Guernsey, Maj-Gen A. P. D. Telfer-Smollet and Victor Carey.

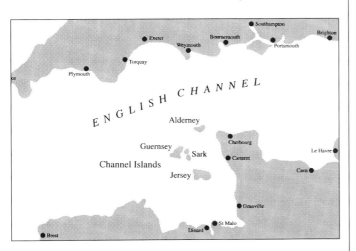

GEOGRAPHY

There are four main islands — Jersey, Guernsey, Alderney and Sark — with lesser islets (eg Herm, Brechou, Jethou and Lithou), plus a labyrinth of rocks and reefs. They lie off the north-west coast of France, some 60 miles from the nearest part of England. Total land area is roughly 75sq miles, Jersey and Guernsey being some 45 and 24sq miles in area respectively. Both capitals are seaports — Jersey's St Helier and Guernsey's St Peter Port — the latter having the better deep-water harbour, because the sea bed around St Helier slopes too gently.

Populations in 1939 were about 50,000 in Jersey and 40,000 in Guernsey. Alderney was next in size, the population being 1,500, and Sark had just 600 inhabitants. Some of the population were expatriates from the United Kingdom, others were itinerant workers — mainly from France and Ireland, although some came from further afield. However, the majority of the populations were born and bred Islanders. After the war began there were only a few Jews who remained on the Islands, the majority having chosen to move to England.

The mild climate and productive soil have always helped to make the Islands a good place to live; indeed, Adolf Hitler, although he never visited the Channel Islands, became enamoured with them — so much so that he decided they would not be returned to the United Kingdom nor joined to France following his victory, but would rather remain a part of Germany. They would be perfect holiday islands for the victorious German people to enjoy for ever as a 'constitutional nature reserve'!

THE SITUATION IN JUNE 1940

On the afternoon of 21 June 1940, one of the most beautiful days of that momentous summer, a Nazi motorcade arrived at an old wooden railway dining car, standing in a small circular clearing in the middle of the forest near Compiègne, some 50 miles north-east of Paris. Adolf Hitler got out of his gleaming Mercedes and, accompanied by Göring, Brauchitsch, Keitel, Raeder, Ribbentrop and Hess, walked over to a large granite block which bore the following inscription: 'Here on the Eleventh of November 1918 succumbed the criminal pride of the German Empire — vanquished by the free people which it tried to enslave.'

One observer reported that Hitler's expression was 'afire with scorn, anger, hate, revenge and triumph'. He had deliberately chosen the railway carriage, the location of the signing of the hated Versailles Treaty, in order to rub as much salt as possible into the wounds of the shattered French. The new armistice

Opposite above: A triumphant Adolf Hitler and his entourage outside the railway carriage at Compiègne on 21 June 1940, when the instrument of surrender was signed by the French. It was the same railway carriage that was used by Marshal Foch to accept the German surrender in 1918. *Author's collection*

Opposite: German Panzers reach the English Channel, 10 June 1940. Tanks belonging to Gen Erwin Rommel's 7th Panzer Division reached the sea-front at Petites-Dalles (between Fécamp and Saint-Valery-en-Caux) exactly one month after the start of the offensive. This PzKpfw III belonged to Oberstlt Ligen, commander II./Panzer Regiment 25. *Tank Museum*

'For you the war is over.' Captured Allied soldiers, who had missed the 'miracle of Dunkirk', many of them wounded, were rounded up on the quaysides of the Channel ports and taken back to POW camps where they would remain throughout five long years of war. *Author's collection*

signed in the railway carriage would bring all hostilities to a close at 21.00hrs on 24 June. Thus, in just a few short weeks since the launching of the assault upon the West on 10 May 1940, the Wehrmacht had overrun Holland, Belgium and France, booting the battered — but still defiant — British Expeditionary Force unceremoniously into the Channel to make its hazardous way back to Britain. The might of the German forces now stood, cock-a-hoop, on the Channel coast waiting for that glorious moment when they would be marching against England!

One of the German soldiers who had fought across France, and was now happily ensconced near the 'shimmering white bays' of Normandy, was Maj Dr Albrecht Lanz, a battalion commander of 216. ID. Able, intelligent and well educated, Maj Lanz was a Doctor of Law and Philosophy. On 29 June he visited the Naval HQ in Cherbourg, where he met up with an old naval friend, Kapitänleutnant Koch. 'From my No 3 Company's position, on the Nez de Jobourg, islands can be seen,' he had remarked in the course of their conversation, going on to explain to his friend how he had found out that the nearest island was Alderney — British territory, but presently uninhabited as the population had been evacuated. 'It would be a great thing for us to land there,' he went on and Koch agreed, saying that he also had often wondered why they should not cross the sea and occupy the beautiful Channel Islands. The major problem at that time, however, Koch explained, was the lack of proper shipping. 'With this unsatisfied desire in our breasts we parted, not dreaming that the Occupation would come about sooner than we thought.'

To be left unguarded

Before elaborating on the important role which Maj Lanz will play in the occupation of the Channel Islands, it is first necessary to explain why it was that the Occupation was made so simple and easy to achieve by such a small number of German troops. The reason lies fairly and squarely in the decision of the British Government to leave the Islands unguarded. It was naturally a very difficult decision to make and the deliberations that preceded it were long and drawn out.

Looking back to 1 September 1939, soon after war had been declared and without receiving any proper guidance from London, both Lieutenant-Governors ordered the call-up of the Islands' militia. Some days later, after much dithering in Whitehall, first the War Office concurred, then the Home Office also agreed, once they had accepted the fact that the Army Council had the necessary authority to deal direct with the Lieutenant-Governors in their capacity as General Officers Commanding. This type of indecision and muddle would be the hallmark of London's dealings with the Islands in the early days of June 1940.

Conscription had been introduced into the United Kingdom by the passing of the National Service (Armed Forces) Act by Parliament, just hours after war had been declared. Just as they had done in World War 1, when many men from the Channel Islands had immediately volunteered to serve in the armed forces, the Islanders again unhesitatingly followed suit, authorising that all men between the ages of 18 and 41 would be liable to do military service.

So, as the first months of the strange period which became known as the 'Phoney War' began, there was a constant dribble of manpower away from the Islands as men were called up, thus depleting the strength of the militia. Although both Lieutenant-Governors repeatedly asked for coastal defence and anti-aircraft (AA) guns, their requests fell on deaf ears:

'The formal reply was that coastal guns might be delivered in August 1940, but that it was impossible to quote a date for Bofors, production of which had only just started, or for Bren guns. The War Office airily told the Home Office that the possibility of attack on Jersey was 'somewhat remote', and the Army Council hinted that the weapons might be more useful elsewhere.'[1]

This somewhat offhand and apparently cynical approach was based upon the fact that the 'powers that be' in London had already come to the conclusion that the Channel Islands were not worth defending, because they were of no real strategic value. It was argued that they were wide open to air attack and would need a massive garrison to defend them against an all-out assault by sea and air. Also, such a defence would endanger the lives of the civilian population of the Islands unnecessarily. This thinking led to the removal of what was left of the regular garrison — the infantry battalion on Jersey had been withdrawn years ago in 1925. Now it was the turn of the Guernsey-based battalion to leave, this latter battalion being 1st Battalion The Royal Irish Fusiliers.

Despite seeing the effects of the German Blitzkrieg through France, the view that the Islands were indefensible rapidly changed and it was decided on 12 June, at a morning meeting of the War Cabinet, that, although the Channel Islands had no great strategic importance, approval would be given for the despatch of two infantry battalions to replace the various training establishments there, which should then be withdrawn.

It did not take the War Cabinet long to realise the change of heart was wrong. That afternoon, at another meeting, the full realisation that the Germans would soon be controlling the Channel coast of France struck home and it was appreciated that the Islands would then immediately lose any strategic importance they might have hitherto possessed. The Chief of the General Staff (CIGS) recommended a change of plan, namely the withdrawal of all British troops, whilst the local militia should be ordered to concentrate upon security and anti-sabotage, whilst preparations were made to destroy any airfield facilities which could be of use to the enemy.

The British troops which would have to be withdrawn were:

- Guernsey and Alderney District — some 1,500 men at the 341st Machine Gun Training Centre (on Alderney); detachments of RE, RASC and RAMC.

- Jersey District — some 250 boys at the Army Technical School; detachments of RE, RASC and a Military Hospital.

The CIGS further recommended that the Lieutenant-Governors should be ordered to surrender the Islands if the Germans landed, so as to avoid useless bloodshed. It took the civil servants in London three more days to make up their minds to agree these proposals and to formulate a plan, then on Saturday, 15 June, acting on the assumption that no more troops would be sent from the UK to protect the airfields, the War Office issued orders to the Machine Gun Training Centre on Alderney to use its men to defend the Jersey and Guernsey airfields (they did not consider that the strip on Alderney was worth using), so that they could still be used by the RAF for as long as they needed to support operations in northwest France. Once this need was over, then 'a policy of demilitarisation will rule'.

The Admiralty also wrote to the harassed Lieutenant-Governor of Jersey telling him that they were no longer interested in Jersey and that he had '. . . complete freedom, so far as My Lords are concerned, to take any measures you consider necessary for the immobilisation of aircraft landing facilities.' They were of course thinking only of the Fleet Air Arm and, as Bernard Cruickshank comments in his definitive history of the Occupation, 'It is not clear whether a copy of this single-minded missive was sent to the Air Ministry, which still had a strong interest in keeping the airfields operational, having regard to the needs of Bomber and Fighter Command.' These needs were quite considerable; for example, as the Germans advanced through France, No 17 Squadron, RAF, was forced to withdraw from Le Mans and Dinard, moving its Hurricanes to Jersey, where they were joined by No 501 Squadron from Dinard on 18 June. Both units attempted to cover the evacuation of France from there until they were recalled to mainland UK on the following day.

Guernsey airfield was even busier. The RAF School of General Reconnaissance had been there since April 1940 and did not cease training until 14 June. Two days later all their serviceable aircraft (26 Avro Ansons) flew off, leaving one unserviceable Anson to be destroyed, whilst their ground party departed on SS *Brittany* on the 18th. This left the nucleus of Nos 32 and 64 Fighter Wing Servicing Units which were withdrawn on the 19th. No 17 Squadron operated a detachment of Hurricanes for a short while but then they also departed. Between the 19th and 21st both Jersey and Guernsey Airways, based at Exeter, operated evacuation services from the Channel Islands, carrying 319 people to safety in their DH86s. [2]

In the next barrage of missives from London, the long-suffering Lieutenant-Governors were told that a battery of Bofors LAA guns were, after all, going to be sent for the defence of the airfields in Jersey and Guernsey and that a section of an RE construction company was being sent to Guernsey from Gosport, presumably to prepare gun positions for them — despite the fact that the earlier intention had been to leave airfield defence to the Machine Gun Training Centre! The Admiralty then told them that they might need to use the Channel Islands as staging posts for troops escaping from St Malo. This rapidly became a reality when they were told that they should assemble as many sea-going

boats as possible and be ready to assist with the evacuation. This was done as quickly as possible and, in all, some 18 yachts from the St Helier Yacht Club went to St Malo on 17–18 June and successfully ferried many soldiers to the waiting transports. All the yachts returned safely to Jersey and the Commodore of the Yacht Club received a signal of thanks from the Admiralty.

Just before this evacuation took place, orders were received to stand by to evacuate all troops from Alderney. These orders were received at 05.00hrs on 16 June and two hours later the soldiers were moving to the waiting transport ships. As one can imagine, this caused considerable alarm amongst the local people and especially of course among the soldiers' families. However, their fears were partly allayed when it was explained that they were only going to Jersey and Guernsey. Despite the fact that no formal decision had been made about demilitarisation, the Home Office and War Office continued apace to formulate plans for such an eventuality, deciding to withdraw the Lieutenant-Governors once the last of the troops had left. Other major problems remained unresolved, such as what should be done about the 3,000 young men who were now becoming eligible for conscription.

In the argument about demilitarisation there were many dissenting voices, one of the strongest being that of the Prime Minister, who found it utterly repugnant to consider giving up Crown territory — could not, he argued, the Royal Navy prevent any landing force reaching the Islands? However, he had to agree in the end with the inevitable conclusion that it would be impossible to produce an adequate defence force on land and in the air, without seriously weakening what there was left to defend the British Isles after the serious losses of matériel in France. The Channel Islands were just too far away from England and too near the enemy bases in northwest France, and this would present even the might of the Royal Navy with an impossible task. The Islands would, therefore, have to be abandoned.

Although the decision was now irrevocable, no attempt was made to inform the enemy, obviously to prevent him from interfering with the wholesale evacuation which had now speeded up, as this extract from *Jersey under the Swastika* by Ralph Mollet aptly illustrates:

'*Wednesday, the 19th was the climax. The Lieutenant-Governor informed the Assembly of the States, that the British Government had given him orders to demilitarise the Island immediately, as it was not in the interest of the war to defend the Channel Islands. The Home Office was arranging to evacuate the bulk of those who wished to go; but he felt sure that those who had their roots in the soil would not want to leave . . . When this information reached the public, a considerable amount of panic ensued. A register was immediately instituted at the Town Hall for the names of those who wished to leave the Island and a long queue of people five and six deep extended as far as the Opera House, Gloucester Street, some standing for at least ten hours; 23,063 registered their names, almost two-thirds of whom subsequently changed their minds and decided to remain.*'

Above: 'Rule Britannia!' Guardian of the vital worldwide links and protector of the British Isles, the Royal Navy was still a major force to be reckoned with in World War 2, despite cutbacks after World War 1. *IWM* — HU 56004

Above: Safe and sound in the arms of the law! Two young evacuees from Guernsey are cuddled by a Glasgow Bobby, 24 June 1940. *IWM* — HU24895

Demilitarisation

This is not the book in which to detail all the traumas which the Islands and their inhabitants went through during the days leading up to the Occupation. Suffice to say that the vast majority of those civilians who needed or wanted to leave, left safely, mostly bound for England. This included, of course, all military personnel, their final evacuation taking place on Thursday, 20 June. The SS *Biarritz* arrived at Guernsey very early that morning, whilst the SS *Malines* reached Jersey some four hours later. Both successfully embarked the last of the troops, the two ships leaving on the same tide later that morning. The Jersey Militia went *en bloc* to England, where it was assimilated into the British Army, becoming the 11th Battalion of the Hampshires. The Guernsey Militia was disbanded, but many of its members joined the Royal Artillery and the Hampshires. Alderney was almost completely evacuated, its inhabitants being shipped over to the UK. [3] Finally, instructions were received from London to cut the telephone cable to France. There being no further military duties to perform, the Lieutenant-Governors departed the following day. The Islands were now totally defenceless. The Lieutenant-Governors had been asked to inform the Home Office that the demilitarisation had been completed and that the Islands were now undefended areas. The Home Office accordingly drafted the necessary notice to explain the situation, but, although it was drafted on the 22nd, it was not sent to anyone because it was considered that the Germans might regard it as an open invitation to invade. On the 24th, the Bailiffs received the following message from HM King George VI:

'For strategic reasons it has been found necessary to withdraw the armed forces from the Channel Islands.

I deeply regret this necessity, and I wish to assure My people in the Islands that in taking this decision My Government have not been unmindful of their position.

It is in their interest that this step should be taken in present circumstances.

'The long association of the Islands with the Crown and the loyal service the people of the Islands have rendered to My Ancestors and Myself are guarantees that the link between us will remain unbroken, and I know that My people in the Islands will look forward with the same confidence as I do, to the day when the resolute fortitude, with which we face our present difficulties, will reap the reward of victory.'

Gradually the Islands returned to something approaching normality, as Ralph Mollet explains:

'As the day ended the population became calmer. On the piers and at the airport large numbers of cars were found, abandoned by the evacuees, and were gradually reclaimed by their friends who were looking after their effects. On Saturday, the 22nd the run on the banks still continued, but the panic subsided and calmness became more apparent. Shops reopened, and people paid in money to the banks.'

Alone and defenceless, the Islands awaited their fate.

Above: Evacuated to England. All the members of this little Channel Islands family look lost and bewildered as they arrive in England after a 20-hour boat trip to a West Country port — it was probably the first time they had ever left their island home, 23 June 1940. *IWM* — HU24887

Above: Maj Dr Albrecht Lanz, CO of II./Regiment 396 of 216. ID, is seen here (centre) with Lt Müller (left) and Maj Maas, a fluent English-speaker who would later act as Lanz's interpreter. *IWM* — HU 25919

Chapter 1

Arrival

Evening Press

Home Circle Library
BUSINESS AS USUAL
— AT —
Old Gate House
AND THE BRIDGE,
ST. SAMPSON'S.

SWELLING THE FRUIT
Use Flask Blood and Bone, Blood and Fish, Aeroplane Organic and Special Fertiliser or Aeroplane Invigorator or Aeroplane Extra Special Fertiliser.

W.J. Holmes & Son Ltd.
ESPLANADE. 'Phone 713 3 (lines)

No. 10,971   REGISTERED AT THE G.P.O. AS A NEWSPAPER   POSTAGE 1d.   GUERNSEY, SATURDAY,   JUNE 29, 1940   TELEPHONE 1400 (FIVE LINES)   ONE PENNY

GUERNSEY SUFFERS FIRST AIR RAID

25 KILLED — 33 INJURED

Policeman and Ambulance Driver Among the Fatalities

WEIGHBRIDGE "SQUARE" CENTRE OF WRECKAGE

Left: Headlines in the local newspapers on the 29th told of the previous day's strafing raid, with details of the casualties.

THE BOMBING RAID

'The blood of the wounded and the dying mingled with the juice of the tomatoes, and when I came on the scene just as the last Hun plane faded into the distance, the sight was one I shall never forget; the flames, the bodies, the cries of the dying and injured, and the straggling line of people emerging from their shelter under the pier jetty.' [1]

That is how one eyewitness remembered the Luftwaffe raid on Guernsey, which was the curtain-raiser to Operation '*Grüne Pfeil*' ('Green Arrow'), the German invasion of the Channel Islands. Six Heinkel He111 medium bombers [2] had suddenly appeared without warning over the Islands, after taking off from their airstrip in the Cherbourg area, late on the afternoon of Friday, 28 June 1940. Spraying bullets from their machine guns and dropping some 180 bombs, the enemy aircraft effectively strafed the dock areas of both St Helier in Jersey and St Peter Port in Guernsey, killing a total of 44 people and wounding many more. There were no military casualties as the Islands had been demilitarised some days previously. The only retaliation was light anti-aircraft machine gun fire from twin Lewis guns on the mail steamer *Isle of Sark*, which was at the time embarking passengers for England from one of the jetties at St Peter Port.

In the docks of St Helier, Jersey, it was just as terrifying. Mr E. J. de Ste Croix had been working at the Albert Pier that afternoon, loading potatoes into the small freighter *Hull Trader*, which was one of the last ships to leave the Islands before the Occupation. He had been down in the hold loading barrels of potatoes and recalled later that he remembered seeing German planes flying over on several previous occasions, presumably taking photographs, and how this time:

'They came out of the blue. In fact I don't ever remember the siren going. And then they dropped these bombs which landed across the harbour and did extensive damage. We were ordered out of the ship to take shelter on the pier where best we could. I remember at the time the strange things that men do, under stress, where some men crawled under the tarpaulin. What shelter they expected to find there heaven knows. Others had gathered under the framework of cranes quite out in the open.'

With a number of others, Mr de Ste Croix made for a small shack which was used by the dockers for their tea-breaks and jammed himself between the back of the shack and the wall of Albert Pier promenade. By the time he emerged from this comparatively safe place the aircraft had gone and the ship was already battening down its hatches and preparing to sail. Several people had been killed and wounded in this five to ten minutes of bombing and machine-gunning, which as well as hitting the harbour, '. . . set fire to Norman's timber yard, the Southampton Hotel, the Weighbridge, the Finsbury, the Star Hotel which no longer exists now. They were all extensively damaged. And higher up in Mulcaster Street, I remember the body of Mr Ferrand, mine host of "Daley's Bunch of Grapes", the public house, he was dead in the road where he had been killed.' [3]

Another eyewitness reported seeing machine gun bullets ploughing up the sand on the beach at Havre des Pas; two bombs being dropped on Mount Bingham, killing Mr John Mauger near his house and damaging many nearby houses; two more bombs falling on the Fort and the District Office as well as more that fell in the Old Harbour, which set fire to many small boats. The planes went over the island to St Ouen, then returned to St Helier, machine-gunning the Albert and North Piers and bombing Commercial Buildings. The furze on Fort Regent caught fire and burnt for several days. Finally, after using their machine guns on various parts of the island, they dropped two more bombs, causing more deaths, then machine-gunned the Guernsey lifeboat which was off Noirmont on its way to Jersey, killing Mr Harold Hobbs. The casualties were taken to the General Hospital and many people left St Helier to sleep in the country that night.

Any casualties, especially those amongst innocent civilians, are naturally to be deeply regretted at any time; however, it has to be said that the opening of the German assault on the Islands was a fairly low-key affair compared, say, to the opening assault on France and the Low Countries. As explained in the last chapter, the British Government had declared the Islands to be

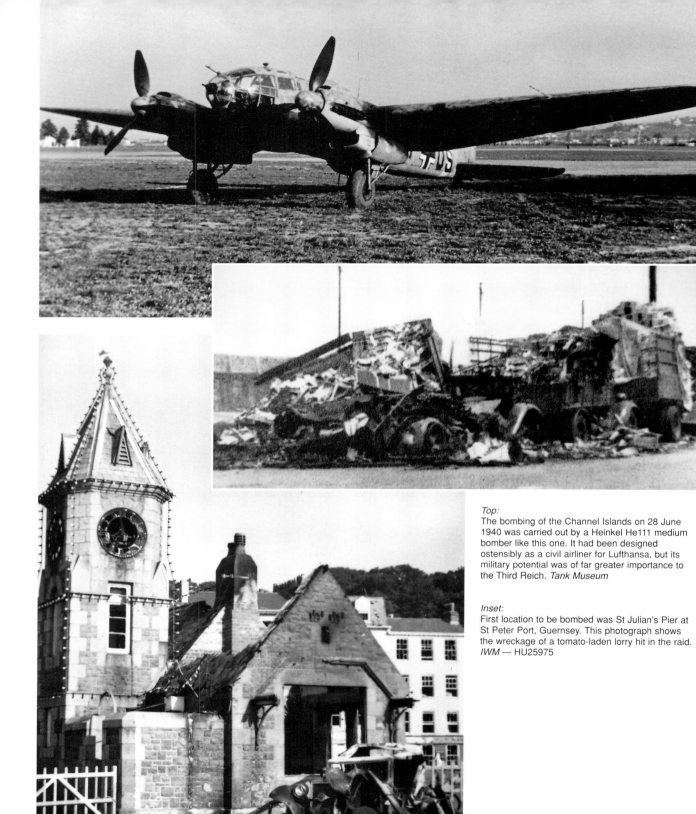

Top:
The bombing of the Channel Islands on 28 June 1940 was carried out by a Heinkel He111 medium bomber like this one. It had been designed ostensibly as a civil airliner for Lufthansa, but its military potential was of far greater importance to the Third Reich. *Tank Museum*

Inset:
First location to be bombed was St Julian's Pier at St Peter Port, Guernsey. This photograph shows the wreckage of a tomato-laden lorry hit in the raid. *IWM — HU25975*

Left:
Another view of air raid damage showing the gutted clocktower and badly damaged car at the junction of St Julian's Pier and the North Esplanade. *IWM — HU 25922*

demilitarised, but had tried to hide this fact from the Germans. In his definitive history, the late Charles Cruickshank makes the point that the Home Office deliberately muddied the waters so that it would appear to the British population — and to the Islanders — that Germany had launched a cowardly attack upon innocent civilians, well knowing the Islands to be undefended. The British Press also seized upon this line; however, as we now know, this was not the case. As we have seen, although the Islands had been demilitarised since the 21st, this information was not broadcast on the radio until the 28th, whilst the more formal process of telling the German government did not begin until the 30th, two days after the raids had taken place. When looked at against these facts, the raid can be seen in its proper perspective. Mr R. W. Le Sueur, who, like Mr de Ste Croix, was born in Jersey, also recorded his thoughts for the IWM's Sound Archive:

'I think it is interesting to record this, on the Friday of the air raid, the air raid occurred about seven o'clock in the evening, on the nine o'clock news, we heard that the Channel Islands had been declared open and would not be defended. On the eight o'clock news on the Saturday morning — I hope this doesn't sound anti-British, but it is factually true — at eight o'clock on the Saturday morning on the same news bulletin, we heard about the bombing.

'Now the reaction in the minds of everybody in the United Kingdom must have been, "There you are, they declare a place undefended on the nine o'clock news on the Friday and now we hear that the place has been bombed and many people have been killed." But it really didn't happen that way.' [4]

AIR RECONNAISSANCE

On 20 June Berlin had sent the following signal to German Naval Group West:

'Occupation of the British Channel Islands is urgent and important. Carry out local reconnaissance and execution thereof.'

Before making any major amphibious or aerial assault on the Channel Islands it was only natural that air reconnaissance would have to take place. This had in fact been going on since about 18 June, first by aircraft of Luftflotte 2 (*Luftflotte* = Air Fleet), then later by aircraft of Luftflotte 3 which took over responsibility to support Operation '*Grüne Pfeil*' from 25 June.

The earlier recce flights had shown no visible signs of occupied artillery emplacements, no aircraft on the airfields, and little sea traffic. However, later sorties had seemed to suggest that there was considerable activity at the main ports, with transport ships and motor vehicles busy at the quays — but were they evacuating civilians and moving produce, or were they reinforcing the garrison and bringing in more arms and ammunition? The general conclusion reached by Admiral Karlgeorg Schuster — the senior German naval commander in France — in conjunction with Vizeadmiral Eugen Lindau was

that the garrison had been reduced by evacuation; there were still some troops, probably with coastal artillery support, but clearly weak AA defences. (Vizeadmiral Eugen Lindau was Flag Officer Northern France, responsible for the planning and execution of the invasion of the Islands.) In addition, protective minefields had probably been laid in certain sea areas. Therefore it would be prudent to send in small-scale raids by armed reconnaissance aircraft, to get the troops on the ground to show their hand and expose their positions.

Both Schuster and Lindau realised that their heads would roll if anything went wrong in this the first German assault on British soil and, although the British Army was in no position to retaliate after the débâcle in France and the RAF was undoubtedly too preoccupied defending mainland Britain to play a major role, the Royal Navy, despite its other commitments, could wreak havoc on any invasion force the Germans might launch. This then was the reason why the raids took place on the 28th and, although there was only minimal opposition (light machine gun fire from the ship in St Peter Port), in their opinion, further armed air reconnaissance would be necessary before a full-scale landing was attempted.

THE INVASION

The original proposal had called for a force of some six battalions to be used — three for Jersey, two for Guernsey and one for Alderney. They would only be lightly equipped because difficulties were foreseen in manhandling any heavy weapons or equipment from ship to shore and then getting it off the beaches. The assault force would also contain a suitable naval ground element, a *Marinestosstruppabteilung* (Naval assault detachment — the Kriegsmarine equivalent of the Royal Marines) and two engineer companies. Due to the shortage of suitable amphibious craft, the assault would have to take place over two days — Alderney and Guernsey being the objectives for Day 1, then Jersey on Day 2. The amphibious landings would be preceded by naval operations to clear gaps through the sea minefields and 'softening-up' air raids on land targets, whilst the actual assault would be supported by Ju87 Stuka dive-bombers which had wreaked such havoc during the Blitzkrieg in France. The Luftwaffe would also clearly play a major role, protecting the convoys, whilst the Kriegsmarine's main task would be to prevent interference from the Royal Navy.

After hearing the results of the raids on the 28th and the lack of reaction from the Islands' defences, it was agreed that the assault force should be scaled down to just one battalion for Guernsey, one for Jersey and a single infantry company for Alderney. The troops would mainly come from 216. ID, which was now stationed in the Cherbourg area, supported by the *Kriegsmarine Abteilung 'Gotenhafen'* (Naval Assault Group 'Gotenhafen' — henceforth referred to as 'Gotenhafen'), and Luftwaffe light anti-aircraft guns, which would have to be withdrawn from the Cherbourg area. The Luftwaffe would also supply constant air cover.

Right:
The assault force was carried in Junkers Ju52/3m transport aircraft, the 'maid-of-all-work' of the Luftwaffe, which always looked as though it was made out of corrugated iron sheeting! In fact it was a very reliable aeroplane and used worldwide.
Hans-Gerhard Sandmann

Left:
Two Ju52/3m crew members, the one on the left is an Unteroffizier and the one on the right an Oberfeldwebel, who wears the Iron Cross ribbon and on his left breast, the Airmen's Commemorative Badge *(Erinnungsabzeichen)*. He wears the comfortable Flying Blouse *(Fliegerbluse)*.
Hans-Gerhard Sandmann

Right:
Members of 216. ID wait to board their aircraft at Cherbourg West airfield, together with their pilots.
Hans-Gerhard Sandmann

Hauptmann Liebe-Pieteritz steals the limelight

The next event in the proceedings was very definitely not planned and took everyone by surprise. A planning meeting, held in Paris on Sunday afternoon, 30 June, had just decided that another armed reconnaissance would be flown the following day, and that one of the aircraft would land at one of the airports to see what the reaction would be. If it provoked opposition, then the full-scale assault would take place as planned; however, if there was no reaction then the army and navy units would be flown in to the two airports.

Just as the meeting was ending, the news came in that a Luftwaffe pilot, Hptm Liebe-Pieteritz, had just landed on the airfield at Guernsey whilst on a routine air reconnaissance, thus pre-empting plans of the high-level planners! He had been leading a flight of four Dornier Do17Ps [5], and on the spur of the moment — and acting entirely on his own initiative — had landed with two of his aircraft (some accounts say he landed alone) whilst the others circled overhead to give him protection.

Hptm Liebe-Pieteritz got out of his Dornier and entered the airport building but found it was empty. His daring sortie was interrupted by the arrival of three RAF Bristol Blenheims, so he hastily got airborne again (one account says he left so hastily that he dropped his pistol in the rush to get airborne!). The Germans claim to have shot down two of the Blenheims in the dogfight which followed; however, other sources say that no losses are reported in RAF records for that day. Whatever happened did not stop the audacious captain from reporting his success to Luftflotte 3, saying that the island appeared to be undefended. This led to a second landing later that evening, when a party of Luftwaffe personnel from *Aufklärungsgruppe* 123 (Recce Group 123) under Hptm von Obernitz and the overall command of a Maj Hessel took control of the airport. The head of the Guernsey police, Inspector William R. Sculpher, then arrived at the airfield, bearing a letter in English (which he had been holding for just such an occasion since the 27th), addressed to: 'The Officer Commanding German Troops in Guernsey' and signed by the Bailiff (Victor — later Sir Victor — Carey). The short letter read as follows:

> 'This Island has been declared an Open Island by His Majesty's Government of the United Kingdom. There are in it no armed forces of any description. The bearer has been instructed to hand this communication to you. He does not understand the German language.'

Top: Airborne at long last! The Unteroffizier piloting the Ju52/3m on the journey to Guernsey. *Hans-Gerhard Sandmann*

Above: 'A few seconds later the machines turned out to sea in a great loop and arranged themselves in ordered formation . . . we could fly only between 25 and 50 yards above the wave-crests.' *Author's collection*

Left: Their first view of the Islands. *Hans-Gerhard Sandmann*

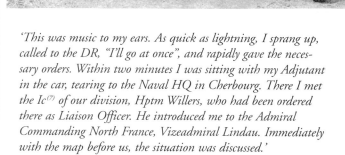

Inspector Sculpher then drove Maj Hessel into St Peter Port to meet the Bailiff. Whilst he was there, Hessel ordered a local shop to manufacture a German Imperial War Flag, which he intended to fly from the signal mast on the airport terminal. Clearly there was now no reason for an operational assault by either sea or air, so the Occupation could proceed without further bloodshed.

Guernsey

In the Introduction, we left Maj Dr Albrecht Lanz, CO of II./IR.396, 216. ID, visiting Naval HQ at Cherbourg and bemoaning the fact that his troops could not 'cross over and occupy the beautiful Channel Islands'. Two days later, on 1 July, whilst he was having breakfast on the spacious glassed-in veranda of his HQ at Urville, a motorcycle despatch rider 'shattered the glorious calm of the morning', bringing an order that Lanz was to report immediately to Vizeadmiral Lindau's HQ in Cherbourg. 'I didn't believe my ears,' commented Lanz later. 'What's this all about Admiral Commanding?' he had asked the DR. 'We're not the Navy after all. You must have come to the wrong address, what should I have to do with the Admiral Commanding North France?' The DR's sunburnt face lit up and he said, with eyes shining, 'We're attacking England, sir, the Islands. A rifle company, a troop of heavy machine guns, and, if possible, infantry guns of the battalion are to be warned immediately to report to the airport at Cherbourg!'

One can imagine how Maj Lanz felt on receiving this exciting news. Later he wrote a report about his introduction to the Channel Islands, which appeared in the 1984 edition of the *Channel Islands Occupation Review* and from which the following quotation is taken, with the kind permission of the Channel Islands Occupation Society. [6] Lanz recalled:

'This was music to my ears. As quick as lightning, I sprang up, called to the DR, "I'll go at once", and rapidly gave the necessary orders. Within two minutes I was sitting with my Adjutant in the car, tearing to the Naval HQ in Cherbourg. There I met the Ic[7] of our division, Hptm Willers, who had been ordered there as Liaison Officer. He introduced me to the Admiral Commanding North France, Vizeadmiral Lindau. Immediately with the map before us, the situation was discussed.'

It was then explained how, the day before, air reconnaissance personnel of the Luftwaffe had landed on Guernsey and encountered no opposition. They were even now holding the airfield without any interference from anyone, so the High Command had decided to take the Islands by a surprise air landing. The troops to be landed would be from 'Gotenhafen' and the Heer units stationed near Cherbourg, which was why Lanz's battalion had been selected. Reports about artillery battery positions being recognised on Guernsey were voiced (little did they realise that these positions were over a hundred years old and occupied by ancient cannons!) and that a British minesweeper had been seen putting into the island the day before, so opinions on the strength of the force needed were still mixed and clearly no one knew for certain whether the Islands had really been demilitarised or not. After considerable discussion it was eventually agreed that just one infantry rifle company from Lanz's battalion, reinforced with heavy machine guns, plus 'Gotenhafen', would be given the task of landing by air in Guernsey, whilst Maj Lanz would be entrusted to prepare and execute the necessary plan. He was also told that nine Ju52/3m transport aircraft had been allocated for the operation, codenamed 'Green Arrow' and would be arriving at the Cherbourg West airfield at Querqueville, at about 09.30hrs that morning. To return to Lanz's narrative:

'As this operation was principally a naval action, Admiral Lindau proposed to put the Assault Detachment "Gotenhafen" in the first Ju52s. Directly the Conference was over we went out to the airfield at which in the meantime the Assault Detachment "Gotenhafen" had already arrived. The allotted groups of my battalion rolled up, at about the same time, to the naval barracks, where 1. Kompanie, whose positions were near the airfield, were billeted. "Don't let too many people be seen on the airfield" was the order, for only two days before, a British plane had disposed of the Admiral Commanding's car, which was on the airfield, diving three times in broad daylight. Quickly various questions were discussed with the Admiral's Chief of Staff. With Oberleutnant Rettighaus, OC of the Assault Detachment "Gotenhafen", dispositions and loading were decided, rifles and heavy weapons separated, and an Officer was entrusted with the supervision of the operation after our departure.'

Top: Maj Lanz, with Maj Maas acting as his interpreter, now began his tour of the Islands to meet local dignitaries. First of all he met the Bailiff of Guernsey, Victor Carey, and this unique photograph was taken secretly whilst the German officers awaited his arrival in the 'large richly furnished living room' — see text. *La Valette Museum*

Above: Later, they would meet the Attorney-General of Guernsey, Ambrose Sherwill, seen here shaking hands with Maj Maas, whilst Maj Lanz salutes, at the Court House, St Peter Port. *IWM — HU25943*

Left: Meanwhile in Jersey, the Bailiff, Alexander Coutanche, and the Attorney-General, Duret-Aubin (far left), first met Staffel Kapitän von Obernitz, while Lt Kern, who had been the first to land on Jersey, looks on with a smile. *IWM — HU 25961*

Also arriving must have been the light anti-aircraft guns, which Luftflotte 3 had given permission to be withdrawn to protect the airfield at Guernsey.

If Maj Lanz had thought he would be given a free hand to carry out the operation, then he was in for a big disappointment, because suddenly a crowd of high-ranking officers descended on the airfield. Among them was the CO of Lanz's regiment (IR 396) Oberstlt Gene, accompanied by his adjutant Oblt Niebuhr, who had just heard that part of one of his battalions was about to depart for the Channel Islands! Also there was an Oberstlt Plocher, Chief of Staff of Fliegerkorps 5, who said that he would be accompanying the assault force. What did not arrive were the promised 'Tante Jus' — as the ugly-looking Ju52 maids-of-all-work of the Luftwaffe were popularly called — so it was fortunate that at about 12.00hrs Generalfeldmarschall Hugo Sperrle arrived.

He had been in charge of the German Condor Legion in Spain during the civil war (1936–39), when the Germans had sent troops, tanks and aircraft to help Franco, and now he commanded Luftflotte 3. He immediately took charge of the situation and found out that the Ju52s, which had been flying to France from Mannheim, had been held up by thick ground mist in the Paris area and had had to land at various airfields to refuel, thus breaking up the formation. Gen Sperrle also made use of the delay to obtain an up-to-the-minute report on the situation in Guernsey, by sending off a Messerschmitt

Bf110 twin-engined fighter, to reconnoitre. It returned about an hour later and reported that the German recce personnel were still occupying the airfield, but could not comment on the rest of the island. Then at long last the first two Ju52s arrived, but, although a further half an hour elapsed, there was no sign of the other seven aircraft. Maj Lanz wrote later:

'We could stay no longer. We decided, after discussing it with Oberstlt Plocher to set off in these two machines and get the business started at last. Oberstlt Plocher announced his intention of joining us with his machine and a Radio-Ju. Quickly two platoons of the Assault Detachment "Gotenhafen" were loaded into the two Jus and already the engines were roaring. With many good wishes from all those left behind, who envied us our glorious task, we rolled to the taking-off place. With a drone of engines one Ju followed the other across the field. Soon the ground vanished beneath our feet. A few seconds later the machines turned out to sea in a great loop and arranged themselves in ordered formation . . . We had scarcely left the Mainland when there was a slight jolt to the stomach, and the Jus dived down towards the foaming waves for we could fly only between 25 and 50 yards above the wave-crests in order to keep out of sight of British fighters and remain hidden. Evenly the engines droned their former song, already in the distance the first contours of the longed-for Island began to show themselves. Then someone began to sing and in a moment the whole of the occupants of the aircraft joined in. With steady voice and shining eyes the battle song

Below: The Dame of Sark, Sibyl Hathaway, was also visited by Maj Lanz and party at La Seigneurie, but was not intimidated by them! *IWM* — HU 25974

resounded through the aircraft: "Wir denn fahren gegen England" (For we're marching against England). Now at last we really were. An unforgettable moment. We still did not know what to expect, battle or peace.'

Lanz's aircraft was the first to land, and he and his adjutant were the first of the party to jump out of the plane, 'I didn't want anyone to take that pleasure from me. Now we had British ground beneath our feet. It was now 14.45hrs. Rapidly each platoon received its orders.'

The new arrivals were met by a smiling Maj Hessel, the OC of Aufklärungsgruppe 123, who told them that everything was quiet both here on the airfield and down in St Peter Port. Then, a few minutes later, at about 15.00hrs, they hauled up the flag 'sewn with British hands', which now was flying for the first time over British territory, a visible symbol of the Germans having taken over Guernsey. Lanz goes on to explain how a few days later he had paid the bill and given it to Maj Hessel so that he could hang it with the flag in the Officers' Mess of his recce squadron — a unique document indeed!

Then the other Jus began to arrive in quick succession. At about 16.00hrs, GenLt Hermann Böttcher, divisional commander of 216. ID arrived, accompanied by his deputy and adjutant, together with Admiral Lindau, so that they could all be a part of this historic occasion. Maj Hessel then handed over command of the island, which he had held since the previous evening, to Maj Lanz, because he wanted to get back to France that evening with his recce squadron. There was a mass of civilian cars abandoned at the airport, so Lanz took one and he and Maj Hessel, driven by a Guernsey policeman — presumably Inspector Sculpher — went down into St Peter Port:

'. . . about 5 miles away, through narrow roads, mostly with fences, hedges and walls on either side, continually bending, devilish difficult to find one's bearings here. Several times thought an approaching wagon was going to crash into us, but that was a typical case of false impression, for here they drive on the left, one must get used to that first, and anyway these fellows drive like the devil.'

Almost certainly Maj Lanz would have been accompanied by the English-speaking MO of 'Gotenhafen', Maj Dr Maas, to act as interpreter, because Lanz spoke little English himself, although the narrative merely says that he was accompanied by an interpreter. Maas had spent some seven years in Africa and made as Lanz recalled: 'an exemplary interpreter. Instead of his medical work, he took over the office of official interpreter and departmental chief for all questions of administration and public relations.' They soon arrived at the Royal Hotel on the Esplanade which Hessel had commandeered the day before.[8] There were hundreds of curious Islanders thronging around the hotel, anxious to see what would happen next. The first list of German Regulations had been published in the previous night's newspaper, so all that remained was for them to meet the Bailiff and explain that Lanz was taking over from Hessel.

Lanz records how they had driven into the park surrounding the Bailiff's house, had rung the bell and been ushered into a 'large richly furnished living room' where he saw 'an old gentleman of 68 in a dark suit'. Hessel explained, via the interpreter, that he had handed over command to Maj Lanz and that he had come to take his leave of the Bailiff and to introduce his successor. In what Lanz describes as being easily his proudest moment of the war, the Bailiff:

'With his arms folded, the old gentleman bowed deeply before the representatives of the German Army. The first time in the history of England that a Governor and the direct representative of His Britannic Majesty has ever bowed to the German Army. He thanked us particularly and repeatedly for the correct behaviour of the German troops and promised to make all necessary for our wishes and regulations to be carried out in the smallest detail. Everything we needed was at our disposal.'

Jersey

Then it was back to the airport, where they found that more '*Tante Jus*' had landed with more troops, so clearly Guernsey was now well and truly occupied. However, none of the other islands had been taken and, as Lanz noted, the island of Jersey, which lay some 16 miles further south, was twice as big as Guernsey and taking it might hold all sorts of new problems. However, he need not have worried as action was already in hand to call on both Jersey and Alderney to surrender. Admiral Lindau had caused a message to be written demanding their surrender[9] and copies had been despatched by aircraft in the early hours of 1 July in pouches with white streamers attached (one source says that the Germans used the sheets from the French officers' sleeping quarters on the airfield they had taken over to make these streamers!). As no reply was received to the messages, two aircraft were then ordered to find out what was going on. The Jersey-bound pilot was a Lt Richard Kern, who, having seen that all seemed peaceful, decided to land at the airport. A German newspaper reporter wrote later:

'Lonely and deserted, the machine rolled over the wide, empty field. Then Lt Kern gripped his pistol and jumped to the ground. He strode towards the administration building followed by the machine, its machine guns at the ready. Nothing happened. Finally, from the airport building emerged an excited man, who to the astonishment of the newcomers, spoke in German. He took the Leutnant to the telephone and got in touch with the Bailiff.'[10]

The Bailiff, Mr Alexander Coutanche, explained that the island was prepared to surrender and that the reason why there were no white flags showing was that they had had to wait for the formal decision of the States and this had only just been given. However, he asked Kern to make sure that Vizeadmiral Lindau was told as quickly as possible. Lt Kern told him that he should assume that from now onwards the Island was under German occupation.

ORDERS OF THE COMMANDANT OF THE GERMAN FORCES IN OCCUPATION OF THE ISLAND OF GUERNSEY

(1)—ALL INHABITANTS MUST BE INDOORS BY 11 P.M. AND MUST NOT LEAVE THEIR HOMES BEFORE 6 A.M.

(2)—WE WILL RESPECT THE POPULATION IN GUERNSEY; BUT, SHOULD ANYONE ATTEMPT TO CAUSE THE LEAST TROUBLE, SERIOUS MEASURES WILL BE TAKEN AND THE TOWN WILL BE BOMBED.

(3)—ALL ORDERS GIVEN BY THE MILITARY AUTHORITY ARE TO BE STRICTLY OBEYED.

(4)—ALL SPIRITS MUST BE LOCKED UP IMMEDIATELY, AND NO SPIRITS MAY BE SUPPLIED, OBTAINED OR CONSUMED HENCEFORTH. THIS PROHIBITION DOES NOT APPLY TO STOCKS IN PRIVATE HOUSES.

(5)—NO PERSON SHALL ENTER THE AERODROME AT LA VILLIAZE.

(6)—ALL RIFLES, AIRGUNS, PISTOLS, REVOLVERS, DAGGERS, SPORTING GUNS, AND ALL OTHER WEAPONS WHATSOEVER, EXCEPT SOUVENIRS, MUST, TOGETHER WITH ALL AMMUNITION, BE DELIVERED AT THE ROYAL HOTEL BY 12 NOON TO-DAY, JULY 1.

(7)—ALL BRITISH SAILORS, AIRMEN AND SOLDIERS ON LEAVE IN THIS ISLAND MUST REPORT AT THE POLICE STATION AT 9 A.M. TO-DAY, AND MUST THEN REPORT AT THE ROYAL HOTEL.

(8)—NO BOAT OR VESSEL OF ANY DESCRIPTION, INCLUDING ANY FISHING BOAT, SHALL LEAVE THE HARBOURS OR ANY OTHER PLACE WHERE THE SAME IS MOORED, WITHOUT AN ORDER FROM THE MILITARY AUTHORITY, TO BE OBTAINED AT THE ROYAL HOTEL. ALL BOATS ARRIVING FROM JERSEY, FROM SARK OR FROM HERM, OR ELSEWHERE, MUST REMAIN IN HARBOUR UNTIL PERMITTED BY THE MILITARY TO LEAVE.

THE CREWS WILL REMAIN ON BOARD. THE MASTER WILL REPORT TO THE HARBOURMASTER, ST. PETER-PORT, AND WILL OBEY HIS INSTRUCTIONS.

(9)—THE SALE OF MOTOR SPIRIT IS PROHIBITED, EXCEPT FOR USE ON ESSENTIAL SERVICES, SUCH AS DOCTORS' VEHICLES, THE DELIVERY OF FOODSTUFFS, AND SANITARY SERVICES WHERE SUCH VEHICLES ARE IN POSSESSION OF A PERMIT FROM THE MILITARY AUTHORITY TO OBTAIN SUPPLIES.

THESE VEHICLES MUST BE BROUGHT TO THE ROYAL HOTEL BY 12 NOON TO-DAY TO RECEIVE THE NECESSARY PERMISSION.

THE USE OF CARS FOR PRIVATE PURPOSES IS FORBIDDEN.

(10)—THE BLACK-OUT REGULATIONS ALREADY IN FORCE MUST BE OBSERVED AS BEFORE.

(11)—BANKS AND SHOPS WILL BE OPEN AS USUAL.

(Signed) THE GERMAN COMMANDANT OF THE ISLAND OF GUERNSEY

JULY 1, 1940.

Above: Orders of the Commandant of the German Forces in Occupation of the Island of Guernsey. *Guernsey Museum and Galleries*

Lt Kern then flew to Guernsey and told Lanz that Jersey was ready to surrender, the formal handing over by the Bailiff being scheduled for 18.00hrs. Lanz recalls:

'That was enough for us. Off we went and even flew over alone to complete the formal surrender . . . twenty minutes later we were circling over the airfield on Jersey. The landing was smooth. As we rolled across the field to the Airport building Haupt von Obernitz came smiling towards us and reported that he had landed with his men on the Island that day and taken possession of it . . . Hptm von Obernitz reported briefly that here on Jersey everything was quiet and under control. Cherbourg was informed quickly through the wireless at the airport and presently, after a short time, the first Jus came directly from Cherbourg, carrying my 1. Kompanie.'

Albrecht Lanz had borrowed the German Imperial War Flag from Maj Hessel, before leaving Guernsey — promising his head as security for it! — so when the last of the company had arrived he organised a proper flag-raising ceremony:

'On the right flank was Oberstlt Plocher with all the other officers present, then a section of the Luftwaffe, consisting of the crews of the Obernitz Squadron, then the men of Assault Detachment "Gotenhafen", and finishing with the whole of 1. Kompanie. Kapitänleutnant Koch, who, naturally, was with us, had the task of hoisting with his own hands the German Imperial War Flag high above the roof of the airport building. I myself gave the orders. With arms at the slope and eyes right, over the airfield rang the command "Hoist Flag!" Slowly and ceremonially over this British territory, also for the first time in history, rose the German Imperial War Flag high upon the mast. Now Jersey too was under German overlordship.'

The indefatigable Lanz had still not finished his first day's work on the Islands. After the ceremony he appointed Hptm Gussek, OC 1. Kompanie, as Island Commander of Jersey, and gave him a quick briefing on the salient points of his new command. In fact Gussek was no stranger to the Island, having been a prisoner of war there during World War 1, incarcerated in a camp established at the foot of Mont à la Brune, St Brelade (see *CIOS Review* No 18, page 63). It was then back to Guernsey for Lanz to deal with the hundreds of administrative matters — not the least being that the Royal Hotel was almost without windows as they had been broken by the bombing attack on the 28th. It was well after midnight when 'this first great day drew to a close'.

Sark

The next few days were equally hectic for Major Lanz. Next on his itinerary was a visit to the little island of Sark, where he was met on landing at the tiny harbour by the Seneschal who took them up to the Seigneurie to meet Sibyl Hathaway, then Dame of Sark, the Island's ruler. She recalled in her autobiography that

Lanz was 'tall, alert, quick spoken, with dark hair and dark eyes. In civilian life he had been a Doctor of both Law and Philosophy, and I believe he came from a family of agricultural machinery manufacturers in Stuttgart. Maas was a Naval surgeon who spoke perfect English and had studied tropical diseases for eight years in Liverpool.' She goes on to say that she judged Lanz to be a fair-minded man, who would never trick anyone by low cunning, but immediately felt there was something about Maas that she did not like — he was just 'too smooth'! They produced a large printed poster in both English and German, headed 'Orders of the Commandant of the German Forces of the Channel Islands' and covering such strictures as the times of the curfew (23.00–06.00hrs); the handing in of firearms of all types; forbidding the sale of drinks; the closing of licensed premises; no assemblies of more than five people allowed in the streets; no boats to leave the harbour without an order from the military authority. It also said that they could keep their cameras and wireless, but only until 1941.

'When I had read the notice I turned to Lanz and said in German, "Please sit down. I will see that these orders are obeyed." Both men seemed astonished that I could speak the language and Maas said, "So you can talk German."

"Badly, but well enough to understand it and to make myself understood."

'Then he gave me a wonderful opportunity by remarking, "You do not appear to be the least afraid." Looking as innocent as possible I asked in a surprised voice, "Is there any reason why I should be afraid of German officers?" This question had an immediate effect. They assured me that I was indeed right in my assumption. Their manners suddenly became most affable and Lanz went so far as to say that if ever I found any difficulties I was to communicate directly with the Commandant of the Channel Islands in Guernsey.' [11]

Dame Sibyl continued to take advantage this way to get preferential treatment throughout the Occupation and found that it paid dividends. Invariably she would go over the head of the local Sark Commandant and deal direct with the High Command in Guernsey which soon 'put a stop to any petty tyranny by local officers in Sark'.

The occupation of Sark took place on 4 July (the Dame's husband, an American, commenting wryly that it was 'a hell of a day on which to be occupied!'). A section of ten men under Obergefreiter Obenhauf and the civil administration worked together, whilst the mass of the population 'gratefully recognised the correctness, generosity and obligingness of the occupying troops'. One cannot help but think that the good Maj Lanz saw the world rather through rose-coloured spectacles and had certainly misjudged the true feelings of the fiercely independent Islanders to whom the occupation was an anathema from the outset. He would die far away on a Russian battlefield long before the going really got tough for both the Garrison and the Islanders.

Chapter 2

Military Organisation: Higher Organisations

Before covering the organisation of the occupation forces, it is necessary to explain briefly the outline organisation of the German armed forces (Wehrmacht) and how the various levels of command fitted together in the somewhat complicated family tree which towered above the troops on the Islands. At the top, of course, was Adolf Hitler and then immediately below him the headquarters of the Wehrmacht High Command — *Oberkommando der Wehrmacht* (OKW). This was Germany's supreme command throughout World War 2 and comprised:

- Wehrmacht Operations Office (later renamed the Wehrmacht Operations Staff)

- Office of Foreign Affairs and Intelligence

- Economics and Armaments Office

- Office for General Wehrmacht Affairs

The main task of the OKW was to correlate and supervise the individual strategy of the three Service headquarters:

- *Oberkommando des Heeres* (OKH) — Army High Command

- *Oberkommando der Kriegsmarine* (OKM) — Naval High Command

- *Oberkommando der Luftwaffe* (OKL) — Air Force High Command

Chief of the OKW was Generalfeldmarschall Wilhelm Keitel, who was involved in all of Hitler's strategic decisions. His fawning attitude towards the Führer earned him the contempt of many of his colleagues, who called him 'Lakeitel' — a punning reference to the German word for footman or lackey (*Lakai*).

The OKW's Operation Office — *Wehrmachtführungsamt* (WFA) — had three main branches: National Defence, Wehrmacht Communications, and Press and Propaganda. When war began the WFA was headed by Alfred Jodl, then a GenMaj. After Keitel he was Hitler's closest adviser on all matters relating to top-level Wehrmacht operations. It was his job to keep Hitler informed of all military developments and to pass on Hitler's orders to the various operational commands. Inside the National Defence branch were officers from the OKH, OKM and OKL, who were, in effect, Hitler's working staff. They had to produce the data on which the Supreme Commander could base his decisions and then prepare his directives for the conduct of the war.

DAS HEER (THE ARMY) — OKH

The C-in-C of the OKH was GenOb Walter von Brauchitsch, who held the post until 1941 when Hitler took personal command of the Army. His HQ was divided into a field head-quarters and a home command, the latter stationed in Berlin. The Commander of the Replacement Army (*Befehlshaber des Ersatzheeres*) was appointed to take control of the home command, with responsibility for the General Army Office, the Army Ordnance Office, the Army Administrative Office, the Inspector of Officer Cadet Courses, the Inspectors of Arms and Services, and the Chief of Army Judiciary. The field HQ comprised the Army General Staff and the Army Personnel Staff and was commanded by the Chief of the General Staff, with the *Oberquartermeister* I (OQu I) as his deputy. Subordinate to the OKH were the army groups, followed in turn by the armies, corps and divisions. In occupied France the 'chain' led down through Army Group HQ to HQ Seventh Army (AOK7) thence to HQ LXXXIV Armeekorps and from there to the divisional HQ on the Islands.

If one takes the situation that existed in Northern France from 15 January 1944, when Rommel's HQ Armeegruppe B assumed responsibility for the Atlantic and Channel coasts north of the Loire River, then the various personalities in the chain were:

Oberbefehlshaber West

Commander: Generalfeldmarschall Gerd von Rundstedt
HQ location: Paris

The highly experienced, competent but uninspiring von Rundstedt, who was retired and recalled at least three times during the war, had taken over from Generalfeldmarschall Hermann von Witzleben as OB West on 15 March 1942. He remained in charge until he was sacked in July 1944, but was then reinstated two months later.

Armeegruppe B

Commander: Generalfeldmarschall Erwin Rommel
HQ location: La Roche-Guyon, on the Lower Seine, some 80 miles from the coast

Above:
The Führer in his HQ *Felsennest*, located near Bad Münstereifel, south of Bonn, where he spent part of the time during the Battle for France. Here he is being breifed by GenOb Wilhelm Keitel, Cheif of the OKW. *Author's Collection*

Rommel commanded two armies (the Seventh and the Fifteenth) and also the LXXXVIII Armeekorps on the North Sea Coast (*Befehlshaber Niederländer*). The brilliant, charismatic 'Desert Fox' threw his considerable expertise into strengthening the Atlantic Wall and then, after the Allied landing, to defending it. However, he was never allowed a free hand and was seriously wounded on 17 July 1944, when his staff car was strafed by Allied fighter-bombers near Livarot and paid no further part in proceedings from then on. He was replaced by Generalfeldmarschall Günther von Kluge, who was also at the time OB West, having taken over from von Rundstedt.

As has been mentioned, Rommel had a great aversion to the waste of manpower locked up in the Channel Islands, but was powerless to get them released.

Armee 7 (Channel Coast Brittany — R Seine)

Commander: GenOb Friedrich Dollmann
HQ location: Le Mans

Dollmann was an expert in long-range artillery and a highly experienced officer. However, he had been appointed to command Seventh Army in October 1939 at the age of 57, so he was rather old for the job and in addition was large, corpulent and suffered from heart trouble. Basically he did not approve of Hitler's methods and was sacked by him for losing Cherbourg (von Rundstedt and Rommel had refused to dismiss him). Rommel's Chief of Staff, Hans Speidel, encapsulated Dollmann's views when he wrote of him, 'The methods of Hitler had wounded him deeply, both as a soldier and a man.' Dollmann died of a heart attack at his battle headquarters on 29 June 1944, a few days after he lost Cherbourg.

LXXXIV Armeekorps

Commander: General der Artillerie Erich Marcks
HQ location: St Lô

His corps would bear the brunt of the D-Day landings and would later be destroyed in the Falaise pocket. Despite having a wooden leg (he had been injured in Russia), Knight's Cross holder (with Oak Leaves) Erich Marcks was an energetic, capable and well-liked commander who had commanded LXXXIV Armeekorps since 1 August 1943. He foretold that the Allied assault would come in Normandy and was killed near Carentan on 12 June 1944, when cannon fire from a strafing fighter struck his car. Interestingly, he was born in Berlin on 6 June 1891, so he was celebrating his 53rd birthday when the Allies launched their assault on Normandy: what a birthday present! He shared his birthday with Rommel's wife Lucie and got on well with Rommel who wrote of him, 'We get on well together, although we're two very different sorts.'

Then came HQ 319. ID in Guernsey, the other divisions in Marcks' LXXXIV Armeekorps, as at 6 June 1944, being 243., 352., 709. and 716.IDs.

DIE KRIEGSMARINE (THE NAVY) — OKM

The C-in-C of the German Navy was Admiral Erich Raeder who had undoubtedly been the main architect in the rapid

Right: Generalfeldmarschall Gerd von Rundstedt (centre of group with light facings on the lapels of his greatcoat) was Oberbefelshaber West, and his HQ was located in Paris. He is seen here with other senior officers and staff, inspecting part of the Atlantic Wall defences. *IWM — HU 17160*

Below: Armeegruppe B was commanded by the charismatic Generalfeldmarschall Erwin Rommel, hero of North Africa and the youngest field marshal in the German Army. Despite his undoubted influence with Hitler, he could not get him to take sufficient interest in defences in the West. Here Rommel (with baton) inspects part of the Atlantic Wall. *IWM — HU 3060*

prewar expansion of the Kriegsmarine, including the launching of the pocket battleships, new submarines and the build-up of the naval air arm. Under Raeder, the OKM was concerned with strategic and operational planning, keeping under its direct control the raiders plus their intelligence and supply systems. Initially below the OKM were two commands: *Kriegsmarinegruppe Est* (Naval Group East) and *Kriegsmarinegruppe West* (Naval Group West), each of which was responsible for all naval operations in their respective areas and for the safety of coastal waters. Because most of the larger ships operated in the North Sea, Group West under Admiral Theodor Krancke, became the most important part of the navy and this inevitably led to friction with the OKM. Krancke had previously been Permanent Representative of the Supreme C-in-C of the Navy at Hitler's headquarters from January 1942 until March 1943, then moved on to become Supreme C-in-C of Naval Group West; prior to this he had been 'Admiral Norway' and before that had taken the pocket battleship *Admiral Scheer* on its most successful cruise of the war.

The naval network in France was vast and covered a multiplicity of naval artillery and AA detachments (*Marinenartillerieabteilung und Marineflakabteilung*), as well as a mass of ports and naval bases. From Group West command went down to the Admiral in command of the Channel Coast (*Kommandieren Admiral Kanalküste*), below whom the coast was split into a number of Sea Defence Areas (*Seeverteidigungsbereiche*), each commanded by a *Seekommandant* — normally abbreviated to SEEKO. Until the summer of 1942, the Channel Islands came under SEEKO Cherbourg but that July the Islands became a Sea Defence Area in their own right, with Kapitän zur See Julius Steinbach being appointed as Naval Commander of the Channel Islands (*SEEKO-KI*). He would stay in that post for two years before being replaced by Vizeadmiral Friedrich Hüffmeier, a fervent and ruthless Nazi, who always had designs upon becoming 'top dog' on the Islands and eventually succeeded in February 1945. From then on the Kriegsmarine influence in the Islands increased considerably, with naval officers being given many of the key appointments. This followed the national trend, as Hitler felt he could no longer trust the army generals after the attempted assassination of 20 July 1944.

DIE LUFTWAFFE (THE AIR FORCE) — OKL

The Luftwaffe — German Air Force — was directed by the *Reichsluftfahrt Ministerium* (Air Ministry) which was divided into two main parts: the OKL which was concerned with the command of the air force; and the office of the *Reichsminister der Luftfahrt* (Minister for Air), which dealt with the purely administrative matters such as financial control and aircraft production. Reichsmarschall Hermann Göring was both C-in-C of the Air Force and Minister for Air. The OKL was divided into a number of directorates which were grouped under the Chief of Operations Staff, the Chief of the General Staff and the Quartermaster General thus:

- Chief of Operations Staff — Operations, Training, Intelligence
- CGS — Historical
- QMG — Organisation, Movements, Equipment, Personnel

The Chief of Operations Staff was responsible for the implementation of air strategy as laid down by the CGS as well as being responsible for operations. The CGS also controlled various inspectorates dealing with such flying subjects as flight safety, fighter tactics, etc.

Luftflotten (Air Fleets)

In 1939 all operational flying units were divided between four Luftflotten, each being a balanced force of fighter, bomber, reconnaissance, ground-attack, and other aircraft. They covered north and east Germany, northwest Germany, southwest Germany, southeast Germany, Austria and Czechoslovakia respectively. More air fleets were formed as the war progressed. Each air fleet was divided into several *Luftgaue* (Air Zones) with an HQ responsible for providing the men for the technical and administrative tasks at the airfields in their zone. In parallel with the Luftgau organisation was the *Fliegerkorps* (Air Corps) which operated the aircraft. The basic flying unit was a *Gruppe* (Group) of 30 aircraft and normally occupied one airfield. A Gruppe comprised the *Staffeln* (Squadrons) each with a nominal strength of nine aircraft with air crews, technical and signal ground personnel.

Command structure

From the OKL command of air forces in the Islands' area went down to Luftflotte 3, commanded by Generalfeldmarschall Hugo Sperrle, who had commanded the Condor Legion in Spain, then Luftwaffengruppe 3 (which became Luftflotte 3 just before the outbreak of war). His Luftflotte had provided the air support for the powerful armoured thrust which had sliced through southern Belgium and northern France, splitting the Allied armies in two. He would also command Luftflotte 3 during the Battle of Britain and the long period of night attacks that followed.

In the spring of 1941, a large proportion of his aircraft were extracted from his air fleet and transferred over to the Eastern Front to support the attack on Russia. Nevertheless, Sperrle continued to maintain steady pressure on the British Isles with his much reduced bomber force, successfully tying down many British fighter squadrons and considerable manpower on AA gunsites defending the UK against these raids. However, from D-Day onwards, Luftflotte 3 was almost completely overwhelmed by the Allied air forces and could do little to influence events any further — Rommel went so far as to make a formal complaint to the OKW about the total lack of Luftwaffe support. In August 1944, Sperrle was transferred to the reserve. From Luftflotte 3, command went directly to the *General der Luftwaffe Kanalinseln* (Air Force Commander Channel Islands), whose responsibilities covered the important AA (Flak) batteries on all the Islands, as well as the aerodromes, all flying and aircraft maintenance.

Chapter 3
Military Organisation: The Years of Occupation

THE OCCUPATION FORCES

As we have seen from the first chapter, the ground force which had initially occupied the Channel Islands was based upon sub-units of 216. ID. However, in addition to army units there were also naval and air force elements with their own tasks to perform. Before looking at all of these units in more detail in this and succeeding chapters, it must be emphasised that, although these were the first units of the Wehrmacht to land, they were not all destined to remain on the Islands for the entire period of the Occupation.

Troop movements, caused in particular by the effects of the opening of the war against Russia in the East, which began with Operation 'Barbarossa' in June 1941, caused continual changes to the manpower structure in all other areas from then on, including from time to time even in the Channel Islands garrison. One of the main effects was to withdraw fit, well-trained soldiers and replace them with older, less well-trained and, in some cases, non-German troops. This was also true — but in reverse — concerning the effects of Adolf Hitler's decision, made in June 1941, to fortify the Islands, as this increased the size and armaments of the garrison. Efforts were made at various levels, even up to army group, to remove some of the garrison, especially after D-Day, but this was always strongly resisted at the highest level.

Three divisions were involved in providing troops for the Islands' garrisons: the 216. ID, then the 83. and 319. IDs. In addition, as well as more fighting men from all three Services entering the garrison, the military and civilian administrators also arrived. This organisation, which was known as FK515 (*Feldkommandantur* (FK) = Field Command), began to make its presence felt in mid-August 1940, establishing its headquarters in Jersey, while the Army HQ was in Guernsey. This duality of power bases would prove both a help and a hindrance to the running of the operational and administrative tasks on the Islands.

The five years of Occupation can best be broken down into three periods:

From 1 July 1940 to mid-August 1940

This was the initial period when 216. ID troops were in charge of the Islands on their own (apart from the Kriegsmarine and Luftwaffe elements which had landed with them), carrying out all operational and administrative tasks.

From mid-August 1940 to late 1941

During this period FK515 arrived to take over the administration of the Islands on 9 August; Hitler issued his fortification order (15 June 1941), followed on 20 October 1941 by his fortification directive which spelt out exactly what had to be done. These events led to a considerable influx of both military personnel and civilians into the Islands, some merely visiting to survey and plan what had to be done to strengthen the Islands' defences, others to remain permanently. 216. ID officially handed over to 319. ID at 01.00hrs on 30 April 1941 and was partly withdrawn. Some 83. ID units took over on Alderney for a short period, whilst some 216. ID units remained on the Islands for most of the summer. In order to make the very complicated reinforcement/replacement programme a little easier to follow, the layout of 319. ID has been described in Period 3, although of course it had started much earlier in 1941.

From late 1941 to 9 May 1945

During this period the size of the garrison reached its maximum; forced and slave labour was brought in to complete the massive defences, then shipped back to mainland France when their tasks were completed; post D-Day, everyone — garrison and civilian population alike — had to face the rigours of the 'Hunger Winter'.

Below: Maj Lanz, first commander of the Channel Islands, arrives at the door of his office, in the former Channel Islands Hotel on Glategny Esplanade, Guernsey. Note the Kommandantur's flag on the mudguard of the Wolseley, the AA recommendation and the 'Old Bill' opening the car door! *IWM* — HU 3616

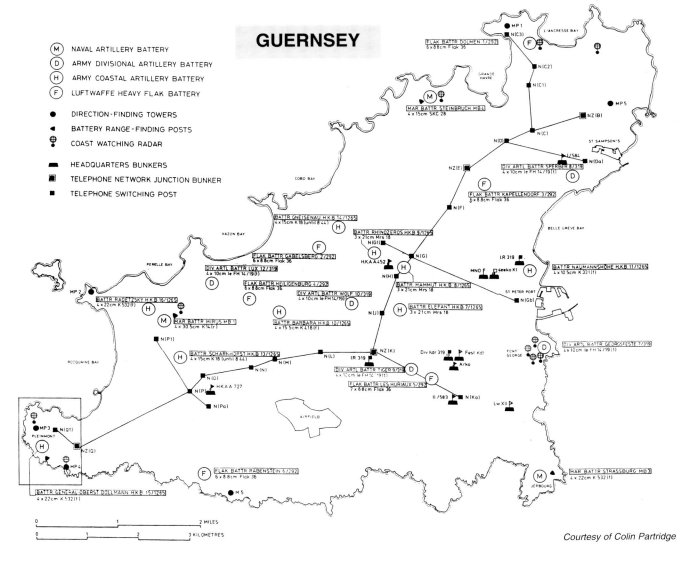

GUERNSEY

M NAVAL ARTILLERY BATTERY
D ARMY DIVISIONAL ARTILLERY BATTERY
H ARMY COASTAL ARTILLERY BATTERY
F LUFTWAFFE HEAVY FLAK BATTERY

● DIRECTION-FINDING TOWERS
◄ BATTERY RANGE-FINDING POSTS
⊕ COAST WATCHING RADAR

▬ HEADQUARTERS BUNKERS
◼ TELEPHONE NETWORK JUNCTION BUNKER
▪ TELEPHONE SWITCHING POST

Courtesy of Colin Partridge

Period 1:
1 JULY 1940 TO MID-AUGUST 1940

Once the assault force had spread itself over the Islands, the dispositions of the garrison were as follows:

Heer units

GUERNSEY
Inselkommandant (Island Commandant): Maj Dr Albrecht Lanz

I./IR 396, 216. ID (see Box 1), less detachments detailed below, plus Quarter of *AT Kompanie* (Anti-Tank Company) IR 396

JERSEY
Island Commandant: Hptm Erich Gussek

1 x *Schutzen Kompanie* (Rifle Company) of I./IR 396, 216. ID
Half of the *Maschinengewehr Kompanie* (Machine Gun Company), IR 396

Quarter of AT Kompanie (Anti-Tank Company) IR 396
1 x *Pionier Zug* (Engineer Platoon) of 4.Pi./216. ID
Platoon of *Radfahrer* (cycle-borne infantry) [1]

ALDERNEY
Island Commandant: Unterfeldwebel Schmidt

1 x Infantry platoon, I./IR 396

SARK
Island Commandant: Obergefreiter Obenhauf

1 x Infantry section (*Gruppe*), I./IR 396

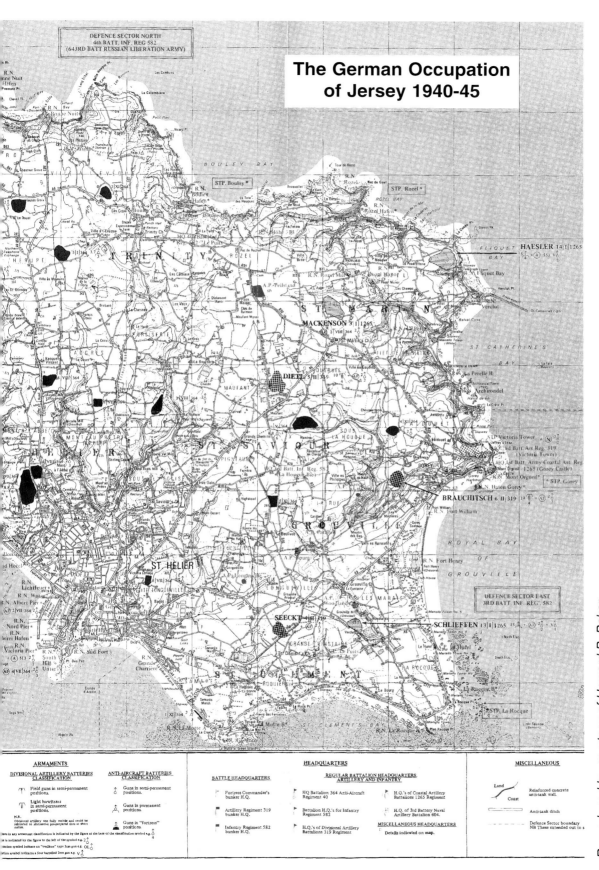

The German Occupation
of Jersey 1940-45

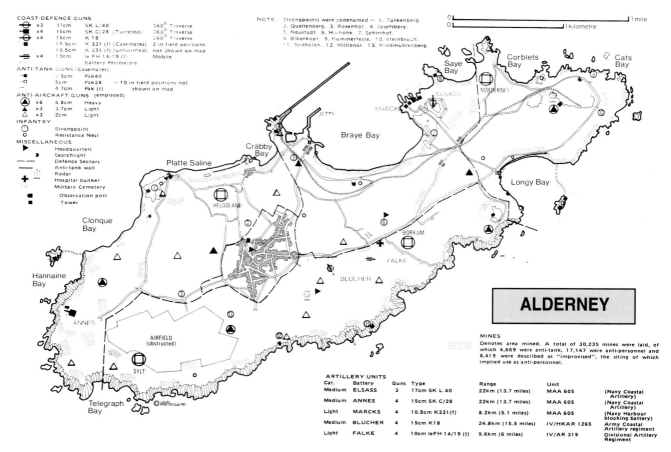

ALDERNEY

MINES
Denotes area mined. A total of 30,235 mines were laid, of which 4,669 were anti-tank, 17,147 were anti-personnel and 8,419 were described as "improvised", the siting of which implied use as anti-personnel.

ARTILLERY UNITS						
Cat.	Battery	Guns	Type	Range	Unit	
Medium	ELSASS	3	17cm SK L 40	22km (13.7 miles)	MAA 605	(Navy Coastal Artillery)
Medium	ANNES	4	15cm SK C/28	22km (13.7 miles)	MAA 605	(Navy Coastal Artillery)
Light	MARCKS	4	10.5cm K331(f)	8.2km (5.1 miles)	MAA 605	(Navy Harbour blocking battery)
Medium	BLÜCHER	4	15cm K18	24.8km (15.5 miles)	IV/HKAR 1265	Army Coastal Artillery regiment
Light	FALKE	4	10cm leFH 14/19 (t)	9.6km (6 miles)	IV/AR 319	Divisional Artillery Regiment

Courtesy of Colin Partridge

216. Infanterie Division

The home station of the division was Hameln, in Wehrkreis XI[2] and the division was made up of Landwehr personnel from Hanover, Brunswick and Anhalt.[3] It was a third wave[4] division having been formed on 29 August 1939. It had fought throughout the campaigns in Poland and France, during the latter campaign as part of the Sixth Army, finishing up around Cherbourg, in June 1940, so it was the obvious division to be chosen to send units to the Channel Islands. Its basic composition was:

IR 348

IR 396 (I.Btl of this regiment was commanded by Maj Lanz and chosen for the invasion of the Islands)

IR 398

AR 216

216 Reconnaissance Battalion

216 Anti-Tank Battalion

216 Engineer Battalion

216 Signal Battalion

GenLt Hermann Böttcher commanded the division from August 1939 until October 1940, when GenMaj Kurt Himer took over. After serving in the Channel Islands the division was sent to the Russian Front. On arrival, whilst it was disembarking from the troop trains at Sukhinitch, one of the Fourth Army's main ammunition dumps, it was surrounded by Red Army troops of the Soviet Tenth Army, who attacked on 3 January 1942, before hardly any of the troops had detrained (just divisional headquarters, one and a half battalions of IR 396 and one battalion of IR 398). With only some 4,000 divisional troops, together with 1,000 supply troops and some Soviet volunteers, the Channel Island veterans held off all the assaults and saved the town. They were at the time commanded by GenLt Baron von und zu Werner Gilsa, who had taken over from GenMaj Himer (who was later killed at Sevastapol in 1942). Gilsa went on to command LXXXIX Armee Korps and later Korps Gilsa, and was awarded the Knight's Cross with Oak Leaves. His division was rescued from Sukhinitch and went on serving with Army Group Centre. Later in the campaign, in July 1943 it suffered very heavy losses at Kursk, and was so badly reduced that winter that it had to be disbanded. Survivors were absorbed into 102. ID.

Kriegsmarine units

Naval Assault Group 'Gotenhafen'
As soon as Operation 'Green Arrow' had been successfully concluded, the group was withdrawn for 'special employment in Paris'.

Harbour Supervisory Staff
These naval personnel had taken over the port installations on Jersey and Guernsey, requisitioning several small boats and taking over the cable stations.

Cable laying
The undersea cable, which had been laid by the GPO as late as May 1940, was connected from Fliquet, Jersey, to Pirou on the Normandy coast. The Kriegsmarine made several attempts over the years of occupation to lay a cable from Alderney direct to Cherbourg; however, due to the rip of the tide, it was always torn out.

Luftwaffe units

During the early months of the Occupation the Luftwaffe personnel outnumbered those of the other two services. This was particularly because the airfields were used for staging and refuelling by German aircraft taking part in the Battle of Britain. For example, there were:

- LAA units. In his report, Admiral Lindau states that there were initially six 2cm and six 3.7cm light anti-aircraft guns on each of the two main islands, making a total of 24 LAA guns, which were also suitable for firing against sea targets.

- Reconnaissance Group 123 (Aufklärungsgruppe 123). Hptm Obernitz and his group were based on Jersey.

- Fighter Group 53 (Jagdgruppe 53) was based on Guernsey.

- Airfield construction companies (*Luftwaffe Baukompanie*) were located and busy on both the main airfields, carrying out enlargement work.

Period 2:
MID-AUGUST 1940 TO LATE 1941

In August 1940, the position of the Channel Islands within the German occupied territories in Europe was regularised by officially incorporating them into the French Department of *Manche* (Channel) as a sub-district of Military Government Area A. This led to the sending of a Field Command, plus the necessary staff, to administer the daily life of the Islands. The working of this Field Command (FK515) is covered in a later chapter. Suffice to record here that the personnel was made up of mainly German civil service bureaucrats, divided into departments dealing with such matters as the running of agriculture, power, transport, etc. FK515 established its headquarters in Jersey at Victoria College House, St Helier. It also had offices in Guernsey and Alderney, plus an 'outpost' in Sark.

The head (*Feldkommandant*) of FK515 was Oberst Friedrich Schumacher, who arrived on 9 August 1940. His organisation had two departments, military and civil, just as were to be found in higher headquarters in other occupied areas. The staff of FK515 was comprised of civilian personnel who wore uniform, were issued with pistols and ammunition and did a certain amount of regular military training. As Charles Cruickshank points out, there was considerable antipathy between FK515 and the troops of the garrison, but infighting such as this was not unique to the Channel Islands. However, because in the Islands the two organisations were working cheek by jowl and

the need for a large garrison grew rather than diminished, FK515 personnel:

'. . . *resented this, particularly those of them who were civilians in uniform who bore no great love for combat troops. The Wehrmacht for their part made no secret of the fact that they despised the military government officials. Since they had little to do other than fire the anti-aircraft and coastal guns from time to time there was plenty of opportunity for mutual resentment to build up.*'[5]

Schumacher would remain until October 1941, when he was replaced by Oberst Friedrich Knackfuss, who remained in charge until February 1944, then being replaced by Maj I. V. Heider, when it became a *Platzkommandantur*.

A military commander arrives

On 19 September 1940, Oberst Graf Rudolf von Schmettow set up his HQ as *Befehlshaber der britische Kanalinseln* (BdbK) — Commander of the Channel Islands (henceforth Befehlshaber) — above the two island commanders Lanz and Gussek. His HQ was on Jersey, initially at 'Monaco' on St Saviour's Road, St Helier, but it later moved to the Metropole Hotel in Roseville Street.

When 319. ID arrived in mid-July 1941, the divisional commander (GenMaj Erich Müller) was senior to von

Schmettow, so he became BdbK, with his HQ in Guernsey. As we shall see later, when Müller was posted to the Eastern Front in 1943, von Schmettow was not only promoted to command 319. ID, but also became BdbK, with his HQ very firmly in Guernsey and located in a large Georgian house called 'The Oberlands' at La Corbinière. In the grounds the OT constructed two command bunkers and a barrack block to house the soldiers.

Count Rudolf von Schmettow was born in Berlin on 8 January 1891, had joined the army in 1909 and was commissioned in 1911 into the cavalry (Cuirassiers). Prewar, he served in the Reichsheer, was an Oberstleutnant in 1935 and promoted Oberst in 1938. He began World War 2 commanding IR 164 in 62.ID, which fought well in Poland and France. He was a nephew of Generalfeldmarschall von Rundstedt, was the holder of the German Cross in Gold and was by all accounts a pleasant man — Baron von Aufsess calls him 'the little Saxon', who stuttered when he got excited, whilst Ambrose Sherwill described him in a letter to the Home Office as being 'a man of great charm and humanity'.

Werner Wagenknecht, a medical sergeant whom we will meet in Chapter 4, also had a high opinion of his commander: 'The General of the occupation division walked without an escort and always had chocolate and sweets in his pockets for the children.'

He certainly built up a reputation for favouring the Channel Islanders and his almost lenient attitude made him the target of Vizeadmiral Hüffmeier — who had been appointed as his Chief of Staff and then plotted to oust him. Hüffmeier eventually succeeded on 28 February 1945, when von Schmettow announced that he was giving up command of the 319. ID and retiring to Germany on health reasons, where he would be transferred to the reserve.

Extra troops arrive

At the same time as the BdbK was established, two new units arrived to strengthen the garrison. Once they had arrived, then the original infantry companies from IR 396 were recalled to the mainland. These new units were *Maschinengewehr Bataillon* (Machine Gun Battalion) 16 and *Panzerjägerabteilung* (Anti-tank Battalion) 652. These new units were not an integral part of 216. ID, but rather both were GHQ troops that could be attached to any division for special duties. In his article on 216. ID, Michael Ginns explains that MG Btl 16 had been formed in March 1940, to man machine gun posts in the Eifel district of Germany's frontier with Belgium. The average age of the troops was 32 years and it had taken part in the Battle of France as part of 1. Kavallerie Division. It was then transferred to 216. ID and moved to Guernsey, where it established its HQ on 13 September 1940. It would remain there for only a year before moving to Jersey where it stayed for the rest of the war. Unfortunately, little is known about the origins of the anti-tank battalion, whose guns (3.7cm Pak 35/36) were the largest artillery present on the Islands at that time, backed up by similar calibre weapons belonging to the Luftwaffe.

Home Defence battalions

In addition to manning shoreline defensive positions, the garrison troops now had to take on the tasks of guarding fuel points and stores dumps, plus more headquarters and even the residence of the Befehlshaber. As might have been expected, there just were not enough soldiers to tackle these extra tasks, so men of an older age group who made up the *Landschutz Bataillonen* (Home Defence battalions) were drafted into both Jersey and Guernsey. Another problem was the constant changeover of personnel between Islands which caused endless turbulence and difficulties. This was recognised and led to more reinforcement. By early 1941 the following reinforcements had arrived:

Guernsey: I., II., III./IR 398 to supplement MG Btl 16.

Jersey: HQ Coy of I./IR 398, all of IV./IR 398, half of the AT company of IR 398, plus the HQ and two companies of Engineer Btl 216.

Alderney: None, still defended by just one platoon; however it was now from IR 348 (based on Cherbourg).

83. ID takes over in Alderney

83. Infanterie Division

83.ID's home station was Hamburg in Wehrkreis X, which covered Schleswig-Holstein, northern Hanover and, from 1940, part of Danish Slesvig. Its basic composition was:

IR 251
IR 257
IR 277
AR 183
   183 Reconnaissance Battalion
   183 Anti-tank Battalion
   183 Engineer Battalion
   183 Signal Battalion

Formed in the mid-1939 mobilisation from reservists, 83. ID fought in Poland and then France. After going home for Christmas 1940, it came back to France for occupation duty in the Cherbourg area. As its positions were closest to Alderney, it was decided that when 216. ID units left the island in summer 1941, they should be replaced by units of 83. ID. This, however, was only a temporary arrangement and by early 1942 they had all been replaced by 319. ID.

83. ID, like 216. ID, was transferred to the Russian front, fighting in Army Group Centre during the defensive battles of 1942 and 1943, when it was transferred to Army Group North that autumn. It took part in the withdrawal from Leningrad, the retreat through the Baltic States and the battles of the Courland Pocket. It finally surrendered to the Red Army in May 1945.

Its commander in France was GenLt Kurt von der Chevallerie, holder of the Knight's Cross with Oak Leaves; later, in Russia, GenLt Theodor Scherer, also a holder of the Knight's Cross with Oak Leaves, commanded 1942–44.

Geographically, Alderney was nearer to France than it was to the other islands, being only 15 miles from Cherbourg, yet 25 miles from Guernsey and 40 miles from Jersey. It therefore seemed more logical to the Germans that Alderney should be garrisoned by the division occupying the Cherbourg area, which was 83. ID, once 216. ID had been posted to the Eastern Front. Therefore they also took over Alderney and, according to the late Theodor Pantcheff, had a garrison of some 450 there in June 1941.

At the end of July, the reinforced 5. Kompanie of IR 277 arrived under Hptm Carl Hoffmann who became Island Commandant, with his HQ at the Connaught Hotel. By November 1941, there were over 2,000 German servicemen on Alderney — over 1,100 Heer, some 200 Kriegsmarine and 1,100 Luftwaffe. These figures were soon to pass the 3,000 mark and, in addition, the first OT labour contingent was about to arrive.

Hoffmann would soon lose his post as Island Commandant to Oberstlt Gleden and a few weeks later, in January 1942, the command of the island passed over to 319. ID.

Visits by planning teams

One of the most important visitors to the Islands was GenMaj Rudolf Schmetzer, Inspector of Fortifications at OB West (*Inspekteur Landbefestig West*), and his Fortress Engineer Staff, who carried out a careful study of the Islands. He quickly realised that if guns of sufficient calibre and range were positioned on the Islands and on the adjacent French coast, then not only would they be able to protect the Channel Islands, but also the Bay of St Malo, thus obviating the necessity to fortify heavily the Cotentin Peninsula. This appealed to Hitler and, as we shall see, led to the vast array of heavy coastal artillery which arrived on the Islands. Another important visitor was Dr Fritz Todt, who came in November 1941 and whose Organization Todt would undertake the fortification programme using some 16,000 forced labour workers. This is covered in a future chapter.

Left:
The Town Hall in York Street, St Helier, became the first German HQ in Jersey. It was swiftly named by the locals: the 'Rat House' (the German for town hall is *Rathaus*)! *IWM* — HU 5790

Below:
Under new management. Fort George near St Peter Port was used by the Germans as a barracks and also as the location for one of their military cemeteries. It was badly bombed in 1944. *IWM* — HU 29169

319. Infanterie Division

The home station of this division was Kassel in Wehrkreis IX, which covered Hessen and part of Thuringia. Its basic composition was:

IR 582

IR 583

IR 584

AR 319

AR 319 Reconnaissance Company

319 Anti-tank Battalion

319 Engineer Battalion

319 Signal Company

(See next chapter for details of reinforcements received whilst serving in the Channel Islands)

319. ID was formed at Gera on 15 November 1940, as a division in the 13th Wave of conscription, which was aimed at creating nine new divisions for employment in occupied Western Europe. The core of these new divisions was a cadre of experienced officers and NCOs who had all seen action in Poland and/or France. The cadre for 319. ID came from units of all types in 87., 169., 299. and 351.IDs. They were under training in their Wehrkreis from November 1940 until March 1941, then, the following month, moved to France.

319. ID officially took over from IR 216 at 00.01hrs 30 April 1941, although there were some sub-units of IR 216 which remained for most of the summer of 1941. 319. ID was responsible from then on for all the Channel Islands (but see below for the special situation in Alderney). For a while it was also responsible for St Malo and a sector of the French coast. When Hitler became convinced that the Allies would have to take the Islands before they could land on the French coast, 319. ID was massively reinforced until it was easily the largest infantry division in the German Army. The detail of this build-up has already been covered, but as we will see, Russian and Georgian volunteers were included in the reinforcements.

Isolated when the Allies landed in Normandy, the division remained marooned after the Normandy front collapsed, although some troops were transferred back to the mainland and fought in the battles of mid-1944, III.Pi/319. ID, for example, being captured in Cherbourg. The majority stayed on the Islands throughout the 'Hunger Winter' and surrendered at 07.14hrs on 9 May 1945, seven hours after the official end of the war in Europe. Throughout the months that he was in charge of Army

Group B, Rommel had tried to get the enormous garrison reduced, requesting that it be returned to the mainland. He dared to put his request directly to the Führer, who abruptly told his favourite field marshal that the matter was closed and he was not to ask again! The fate of the garrison was very clear to the rest of Army Group B and GenLt Hans Speidel, Rommel's Chief of Staff, comments caustically in his book *We defended Normandy* that the average soldiers: '. . . with their sure instinct for the incongruous, had nicknamed the 319. ID the "Canada Division" — as they reckoned that it was sure to go into the Canadian prisoner-of-war camps!'

During its sojourn in the Islands the division was commanded by GenLt Erich Müller (1942–43) who had been commanding since November 1940. Holder of the German Cross in silver, he went on to be the Commandant of Danzig and later commanded 603.ID until he was captured in August 1944. He ended up in a Russian POW camp where he remained until 1955.

No such fate befell his successor, GenLt Graf Rudolf von Schmettow (1944–45), holder of the German Cross in gold, who was summarily 'retired' when Vizeadmiral Hüffmeier took over as BdbK, but survived the end of the war and visited the Channel Islands as a tourist postwar! Finally there was GenMaj Rudolf Wulf, holder of the Knight's Cross with Oak Leaves, who took over on 1 March 1945 and surrendered with his division at the end of the Occupation.

The three infantry regiments of 319. ID (IRs 582, 583 and 584) eventually ended up with IR 582 stationed in Jersey and the other two IRs both in Guernsey. However, they did not go directly to their final locations. Troop movements began at 00.01hrs on 1 May 1941 and, because of the double banking which is always necessary during such a complicated handover/takeover, additional property had to be requisitioned and troops temporarily billeted in civilian houses. At first it had not been intended to move the complete division to the Islands, so the divisional HQ and engineer battalion (Pioneer Battalion 319) remained at Granville in Normandy, together with IR 583, which held defensive positions there, centred around the River Vire area. Main initial moves were:

- PzJgAbt 652 moved to France from Jersey and is replaced (temporarily) by one battalion of IR 584, which eventually then moved on to Guernsey.

- IR 582 moved into Jersey.

- IR 584 moved into Guernsey and was joined by its missing battalion from Jersey (see above).

- MG Btl 16, which was part of the island's garrison with 216. ID, moved to Jersey once the three new Infantry Regiments of 319. ID had got themselves properly established in their permanent locations. The MG battalion stayed on Jersey for the rest of the war.

The strength of the garrison and sample weapon strength

Table 1:
Personnel Strength of the Channel Islands Garrison as at 30 September 1944

Branch of Service	Guernsey	Jersey	Alderney	Total
ARMY Infantry	4,150	3,900	800	8,940
Anti-tank	430	360	-	790
Tank	180	130	20	330
Artillery	520	820	70	1,410
Coastal Artillery	1,130	1,120	150	2,400
Engineers	90	360	10	460
Signals	180	120	70	370
Supply Troops	720	1,150	200	2,070
AIR FORCE	1,850	1,450	1,050	4,350
NAVY	1,420	1,890	150	3,460
CONSTRUCTION TROOPS	310	150	150	610
ARMED FORCES TOTAL	10,980	11,450	2,670	25,100
ORGANIZATION TODT	260	170	40	470
GRAND TOTAL	11,240	11,620	2,710	25,570

Table 1 gives details of the personnel on the strength of 319. ID and other units as at 30 September 1944. The source of this information and for most of the facts and figures in this chapter is an article by Michael Ginns, which appeared in *CIOS (Jersey) Review* No 19, dated April 1991, and I am most indebted to him and the Society for allowing me to use this information. Table 2 gives a sample weapon strength of 319. ID as at 1 August 1943, again from the same source.

Table 2: **Sample Weapon Strength of 319.Infantry Division as at 1 August 1943***

Type of weapon	Qty	Type of weapon	Qty	Type of weapon	Qty
Rifles	9,476	Field guns 8cm FK 30(t)	12	4.7cm Pak 36(t) coupled with MG37(t)	36
Pistols	1,450	10cm leFH 14/19(t)	40	4.7cm Pak 36(t) SP	9
Machine Pistols	840	Grenade launchers	15	5cm Pak 38	27
LMG (MG34)	560	**Fixed Fortress Weapons**		7.5cm Pak 40	NIL
Heavy MG		Machine guns:		Field guns:**	
MG34	10	MG08	43	7.5cm FK 231(f)	6
MG08/15	18	MG34	364	10cm leFH 14/19(t)	4
MG08	9	MG311(f) in tank turrets	49	Fortress guns:	
MG26(t)	1	MG257(f)	30	10.5cm K 331(f) in casemates	35
Mortars:		Mortars:		10.5cm K 331(f) on pivots in open positions	37
Light (5cm Gr.W.36)	6	light Gr.W.36	75	Flamethrowers:	
Heavy (8cm Gr.W.34)	108	fortress Gr.W.210(f)	50	small	15
Small Flamethrowers	6	Ladungswerfer 20cm	30	medium	70
Anti-tank guns:		Light infantry guns		Defensive Abwehr 42	380
3.7cm Pak 35	30	7.5cm leIG 18	12	Searchlights:	
5cm Pak 38	9	Tank guns in turrets 3.7cm Kwk 144(f)	29	20-40cm	102
4.7cm Pak 36(t) SP	15	Same coupled with MG 311(f)	22	60cm	34
Light infantry guns	8	Anti-tank guns:			
AA guns 2cm	12	3.7cm Pak 35	42		

*This is merely the total for that day and numbers were always fluctuating, normally upwards.
**The turrets were from French R35 and FT17 tanks
(t) = of Czech origin; (f) = of French origin

Reinforcements

Infantry

As a result of Hitler's order to make the Islands into an impregnable fortress, the complete 319. ID was ordered to the Islands in the late autumn of 1941. HQ 319. ID, therefore, moved to Guernsey, to be followed by IR 583 (it had one company missing, so it was made up to strength by transferring 5. Kompanie of IR 596 from 327.ID which had been in eastern France since the early autumn). Further reinforcements included two battalions of ex-Red Army soldiers, who had switched their allegiance — *Ostbataillon* (Eastern Battalion) 823, composed of men of the Georgian Legion went to Guernsey and Ostbataillon 643 of the Russian Liberation Army went to Jersey. They did not operate as a single unit, but were rather used to make up in numbers for the inevitable lack of operational experience by the new recruits and the 'middle-age ailments' of the older men in the infantry battalions of the garrison. Attempts were also made to recruit Russians from amongst the slave workers, but with little success.

Lack of seasoned troops

It was estimated that, even before the time of the Normandy invasion, only 30% of the original 319. ID personnel were still serving in the Islands, so great was the turnover and the needs of the Eastern Front. This fact was noted by GenOb Alfred Jodl in his diary on 9 January 1944, during a visit he made to the area between the mouths of the Scheldt and the Seine, which was generally considered by OKW to be the most likely area for a landing. Jodl had wished to get a personal impression of the state of the defences in the west. Walter Warlimont quotes him in his book *Inside Hitler's Headquarters 1939–45*, '9 January: Withdrawals to the East have been on a vast scale. 319. ID in the Channel Islands has only 30 per cent of its original establishment.' Jodl also made such overall comments as 'The best people have been removed . . . Re-equipment is producing chaos . . . There is chaos in Cherbourg with the three Services alongside each other . . . situation in Brest bad.' Later on in his book Warlimont is damning about various decisions which Hitler made and upon which he would then not bend. For example, he says — quoting from late 1944 — that Hitler had 'wrongly, uselessly and entirely for prestige purposes, left a complete infantry division on the Channel Islands; its withdrawal was now out of the question'. Even as late as March 1945, Hitler was still saying that he wanted to hold the Channel Islands 'for a further year'.

Opposite: A German sentry on duty at the 'Rat House' entrance in York Street, St Helier, which became the office of the Kommandantur, Jersey. *IWM — HU 5185*

Above right: In this peaceful street scene taken in St Peter Port in the summer of 1940, one can see German soldiers mingling with the civilian population. *Hans-Gerhard Sandmann*

Right: The Crown Hotel, St Peter Port, became the German Naval Headquarters. It would be from this location that Vizeadmiral Hüffmeier would set out to sign the surrender in May 1945. It is now the Royal Channel Islands Yacht Club. *Hans-Gerhard Sandmann*

Supporting Arms

Artillery

It was not only the infantry of the incoming division that was short of both manpower and weapons. The divisional artillery regiment (Artillerie Regiment 319), which also had been woefully undermanned, was first brought up to full strength, then given a further battalion of 12 guns. All its weapons were of Czech origin rather than German, so instead of the normal 10.5cm gun-howitzers, its 12 batteries were equipped with either the 8cm FK 30(t), which had been the Skoda 76.5mm M.30(NPK), or the 10cm leFH 14/19(t), which had been the Skoda 100mm Model 14/19. This extra battalion was most necessary as the division had to spread itself over all three islands.

The artillery did not arrive all at the same time and there was, of necessity, a certain amount of moving around to cover the perceived threats until full strength was achieved, as will be explained in the next chapter. The anti-tank artillery had a similar problem. PzJgAbt 319 was concentrated in Jersey, where it provided a mobile reserve, being reinforced with some SP artillery. [6] However, it could not be spread to Guernsey without becoming too weak a reserve, so a second anti-tank battalion was brought in, PzJgAbt 225 from 225.ID, which was then also on occupation duty in France (the rest of this division was one of a number hurriedly sent off to reinforce the Eastern Front in January 1942, so the anti-tank gunners had a lucky escape!). Both anti-tank battalions were obvious choices as mobile reserves for the two islands and were soon renamed accordingly: PzJgAbt 225 became *Schnell Abteilung* 450 (*Schnell* = fast) on 3 October 1942 and PzJgAbt 319 became Schnell Abteilung 319 on the same date.

Additional artillery

As well as the integral divisional artillery, various coastal artillery units were sent over to man the mass of coastal guns that were pouring into the Islands. They arrived at various times in May 1943 and were merged together to form *Heeres Küsten Artillerie Regiment* 1265 (*Heeres Küsten Artillerie* = Army Coastal Artillery). See the next chapter for full details of this unit.

Tanks

As will also be explained in detail in the next chapter, 213 Tank Battalion (PzAbt 213), equipped with French Char B1 *bis* heavy tanks was sent to the Islands in March 1942, part to Guernsey and part to Jersey, where they were attached to the respective mobile reserves.

Changes of command

There were a fair number of changes of commanders among the top echelons of the garrison, and while some have been mentioned elsewhere, it would be useful to list the main ones:

July 1941:	Alderney became a separate command under Hptm Carl Hoffmann.
18 October 1941:	Oberst Friedrich Knackfuss replaced Schumacher in charge of FK515.
20 October 1941:	GenMaj Erich Müller became Befehlshaber.
February 1942:	Oberstlt Zuske took over command of Alderney.
November 1943:	Oberstlt Schwalm took over command of Alderney from Zuske.
3 March 1944:	Maj Heider replaced Oberst Knackfuss in charge of FK515.
September 1944:	Vizeadmiral Hüffmeier became Chief of Staff to von Schmettow instead of Oberst Graf von Helldorf.
28 February 1945:	Vizeadmiral Hüffmeier eventually replaced GenMaj Graf von Schmettow as Befehlshaber.
	Korvettenkapitän Kurt von Kleve became the Platzkommandant Jersey in place of Maj Heider and Kapitän sur Zee Reich became Platzkommandant for Guernsey.
	GenMaj Dini became Hüffmeier's Chief of Staff.
15 March 1945:	GenMaj Wulf became commander of 319. ID.

Alderney, a special case

While many of the changeovers outlined above were taking place, Alderney continued to be garrisoned from Cherbourg by 83.ID. However, by the end of the winter of 1941–42 the casualties on the Eastern Front had mounted so alarmingly that various divisions, including 83.ID, were despatched to Russia. 320.ID took its place and sent III./IR 587 to garrison Alderney. However, this was not to stay for long, as 320.ID had soon to spread itself all over the Cotentin Peninsula to take over from 711.ID which had been defending the east coast and now found itself on the way to Russia as well. This meant that 320.ID could no longer spare troops to defend Alderney and withdrew the battalion of IR 587 to the mainland. Responsibility for Alderney was passed to 319. ID, who sent III./IR 583 to take over, together with one platoon of engineers from PiAbt 319.

Sark

Dame Hathaway's tiny island still had the smallest garrison, but it had been increased to a reinforced infantry company from Guernsey.

Rotation

The barren, windswept island of Alderney, minus its civilian population and housing slave workers and an SS Concentration Camp, was considered to be the worst possible posting within the Islands — although, as we shall see, some servicemen liked it because discipline was a little more relaxed (for them, I hasten to add, not for the unfortunate slave labourers). However, in general terms, the troops did not like the posting and, in order to maintain morale, they were rotated roughly on a three-month cycle. Heer exchanges took place with Guernsey, Luftwaffe AA gun crews appear to have been rotated with crews from mainland France, but the Kriegsmarine stayed put — perhaps the advantage of being able to go to sea made up for the loneliness.

Right:
'Stop me and buy one!' Even German soldiers liked ice-cream!
IWM — HU 66488

Below:
Some of the staff at Government House, St Saviour's, Jersey, which was the residence of the commander of the island throughout the Occupation. *Société Jersiaise*

German soldiers now lived in requisitioned houses all over the Islands. Here a trio dine alfresco, listen to the gramophone and act the fool in the fresh air just outside their billet. Billeting costs, including the use and repair of the buildings, was to be paid for by the Island authorities, and householders received a small billeting grant (1s 6d per soldier, plus a further 1s for each subsequent occupant). Damage to property varied considerably. *Hans-Gerhard Sandmann*

Left:
Walking in St Peter Port. Two soldiers enjoy a stroll beside the harbour. *Hans-Gerhard Sandmann*

Left:
Enjoying the sea air. A group of Occupation soldiers get some sea air and perhaps think wistfully of their homes far away. *Hans-Gerhard Sandmann*

Above: Another billet and this time a requisitioned car to boot. There were some 12,000 motor vehicles on the two main islands and by 1942, apart from a few well-hidden ones, the vast majority were in German hands. *Hans-Gerhard Sandmann*

Left & above: Another example of a requisitioned civilian car (a Morris). The German purchasing commission requisitioned all civilian vehicles up to five years old. They also requisitioned tyres, brought in their own road signs and made everyone drive on the right-hand side of the road. *Hans-Gerhard Sandmann*

Right:
Bicycles were also requisitioned under Article 53 of the Hague Convention despite considerable protests. When Guernsey failed to supply the requisite number (100), the Nebenstelle (the Guernsey branch of FK515) accused the authorities of sabotage and threatened to hold the President of the Controlling Committee personally responsible; this quickly produced them.
IWM — HU 25960

Below: The Germans also relied heavily on horse-drawn transport. This photograph was taken at Carmel St Martin's, Guernsey.
IWM — HU 25969

Above:
The main infantry garrisons
were supported by other arms, including
tanks. First to arrive were some of the
captured tiny World War 1 French 7-ton
FT17/18s — known in German parlance as
Panzerkampfwagen FT17/18 730(f). This
one was photographed secretly in La Rue
Cauchée, St Martin's, Guernsey.
IWM — HU 25951

Left:
An old castle entrance
gate has a new guardian.
Hans-Gerhard Sandmann

Above:
Reinforcements came not only from the German Heer proper, but also from the Führer's 'Foreign Legions', such as this gun crew of men from the 823 Georgian Battalion, manning a 10.5cm K 331(f) gun at Widerstandsnest Heilingenbucht, in the harbour at Saint's Bay, Guernsey. The insignia of the unit can just be seen on the arm of the soldier with his right arm raised.
IWM — HU 29157

Right:
'Zutritt Verboten!' This sign, which has been preserved in the Occupation Museum, Guernsey, must have been repeated in many places all over the Islands.
Brian Matthews

Above: As well as requisitioning property for billeting soldiers or for operational reasons, other buildings were taken over for recreational purposes. This is Soldatenheim 3 at Grande Rocques, Guernsey, which is now the Wayside Cheer Hotel. See Chapter 8 for full details of the functions of these 'Soldiers' Homes'. *Hans-Gerhard Sandmann*

Above: 'Boots, Boots, Boots, Marching Up and Down Again!' The Germans did quite a lot of 'Showing The Flag' marches around the towns in the Channel Islands in the early days, like this squad of Luftwaffe personnel, who, apart from the officer at their head, are wearing the pre-1940 Flight Blouse open at the neck and without visible buttons. *IWM — HU 5191*

Chapter 4

The Soldier

HAND-PICKED?

'One of the most persistent of the many myths and legends that the Occupation generated was that the first German troops to land in the Channel Islands were obviously hand-picked because they were all so good-looking, disciplined and polite. Nothing could be further from the truth!'

In an article in *CIOS Review* No 18 of December 1990 about Operation 'Green Arrow' and the arrival of 216. ID in the Channel Islands, Michael Ginns, one of the most respected of Channel Islands historians, begins by using the sentence with which I have opened this chapter. In his article he goes on to explain how it would have been quite impossible for the Germans to have carried out such a procedure even if they had wanted to do so. The choice of first 216. ID, then 83. ID and finally 319. ID as the sources of the major ground units to be sent to the Channel Islands was based purely on operational requirements. Mr Ginns further makes the point that in June 1940, almost the entire German Army was comprised of:

'. . . healthy, well-disciplined young men. The pre-Occupation purveyors of rape, pillage and wholesale looting rumours were sadly disappointed when it was found that the newly arrived troops went around saluting everything that moved, paying for all the items they obtained in the shops and patting small children on the head.'

The same was true of the young Kriegsmarine sailors and Luftwaffe pilots and ground crew who served on the Islands. Naturally there were problems — as one would expect when peaceful, hard-working and somewhat isolated communities are suddenly invaded by groups of uniformed, armed foreigners intent on imposing their will upon them. However, also as one might have expected, it was the German civilians of FK515 and Organization Todt, together with the notorious SS, who were to blame for the vast majority of excesses that took place on the Islands, especially on Alderney, and not the average German soldier, sailor or airman. Those first arrivals undoubtedly left a lasting good impression on the locals, as Mr de Ste Croix has expressed (despite having been bombed in Jersey harbour!). When asked what kind of visual impression they made, he replied:

'Oh, very good, I thought so — I mean they were obviously hand-picked to do the job they were going to do. They were very smart, very correct, polite. I think there was a totally different occupation in the Channel Islands generally to what there was on the Continent. I think there was just that little bit of difference because they knew these places were British, that's my impression.'[1]

Even such an astute person as Dame Sibyl Hathaway of Sark was convinced that the soldiers had been hand-picked, for she wrote in her autobiography:

'We found out later that the first troops sent to occupy the island were specially picked to impress on the British people that the Germans were well-behaved, well-disciplined and withal kind-hearted. The behaviour and discipline of these troops was excellent, and it was rare to see a drunken German soldier in those early days.'

MORALE

Many generals, including the late Field Marshal Montgomery, considered morale to be the most important single factor in war. It can best be described as a serviceman's attitude to life and to his comrades. High morale enables a soldier to endure any hardship or risk, inspiring others to do the same. The majority of the Islands' garrison was in an almost unique position as far as morale was concerned. Immune for years from most of the nastier aspects of the war, they had to face their own morale-sapping problems — such as boredom and isolation, being confined to just one of a number of small islands — something which most of them had never had to experience before in their lives. In the last period of the occupation, after D-Day, they also had to face a severe shortage of food and the knowledge that their eventual capture was inevitable if they did not first starve to death. These were grim enough realities for anyone to have to face, despite the fact that they were still not subject — except in a few isolated cases — to actual bodily harm or death from enemy action.

THE GOOD TIMES

When the Occupation began, German military morale was of a high order. Boosted by a seemingly endless string of victories — in Poland, Norway, Denmark, Holland and Belgium, culminating in France's capitulation — the average German soldier, sailor and airman had unshakeable confidence in the Führer and the rest of his leaders, who, apparently, could do no wrong.

The younger servicemen were mostly thoroughly Nazi-minded anyway, having spent the most impressionable years of their lives under the Nazi regime. Their early training in the Hitler Youth organisation (*Hitler Jugend*) [2] and subsequent compulsory participation service in the State Labour Service (*Reichsarbeitdienst*) [3], had sown the seeds of unquestioning obedience to orders and loyalty to their unit, the armed forces, their country and, above all, to their Führer and the Nazi regime.

Nearly every one of them was confident that the war would soon be over, once England had been defeated — and, of course, taking the Channel Islands was the first important step in that final conquest! Shortages back home and air raids were still too infrequent to give rise to disquieting letters from their loved ones — or to the heavy censoring of their mail. Add to this the fact that the Channel Islands were beautiful, with shops crammed with food and luxury goods unobtainable back home and the men must have thought they had arrived in paradise!

Befehl ist Befehl!

In their dealings with the civilian population, the average German serviceman was governed by how he himself had been taught to behave — namely, instinctive obedience to orders. 'Befehl ist Befehl!' (An Order is an Order!) was the explanation given time and time again when a new regulation was queried, and whilst some of the orders issued were stupid and others onerous, this immediate German reaction to their queries and complaints at least made it easier for the Islanders to deal with them. Raymond Falla commented that he did not find the Germans too hard to deal with, because of this almost blind obedience:

'"Orders are Orders, Mr Falla," they would say, and once they knew what the order was, the German mind did not deviate. He doesn't react to changes of circumstance very quickly, so you were safe in spoofing them a little bit.'[4]

THE BAD TIMES

As the years of the occupation dragged on, the monotony of the tasks of the garrison clearly started to become more irksome. However, whilst the links with mainland France remained open and it was still possible to go home on leave and to receive regular mail from their loved ones, life for the garrison was not too bad. The Allied invasion of Normandy stopped all that, effectively cutting off the Islands and creating a siege mentality. Things became worse as the weeks passed and food became scarcer and scarcer. One soldier, Erwin Albert Grubba, told the Imperial War Museum about his memories of what he described as being the 'Hunger Winter'.

'The last winter — 1944–45 — obviously when the invasion had passed us by, so to speak. And we were cut off. No supplies, no letters, no news came through, and, really, rations were right down to the bare minimum. And people were really hungry; very great problems with the middle-aged groups, the mid-thirties, and people with stomach troubles and ulcers. There were quite a few dying. It was a very difficult position. And, naturally, the civilian population wasn't any better off, unless of course they were farmers and had a few spuds. But even they could have been pinched, dug out in the middle of the night. At risk of life and limb that is, or court-martial. So it sounds ridiculous in a war when the

rest of Europe was up in flames — I had guard duties to guard glasshouses, greenhouses with grapes, from intruders who might have pinched them. I slept in a greenhouse many a night, on a bunk, with my Schmeisser[5] underneath my feet — just in case there was anybody marauding and intruding.

'That, of course, was the last winter, the grim period, when it was very tough. Fortunately, the military authorities stepped in . . . and arranged for a ship from Portugal to bring from New Zealand and Australia, food parcels. And they were of course guarded by the German Army at the dockside. And absolutely fair, distributed to civilians. And not a single German soldier got a parcel. And the civilians appreciated that, no doubt, and knew that would be the correct way. Having said that, of course, I benefited from them because of that family [Ed: this was a family in Vazon Bay, who had earlier invited him in for a cup of tea]. When they got their parcel, they said, "Come on, have a real cup of tea now." And my first bar of Cadbury's chocolate, which she broke for me. And they had condensed milk — you know, Libby's milk — the sort of thing that was almost worth its weight in gold.'[6]

ORGANISATION OF AN INFANTRY DIVISION

Before looking in detail at some of the units and their tasks through the eyes of the soldiers who served in the Channel Islands, it would be useful to fix in our minds the basic organisation of the German infantry division, c1940. This will help to explain how the longest serving division on the Islands, 319. ID, was enlarged to perform the additional tasks it had to face, yet still had to be classed as an infantry division and not as a fortress division which it undoubtedly became in all but name.

Despite the fact that the Panzer divisions had played such a major role in overwhelming Poland and France in 1939 and 1940, there were more infantry divisions than any other type in the German Army at that time, and like the infantry in every other army in World War 2, they provided the backbone of the German ground forces. Each infantry division basically consisted of three infantry regiments, each of three battalions with three rifle companies, plus supporting weapons. They marched into battle and much of their larger weaponry and stores vehicles were horse-drawn. Divisional units included an artillery regiment of four battalions — three being equipped with light FH18 field guns whilst the fourth had medium sFH18 howitzers — an engineer battalion, a reconnaissance battalion, an anti-tank battalion, a signal battalion, plus the usual administrative units such as supply, repair and medical. Appendix 1 on page 243 shows the outline standard organisation. As will be seen this is the actual organisation of 216. ID as at 1 September 1939. The normal infantry division had nearly 5,400 horses and under 1,000 motor vehicles of all types, which shows the German Army's dependence on the horse. It is fortunate, therefore, that most of these draught animals did not accompany the units who came to the Islands as it would have required a staggering 50 tons of hay and oats every day to feed them, not to mention the hours that had to be spent watering, grooming and exercising them, whilst a sophisticated veterinary service was needed to look after their health.

Of course some of the soldiers of 216. ID and those who followed them, found themselves carrying out very different duties to those for which they had been trained. There were no battles to fight, although they had always to be ready for action at short notice in order to repel invaders. Instead they had to deal at firsthand with a civil population who were in the main, distinctly unfriendly if not openly hostile towards them. Being an 'Army Occupation' put all manner of new pressures onto the ordinary soldier, especially before the arrival of the civil servants who were supposedly trained in handling civilians. As we shall see, this affected not just the more senior officers like Maj Lanz, but also many of his men as well in one way or another.

Although 216. ID was a standard infantry division, 319. ID was very different from the norm. It had been considerably reinforced and given weaponry more suited to its coastal defence role. Some of this was of foreign manufacture: for example, its artillery regiment had four battalions entirely equipped with Czech guns (either 8cm or 10cm).

A SOLDIER'S LIFE

Despite the fact that garrison life could never be called enjoyable, it was infinitely better than the horrors of the Russian Front which the 'well-behaved, good-looking and disciplined young soldiers' of 216. ID would have to experience at first hand all too soon after leaving the Islands. As Michael Ginns questions, did they 'look back with longing to the few short months they had passed on the golden beaches and leafy lanes of Guernsey and Jersey?' I'm sure that they did.

Some German soldiers had the pleasure of serving on the Islands after experiencing the rigours of the Eastern Front. One such soldier was Erwin Grubba, who has just been recounting his difficulties during the 'Hunger Winter'. Grubba had been born in Marienburg in East Prussia in 1925, so he had not been old enough to be called up until the spring of 1943 and had first served with a labour battalion in Poland for a few months before returning to Germany to train as a *Panzergrenadier* (mechanised infantryman) at Spandau Barracks, Berlin. He was then sent to fight in Russia, commenting that it was like being sent to Hell — not only was the weather appalling, but also the Red Army had the sinister reputation of never taking any prisoners. So he was undoubtedly fortunate to get dysentery in his last operational location and to be put on a train heading west. 'Little did I know,' he said later, 'that it was my road to Salvation!'

He travelled by cattle truck — with 40 others all lying on filthy straw — out of Russia, through Poland and on through Germany and then into France. Finally they reached Paris and were de-loused at a station just south of the capital, before going on to

Above: This photograph of Hans-Gerhard's father Gerhard, many of whose photographs are in this book and who served from 1939 with 216. ID in France, Guernsey and Russia, was taken in 1944 soon after he was captured. He wears the M1938 field cap (*Feldmütze*), M1936 field-grey uniform (tunic and trousers), the tunic having a dark green collar bearing the collar bars (*Litzen*) and edged with the NCOs' 9mm braid (*Tresse*), whilst the ribbon of the Iron Cross, 2nd Class can be seen below his second button. On his feet are his leather marching boots. By the time he was captured, near Chalons on 1 May 1944, Gerhard had reached the rank of Oberfeldwebel and had been awarded the Iron Cross, 1st Class in Russia, on 27 Jan 1942.
Hans-Gerhard Sandmann

St Malo, where they de-trained and were put into tents in a big sports stadium. A few days later, someone said: 'Well, you lot are going over to the Channel Islands.' The Germans were busy strengthening the Atlantic Wall defences in preparation for the invasion which they all knew was coming. They were taken by sea, in a convoy protected by barrage balloons, to join an infantry unit which was responsible for the area around Vazon Bay, Guernsey, with its Btl HQ at St Martin. The defences at Vazon Bay were the northernmost infantry sector of the island. To the north and south they were flanked by Strongpoint Rotenstein at Fort Hommet and Strongpoint Reichenberg at Fort Richmond

Above: Two officers of 216. ID in greatcoats, wearing their leather belts over the top — note the cross-strap on one and the pistol holster on the other — talking with two warrant officers. The one on the right is '*der Spiess*', a colloquial name for the senior sergeant-major, and wears the black wound insignia (marking one or two wounds suffered in combat) on his left breast pocket.
Hans-Gerhard Sandmann

Left: This group of men of 216. ID, standing at the entrance to their billet, wear an interesting mix of uniforms, including unbleached denim fatigue jackets, normal uniform, whilst one is in his pullover.
Hans-Gerhard Sandmann

(see map of Guernsey at start of book). The beach area of the bay was protected by four lesser strongpoints (Krossen, Margen, Rundbucht Mitte and Rundtfurm). As well as the artillery support the infantry would receive from the Island's heavy gun batteries, they would also have been able to call on the four casemated 10cm field guns of Batterie Lux, which were sited below the ridge at Mont Saint. Grubba recalled:

> '*My first impression of the Channel Islands was the peaceful atmosphere, in the morning, arriving at St Peter Port and seeing the first British "bobby" in a dark blue uniform with his tall hat. And notices advertising Fyffe's bananas and Mazawatee tea. I knew then I was on a good ticket here!*' [7]

Grubba soon settled down to the routine with 'stand-to' every morning, parades, drill and night duties, most of which were guard duties in shifts. 'You went on duty and manned these concrete bunkers at night time. And you went off again at six o'clock in the morning and took your guard duties as they came.' As well as foot drill, there were a great number of military exercises (manoeuvres) which increased — much to the annoyance of the Guernsey farmers — as the fear of invasion became more acute. Then 'anti-parachutist' devices (Grubba rightly called them 'bombs' because they were mostly unused aerial bombs) were tied to stakes and rammed into the ground all over the fields. The farmers were even more worried with these

new devices, in case any of their precious animals blew themselves up! He describes the attitude of the local people as being 'absolutely correct'. He could speak some English and soon made contact, going into the shops buying fruit and vegetables:

> '*They were downright loyal to the Crown. Of course they didn't owe anything to Westminster and Parliament, but they were direct subjects to the Crown and loyal to the King and Queen . . . they told you, "We're not British, we're Guernsey people, but we're loyal to the King and of course we naturally hope and pray for an Allied victory." They made no bones about that. And somehow that created a mutual respect because one felt that they were neither collaborators or cringers or taking advantage of the situation. I think they behaved extremely well and they were sensible too. They said: "Well, while we're occupied we'll have to carry on. Electricity has to go, traffic has to flow. It's no good doing acts of sabotage" . . . they had a sensible attitude, saying: "Well you lads are also here, not because you wanted to come. You were forced to join and come and occupy the Islands. And you want to go home as much as we want you to go home."*'

He also recalled a farmer near his quarters with whom he was friendly, saying: 'I love your singing when you march off in the morning to your exercises. It sounds great. But, by gum, I wish you would go all the same. Because it'll be nice to be free again!' [8]

Medics

Werner Rang served in Guernsey as a medical sergeant in Sanitäts Kompanie 319 and in Sark for six months. He was born in Thuringia in March 1920, so he was some five years older than Grubba. After leaving school in 1935, he had worked in a bank until his call-up in 1939. He joined at Herford and, after a short period of infantry training, was posted to the Medical Corps and did his preliminary medical training in a hospital in Kassel, then in Geissen in Hesse, working mainly in the surgical department. He saw active service in France with 169. ID, then after some leave, was posted to Metz, again working in a hospital. Then he was posted to 319. ID and found himself arriving in Guernsey on 8 October 1940 and being delighted with the clean, neat holiday island.

Below: This burial Guard of Honour was made up of soldiers from 216. ID. The funeral was probably for a sailor — note the naval officer by the vehicle carrying the coffin (which looks suspiciously like a captured British Bedford MWD 15cwt truck). They all carry the standard Karabiner 98k rifle. *Hans-Gerhard Sandmann*

His main task was to look after German soldiers, but he also attended privately to civilians — which would stand him in good stead during the 'Hunger Winter', when they gave him food. He was later sent over to Sark for six months, where he met his wife to be, Phyllis Baker, the daughter of a Sark farmer. She was acting as an interpreter for the German army doctors who, because of a lack of civilian medical practitioners, were treating civilians there — they performed their duties with 'a conscientiousness and care still remembered by the population to this day' (to quote from *Islands in Danger*). Bright and intelligent, Phyllis had quickly learnt German and proved an ideal interpreter — until she herself fell sick. Werner Rang was sent round to her house with pills and a thermometer and it was a case of love at first sight! Werner was still serving in Guernsey on VE-Day and remembers being put aboard a troopship at St Peter Port and taken to Southampton. From there he went by train to POW camps at Devizes, Otley (Yorkshire) and finally, Fareham. When he was released in 1948, he went straight back to the Channel Islands to marry his sweetheart and to live there — which he still does. Currently he is working on a book about his wartime experiences and has recorded his memories of his service in the Channel Islands for the IWM Dept of Sound (Accession No 12543/1) from which this short paragraph was culled.

Another erstwhile member of the medical corps was Werner Wagenknecht who came to Guernsey in March 1942, one of a group of reinforcements to 319. ID, whom a drunken sergeant in St Malo had referred to as 'the death squad'! He recalled:

'We sailed on a steamboat (the Bordeaux) during a stormy night. British planes, searchlight beams and German aircraft defence were our company.

'. . . Arrival in Guernsey. This lovely, sunny day in March 1942 is deep-rooted in my heart!
"Sarnia, cherie, gem of the sea, island of beauty my heart longs for thee!"

'The officer in charge of the harbour gave the order that we should report to the Princess Elizabeth Hospital (the main military hospital during the occupation). There we were thoroughly examined and told that the Army medical service had applied for reinforcements and due to my civilian education [Werner had had a good education and had been a professional druggist before his call-up] I was chosen.

'I had no driving licence and no experience as a medical orderly, but that was no problem for the medical officers!'

Quickly Werner was ordered to a training camp, then medical school, where he learned the theory and practice of military medicine, with which he found no difficulty in view of his previous knowledge of civilian medicine. In next to no time he was allocated to the army medical section, ambulance drivers company. Werner worked in the underground hospital as well as the Princess Elizabeth Hospital and recalled some incidents from his medical service on the island:

'One night I helped to free a soldier who had been wounded by mines, still hanging on the barbed wire in the minefield; we brought him back to hospital and I assisted the operating surgeon. Then there was a shocking occurrence. I was asked to escort the sergeant-major to a great room in the hospital, where there were 10-12 unclothed dead bodies, shapeless and swollen, lying on the floor. They worked with the Organization Todt and were French North African forced labourers. During some digging they had found some good-smelling roots which they ate. They collapsed and were brought to the hospital — death through hemlock, reaction like cyanide. They were buried at Foulon cemetery. There we also buried the MT sergeant of our unit. He was walking with his alsatian dog in Fort George. The dog jumped, detonated the fuse of a bomb and only the remains were found.'

Garrison life

Georg Brefka arrived in Jersey in the autumn of 1943 for service with MG Btl 16. After his primary training he had been posted to the Russian Front, but after a few months had fortunately been posted to the West, with a number of other young 18-year-olds. MG Btl 16 had originally been a frontier guard battalion, recruited from the Eifel district of Germany and contained mainly higher age-group men, whilst Brefka and his companions were from the cities like Berlin. '. . . a group of city kids (Berliners) among a lot of elderly country bumpkins!' is how another member of the MG Battalion described them! Georg Brefka was posted to the second company which had its HQ at the La Moye Golf Hotel and was responsible for the south-west corner of the island, the troops rotating around the various strongpoints every three months or so. Nevertheless, Brefka spent most of his time manning a strongpoint at Les Brayes, at the southern end of St Ouen's Bay. In an article by Michael Ginns, which appeared in *CIOS (Jersey) Review* in 1989, Georg Brefka (now deceased) gave an illuminating account of his duties, whilst manning what was known as Resistance Nest Les Brayes:

'The day was long, beginning at 6am and at 10pm we had our rest. At 7am, after breakfast, work began; there was construction of positions, cleaning of arms and ammunition, and training with guns and weapons. About every four weeks there was practice shooting with live ammunition at targets. These were sheets of lead which had been set up in the bay. Sometimes there was also night shooting with the aid of a searchlight.

'At Les Brayes there was a 4.7cm Czech anti-tank gun coupled with a heavy Czech machine gun, a French 3.7cm gun in a tank turret; two German machine guns; a small searchlight and a signalling lamp. Serving the signalling lamp was very difficult — with one hand you turned a handle to activate the dynamo whilst operating the signalling lamp with the other. Nobody was really able to do it properly. In general, training was done in such a way so that every soldier could be used on every weapon. The rust produced by the strong salt content in the air caused great difficulties for the equipment. But the sand was much worse. Since the greater part of the installation lay in the dunes of the Bay, sand was to be found everywhere and always!

'While constructing positions or doing work, barbed wire was continuously being put around the installation. Trenches for communication and protection were dug, improved and camouflaged. Sods of grass were used for camouflage, they were cut out from somewhere on the other side of the road and transported in handcarts. The position was then more difficult to see and the sand from the dunes was also covered up.

'A problem of a particular kind was presented by sentry duty. Normally at night, or during the hours of darkness, three men did sentry duty. One was in front on the road, while the other two patrolled as a double watch throughout the area, ie: the communication trenches at the bunker and as far as the wall at the beach. During the day there was only one sentry who stayed by the entrance on the road.

'I have no pleasant memories of sentry duty! Normally we had to do two turns of two hours and twenty minutes every night — only about every fifth night did we not have to do more than one turn of sentry duty. There were only a few of us, and when we thought that nothing was going to happen, for example, when it was stormy or there was a very high tide, we slept a little while on sentry duty, sometimes sleeping standing without falling down. And all of this despite the fear of a German court martial on the one hand and of British Commandos on the other. We were on the move the whole day and then out twice a night as well, with never a free night. We were all very tired. And we were checked every night. The positions of the Second Company were checked by the First Company and vice versa.

'At Les Brayes there was also a trained dog with a handler and they took part in the checking too. When the tide was low, La Rocco Tower also had to be checked, in case of landings by British commandos. On the tower, a 30.5cm French naval shell had been installed which could be set off from Les Brayes by remote control by means of an electric cable.

'The combat bunker near the slip was only there for emergency and was only used for sleeping. Some of the troops slept in a former anti-tank gun garage which was made of corrugated iron and dug into the sand. For daytime living, and our sparse free time, there was a big wooden hut available and our meals were taken here too. The food was brought from the La Moye Golf Hotel every day by two or three men and carried on their backs in sacks or cans. The route was always through the sand dunes and the hills, to the Company HQ on the other side of the golf links.

'There was no drinking water available in the Resistance Nest. Thousands of bottles of mineral water had to be stored in case of emergency. Normally fresh water was fetched from a deep bunker that had been constructed by the Organization

Todt, in this there was a spring with a hand pump and it was situated about half way to La Pulente on the left-hand side of the road, it must still be there today.

'*Only particularly heavy things were brought from La Moye by horse and cart. A lorry was there for emergency use, but I did not see it being driven until after the capitulation. 'Every Saturday, everybody had to go from Les Brayes to La Moye for a shower — that was an order! The quietest day was Sunday — in the morning clothes were cleaned and tidied; after lunch we were free and some of the personnel were allowed to go to St Brelade's Bay to the church service or the Soldatenheim at the St Brelade's Bay Hotel (see extracts from the Visitors' Book of this establishment when in German use), where there was a very nice bookshop among other things. In addition, field religious services were occasionally held in the wooden hut.'*

By way of comparison, look at the description of another 'Resistance Nest', this time on Jersey, which is to be found in Chapter 9: Fortifications.

BASIC DRESS AND PERSONAL EQUIPMENT

Other Ranks

The *Schutze* (infantry private) of June 1940, wore, like all other German soldiers, the M1936 service uniform both in barracks and in the field. It comprised a thigh-length field-grey tunic and straight field-grey trousers which were stuffed into the tops of black leather, nail-studded jackboots. The tunic had a dark green high collar on each side of which were patches of dark green cloth bearing the traditional Prussian double collar bars (*Litzen*). The tunic had five large metal dimple-finished buttons down the front, one on each of the four patch pockets, and one on each shoulder close to the collar, on which the shoulder-straps fixed. Above the right breast pocket was the national emblem — the straight spread-winged eagle, clutching in its talons a circular wreath containing a swastika — all in white thread on a dark green background. Later the M1943 uniform jacket (*Feldbluse Modell* 1943) was introduced because of shortages of uniform materials. This was very similar but did not have the dark green collar. Trousers had side pockets and a hip pocket.

A leather belt and leather equipment was worn, the belt buckle being of dull white metal like the buttons. The belt plate bore the German eagle and swastika motif, with the words '*GOT MIT UNS*' (God is with us) surrounding them. The shoulder-straps were of dark green cloth, piped in different branch of service colours (*Waffenfarbe*), the main colours being white for infantry, pink for armour, golden yellow for cavalry, bright red for artillery, grass green for armoured infantry, black for engineers, copper brown for reconnaissance units, lemon yellow for signals and light green for Jäger and mountain troops.

Normal head-dress in battle was the M1935 'coal scuttle' steel helmet, but the side cap (*Feldmütze*) in field-grey was often worn. It had a roundel (red, white and black) on the front of the turned-up portion, and on the front of the crown was a smaller version of the breast eagle. As with the field tunic a new pattern of field cap was introduced in June 1943 — the *Einsheitsfeldmütze* — which became widely used throughout the Wehrmacht.

The double-breasted 12-button (two rows of six) greatcoat was of field-grey cloth with a dark green falling collar. One interesting variation was the insignia of the troops of the *Ostbataillonen* (East battalions) who came as reinforcements in September-October 1943. They wore normal German uniform, but with their own badges of rank and their national insignia on one arm. For instance, Btl 823 of the Georgian Legion wore a red shield with white/black bars in the top left quarter, surmounted by the word *Georgien,* whilst the ROA (Russian Liberation Army) Btl 643 wore a blue St Andrew's cross on a white background with the letters POA above — the 'P' being an 'R' in the Russian Cyrillic alphabet. This gave rise to them being known locally as 'Pals of Adolf'!

Basic personal equipment consisted of the belt, a set of black leather 'Y' straps, triple ammunition pouches, entrenching tool, bayonet (84/98) in its black steel scabbard, canvas bread bag, canteen, gas mask in its fluted metal cylindrical case, tent square (*Zeltbahn*) and a canvas pack which contained washing gear, rifle cleaning kit, spare clothing, tinned rations, tent pegs and rope for the tent square.

The large M1939 pack, which contained the remainder of the soldier's clothing, equipment and personal items, was not often worn in action and would be carried in unit transport, which could be motorised or horse-drawn (despite the image of the fully-motorised Blitzkrieg, the German Army relied heavily on horses to draw its artillery and supply vehicles, whilst most infantrymen marched).

Two more vital items that everyone carried were the Service Book and identity discs. In the former, the soldier's record of service was kept. It also contained his photograph, army number, signature, etc. Around every soldier's neck was a two-piece oval aluminium disc, which was inscribed with his name and the number of his field post or replacement troop. When a soldier died, one half was broken off and given to the burial officer to pass on, the other half staying on the body. Squad leaders also carried binoculars, message bag, torch, compass and whistle.

Officers

Officers wore a similar, but much better cut, field-grey tunic of finer material, with more elaborate *Litzen* on the dark green collar. Some officers wore flared riding breeches instead of the more normal straight trousers. They also often wore the service cap (*Schirmmütze*) instead of the side cap or steel helmet, especially when not on operations or training. The cap had a black peak, dark green band and a field-grey crown.

Above:
The 8cm *schwerer Granatwerfer* 34 infantry mortar was in regular service in
most units, although supplemented by other foreign mortars (see text). Here it
is being fired from one of the coastal bunker positions. *IWM — HU 29014*

Opposite above:
Demonstrating the use of the Pistol Signal. The pistol fired flares of four or
more different colours, which burnt for eight seconds and could be seen from a
radius of 1.5–3 miles by day and 10 miles by night.
IWM — HU 28998

Opposite:
Used for blowing gaps in barbed wire entanglements, the *Gestrechte
Ladungen* (Bangalore torpedo), was an ad hoc weapon up to some 10ft long.
IWM — HU 25999

Above: If he is able, this infantryman intends to throw his 'potato-masher' stick grenade cluster *geballte Ladung* (multiple charge) sufficiently far so that it doesn't blow him up as well as the enemy! The weapon, which had a bunch of six heads around the head of a seventh, was meant for anti-tank use only. *IWM* — HU 29000

Above: Even in hilly areas, the Germans relied on a proportion of bicycle-mounted troops, like this company photographed at Vimera, Guernsey. The bicycles were requisitioned from the civilian population.
Richard Heaume

Below: Motorcycle troops (*Kradschützen*) on their machines; the front trio are mounting an MG34 onto the sidecar. These sidecar combinations were mainly built by Zündapp and BMW.
IWM — 29016

Variations in dress

There were of course variations in dress, as will be described in captions to relevant photographs. Perhaps the most striking Army uniform worn in the Channel Islands garrison was the distinctive black uniform of the armoured troops — *Sonderbekleidung der Deutschen Panzertruppen* — which originally consisted of a protective headgear (*Schmütze* — a padded inner head protector) and a flamboyant outer beret, a short double-breasted jacket and long straight trousers, all in black cloth. The *Schmütze* was phased out early in the war and it is doubtful whether any tank crews in the Channel Islands ever wore one, instead they wore the black Panzer *Feldmütze* (field cap). Officers initially wore a black Sam Browne-style belt; other ranks wore the normal black leather belt. As explained below, the black Panzer uniform and 'Death's Head' collar badges were inevitably mistaken for the SS, giving rise to many rumours that there were SS on all the islands, rather than just on Alderney. The crews of the self-propelled anti-tank assault gun units (*Schnellabteilungen* 319 and 450), probably wore the special field-grey uniform which was exactly the same cut and design as the black Panzer uniform, but gave far better personal camouflage to the wearer.

Personal weapons

The soldier's rifle was the 7.92mm Karabiner 98k and, at the start of the war, all members of the 10-man rifle squad (*Schutzengruppe*) carried one. The 'k' stood for *kurz*, meaning 'short'. It had gone into production initially in 1935, many thousands being produced thereafter. It was a good, accurate rifle, but its main disadvantage was the five-round capacity of its magazine. Gradually machine-pistols began to enter service, such as the 9mm Maschinenpistole 38 and its successor the MP40, which was mass-produced and became one of the most sought-after sub-machine guns of World War 2. It was known by the Allies as the Schmeisser, despite the fact that Schmeisser had nothing to do with its design.

Stick Grenade 24 and Hand Grenade 39 were also two basic infantry weapons, as was a pistol (either a Walther P38 or Luger PO8) and the *Leuchtpistole* (flare pistol) 38. The squad's light machine gun was the 7.92mm *Maschinengewehr* (machine gun) MG34, with its 50-round belt, which could be linked to form a 250-round belt. It used the same ammunition as the rifle and had a rate of fire of 800-900 rpm. It had a built-in bipod, but could also be used on a large tripod which could be turned into an AA mount (not much liked, so the machine gunners often used someone else's shoulder). The MG34 was also used in tanks and other AFVs and was a good, well-liked machine gun. Its replacement was the MG42. Gas-operated, its sight range extended from 200 to 2,000 metres. It was probably the best light machine gun of the war, its only drawback being that it got hot quickly, so asbestos gloves were needed to change barrels.

Alternative weapons

While these were the normal basic weapons of the infantry soldiers, they were by no means the only small arms used by the German forces in the Channel Islands. In addition, there were other weapons manufactured in Germany — such as the earlier 7.92mm Gewehr 98 long-barrelled rifle and the shorter 7.92mm Karabiner 98a carbine, which was issued to both signal and engineer units, and carried on vehicles as the weapon for the driver. Then there were the rifles which had been 'acquired' from the conquered countries of Europe — such as the Czech Puska vz.24 (known in German nomenclature as the 7.92mm Gew 24[t]) and the Polish equivalent, the Karabinek wz.29 (called the Kar 29[p]); the French Fusil d'Infanterie mle 07/15, the Fusil d'Infanterie mle 1916 and the carbine version, the Mousequeton mle 1916. These are but a few examples; there were also other French, Belgian, Dutch, Russian and even British rifles used by the Heer, which no doubt found there way into the Islands' garrison. This was also the same as far as pistols and machine carbines were concerned. Finally, in the field of machine guns, the range of different weapons to be found in service on the Islands was staggering, one weapons expert, Terry Gander, listing no fewer than 16 different types of German, Czech, French, Belgian and Polish machine guns which he had located! Not only were these used in normal mountings; some, like the ex-French 311(f) MG, were also employed mounted in tank turrets.

HEAVY WEAPONS

Infantry Guns

Various foreign field artillery guns were taken into service as infantry guns or used to help provide close protection for coastal batteries. These included the French 75, which became known as the 7.5cm FK 231(f), and the Czech 8cm FK 30(t). There were even some British 18/25pdrs, captured from the BEF in 1940, which had become the 8.76cm FK 281(e).

Table 3: **Infantry Support Weapons**

Type	7.5cm FK 231(f)	8cm FK 30(t)	8.76cm FK 281(e)
Wt in action	1,140kg	1,816kg	1,600kg
Shell wt	6.2kg	8kg	11.35kg
Range	11,100m	13,500m	11,000m
Rate of fire	12rpm	10-12rpm	6rpm

Anti-tank weapons

The three main anti-tank guns to be found on the Islands were all German — the 3.7cm Pak 35, the 5cm Pak 38 and the 7.5cm Pak 40. The first of the three was one of the best anti-tank guns of its day, but by the end of 1940 was considered too light in calibre to be really effective, so was widely replaced. The 5cm Pak 38 entered service in 1940 and it could penetrate most Allied tanks of the period 1941-42 (including the Russian T-34). It continued in service for the rest of the war and was not replaced completely by the larger 7.5cm Pak 40, which was to all intents and purposes just a scaled-up version. However, the Pak 40 was undoubtedly an excellent gun and very effective.

Table 4: **Anti-Tank Weapons**

Type	3.7cm Pak 35	5cm Pak 38	7.5cm Pak 40
Wt in action	328kg	986kg	1,500kg
Wt of shell (AP)	0.68kg	2.25kg	6.8kg
AP40	0.354kg	0.975kg	3.2kg
Armour penetration (AP)	38mm at 400yd	61mm at 500yd	106mm at 500yd
AP40	49mm at 400yd	86mm at 500yd	115mm at 500yd

8.8cm Pak 43 L71

Of course the finest anti-tank gun of the war was the dreaded '88' and there were some in Guernsey but not Jersey. The 5,000kg weapon (complete with carriage) could fire both AP and HE, the former having a staggering armour penetration of some 226mm at 500yd — nearly twice that of the 7.5cm Pak 40.

Anti-aircraft weapons

As the photographs show, many machine guns were used on AA mountings, but the most common small AA gun was the 2cm Flak 30, or the 2cm Flak 38. For details of these weapons and other AA, see Chapter 6.

Mortars

As with machine guns, there were both German-made and foreign mortars in service on the Islands. The German ones ranged from the 5cm *leichte Granatwerfer* (light mortar) 36, and 8cm *schwerer Granatwerfer* (heavy mortar) 34, both of which were normal infantry weapons. Both were gradually withdrawn or supplemented by other mortars in frontline service, but remained as battalion weapons in the Channel Islands. There were also foreign mortars, such as the Russian 50-PM 40, which had been captured in large numbers and became known as the 5cm Granatwerfer 205/3(r), and the 82-PM 36, known as the 8.2cm Granatwerfer 274/1(r). Both were in service with the Ostbataillonen (ROA). Another foreign mortar was the French 81mm, known in German service as 8.14cm Granatwerfer 278(f).

As well as these infantry mortars there were three more specialised versions: the 20cm *leichte Ladungswerfer*, a specialised spigot mortar used by engineers to clear obstacles and minefields, which had a limited range (700m) but a heavy projectile (21.27kg). Some 30 of these were installed in various locations around the coast. The second was the very complex 5cm *Maschinengranatwerfer* (mechanical mortar) M19, a large and complicated rapid fire automatic mortar which fired up to 120 rounds per minute, of which only six were installed. It required a large bunker almost 20ft in height to house it and its attendant machinery (interestingly CIOS [Jersey] has completely restored a bunker for one). It would go on and on firing, provided the loader kept feeding in racks of bombs. Range, traverse and firing were all entirely automatic and the mortar was sited so as to cover dead ground that could not be covered by other weapons. Finally, there was the *Festungsgranatwerfer* (fortification mortar) 210(f), which had

previously been used in the Maginot Line and then sent to the Channel Islands, where some 50 were installed. It was a much simpler weapon which was mounted on a concrete plinth in an open pit and had carrying handles fitted. Breech-loaded by hand, the range was adjusted by bleeding off the exhaust gases of the propellant charge.

Flamethrowers (*Flammenwerfer*)

The Germans had various types of flamethrower, some of which were used by the garrison, mainly the defensive types like the early Flammenwerfer 35, which was both heavy and cumbersome, the Flammenwerfer 41 which was lighter and easier to manage and the Abwehr Flammenwerfer 42, copied from a Russian model, which was purely defensive and could be fired remotely. There is no record of any of them being used in action on the Islands.

Mines

Large numbers of mines were laid to cover such vital areas as the potential main landing sites, important strongpoints and bunkers, coastal batteries, etc. A variety of anti-tank and anti-personnel mines were laid, which included *Teller* mines, S mines, *Schu* mines, plus captured French and Belgian mines, shells, concealed charges and numerous other explosive devices. In an article in *CIOS Review* No 19, Terry Gander makes the sum total of such devices a staggering 175,925 — 'mines, improvised devices and charges, most of them concealed and all of them intended to inflict death and suffering . . . a staggering total for such a relatively small area of real estate.'

Armour
Armoured fighting vehicles

Probably the most incongruous weapons to be found in the Channel Islands garrison were the armoured fighting vehicles, made all the more odd by the fact that they were, without exception, captured French equipment and not German AFVs at all. The first armour to appear was a small consignment of World War 1 vintage Renault FT17s, which arrived on all three main islands in the middle of 1941. The FT17 had been designed by Louis Renault and this remarkable little tank was built in very large numbers during the Great War and 'adopted' by many nations all over the world. However, it was hopelessly obsolete by the 1930s. It was armed with a machine gun (8mm Hotchkiss), had a crew of two, weighed 6.5 tons and was powered by a 35hp Renault engine. It was also the first tank in the world to have a fully revolving turret.

Tank Battalion 213 arrives

As we have seen, Hitler's order of October 1941 led to a general strengthening of the Channel Islands garrison, which included sending heavy tanks to boost the little FT17s. Again, however, the choice was captured French equipment in the shape of the Char B1 *bis,* which had been one of the largest, heaviest and best armed tanks of the Blitzkrieg era, but had never had a chance to show its true worth on the battlefield. At 32 tons, with armour 60mm thick, a top speed of 28km/h and mounting both a 75mm gun (low down in the front hull), plus a 47mm gun in its turret and two machine guns, the four-man heavy tank was quite formidable. Large numbers of the 365 Char B1 *bis* — built for French Army service — were captured in a serviceable condition and it was decided to crew some of them with a draft of the new recruits who were then doing their basic training at the 1. *Panzer Ersatz Regiment* (1st Tank Replacement Regiment) at Erfurt in Thuringia. Having completed their basic training, the recruits moved by train to Poissy, near Paris, where they were told that they would become Panzer Abteilung 213, be equipped entirely with French tanks, lorries and motorcycles, and were likely to be posted to North Africa to serve with Rommel's Deutsches Afrika Korps. All this came true except for the posting, which in early 1942 was changed to the Channel Islands. The unit began loading its vehicles at St Malo on 3 March 1942. By the 25th, 15 tanks had been taken to Jersey and 17 to Guernsey, to be joined on 7 June by two more to each island. The total strength of Panzerkampfwagen (PzKpfw) Char B1 *bis* (f), as the tanks were now called, was therefore 36, divided as follows:

Guernsey

Abteilung HQ: 2 x command version

No 2 Kompanie: 12 x normal gun tanks
                5 x flamethrowing tanks

Jersey

No 1 Kompanie   12 x normal gun tanks
                5 x flamethrowing tanks

Note: The flamethrowers had flame guns fitted in the hull in place of the 75mm hull gun and were known as PzKpfw B1 bis mit Flammenwerfer.

Thus began the history of the only Panzer unit to serve on British soil throughout the war, yet destined never to fire a shot in anger! The Guernsey company (2. Kompanie) and unit HQ were attached to Schnellabteilung 450, while those in Jersey (1. Kompanie) to Schnellabteilung 319. The 310 men (180 in Guernsey and 130 in Jersey) were commanded by a Maj Lecht from their arrival until he was posted to the Eastern Front in March 1944; he was replaced by a Maj Kopp.

Life with the Panzers

In a pamphlet entitled *German Armour in the Channel Islands 1941–45*, produced by the CIOS (Jersey Branch) Michael Ginns tells how all aspects of tank warfare were practised, despite the fact that the tanks could only manage about 0.5 miles/gal cross-country and fuel was in short supply! Live-firing practice took place on L'Eree headland on Guernsey, together with manoeuvres, during which there were at least two serious accidents — in one an Obergefreiter was crushed and fatally injured whilst guiding a tank in a confined space, while on another occasion a tank overturned in Talbot Valley trapping the commander who had to have his leg amputated to free him.

In Jersey, the sand dunes of Les Quennevais proved ideal for training, whilst for weapon training a dummy wooden tank was pulled along La Route de Quennevais on a temporary 60cm gauge railway. Infantry/tank co-operation was also practised. In addition to this training, the troops were 'kept busy with the usual routine matters sent to plague soldiers of any army! Mondays was always inspection day when all kit had to be laid out neatly for the Company Commander's perusal, and hair and fingernails had to be short and clean. Vehicle maintenance was essential and every day the Abteilung had to supply two trucks to work as required for the Organization Todt — carrying, for example, sand and stone to building sites all over the island.'[9]

The tank crewmen naturally all wore the distinctive black uniform of the Panzerwaffe, with the unique *Totenkopf* (Death's Head) collar badges, which — as indicated earlier — gave rise to another Occupation myth: that organised units of the SS served in both Jersey and Guernsey, as well as in Alderney. This was not the case; indeed, the SS usually only wore their black uniforms on ceremonial occasions after 1939, whilst the tankmen always wore theirs.

One tank still remains

Almost all the tanks which had been on the Islands were sent back to France to be scrapped or dumped at sea, but one still remains in existence — Tank No 114, which was No 4 tank in the 1.Zug of the 1.Abteilung (Jersey). It was sent to the School of Tank Technology in the UK in May 1946 for investigation and subsequently donated by them to the Tank Museum at Bovington where it still remains on show in the World War 2 Hall. Also on show there is a tiny FT17— although not one that served in the Channel Islands.

Artillery
Army Coastal Artillery Regiment

As already mentioned in a previous chapter, the various coastal artillery units which had arrived piecemeal in the Islands were, in May 1943, formed into a single coastal artillery regiment — Heeres Küsten Artillerie Regiment 1265, with its HQ at 'Tannenburg', Oberlands Road, Guernsey. The CO was ARKO (*Artilleriekommandeur* — artillery commander) Guernsey. There were four battalions in the regiment, two on Jersey and two on Guernsey:

I./HKAR 1265   — HQ at Mont Orgeuil Castle, Jersey

II./HKAR 1265 — HQ at Old Semaphore Station,
                 La Moye, Jersey

III./HKAR 1265 — HQ at Ruette de l'Eglise, Catel, Guernsey

IV./HKAR 1265 — HQ at St Peter's Arsenal, Guernsey

The battalions were divided into 16 batteries, located as follows:

Jersey

Batterie Endrass (No 4 Bty) — 4 x10.5cm K 331(f) field guns, located at Westmount, St Helier, with the task of blocking entry to the harbour.

Batterie Schliefen (No 13 Bty) and *Batterie Haeseler* (No 14 Bty) — both 4 x 15cm K 18 medium field guns, located at Verclut, Grouville and La Coupe, St Martin, respectively.

Batterie Moltke (No 5 Bty) — 4 x 15.5cm K 418(f) heavy field guns, located at Les Landes, St Ouen.

Batterie Ludendorff (No 2 Bty), *Batterie Hindenburg* (No 1 Bty) and *Batterie Mackensen* (No 3 Bty) — all 3 x 21cm Mrs (*Mörser*) 18 — field howitzers near to St Ouen's Church, Route Orange St Brelade and St Martin's Church.

Batterie Roon (No 6 Bty) — 4 x 22cm K 532(f) heavy field guns at La Moye Point, St Brelade.

Guernsey and Alderney

Batterie Naumannshohe (No 11 Bty) — 4 x 10.5cm K 331(f) field guns, located at Cambridge Park, St Peter Port.

Batterie Blücher (No 12 Bty) — 4 x 15cm K 18 medium field guns, located at St Anne, Alderney.

Batterie Barbara (No 10 Bty) — 4 x 15.5cm K 418(f) heavy field guns, located at North View.

Batterie Elefant (No 7 Bty), *Batterie Mammut* (No 8 Bty) and *Batterie Rhinozeros* (No 9 Bty) — all 3 x 21cm Mörser 18 — field howitzers, located at La Chaumière, Les Effards and Beauchamps respectively, all at Catel.

Batterie Dollmann (No 15) and *Batterie Radetzsky* (No 16) — each 4 x 22cm K 532(f)

Heavy field guns — located at Pleinmont Point and L'Eree respectively.

Table 5: **Coastal Artillery Weapons**

Typeand calibre	Country of origin	Weight (kg)	Weight of shell (kg)	Range (m)	Remarks
K 331(f)10.5cm	France	1,320	16.9	12,700	field gun (used for harbour blocking on all three islands)
K 18 15cm	Germany	12,760	43	24,500	field gun
SK L/45 15cm	Germany	NK	45.3	16,000	SK = 'ship's gun' (*Schiffskanone*) a turret-mounted naval gun
K 418(f) 15.5cm	France	10,750	43.1	16,200	field gun
Mörser 18 21cm	Germany	16,700	133	16,700	field howitzer
K 532(f) 22cm	France	25,000	103.5	22,800	heavy gun

Left:
Werner Wagenknecht learnt to drive this truck before progressing onto an ambulance. He is seen here in 1942, 'somewhere on Guernsey'.
Werner Wagenknecht

Fire control

Despite these guns being Army manned and under the command of the various Island ARKOs, it was the naval SEEKO-KI who had the ultimate responsibility for coastal defence, so the Army and Navy units involved in coastal defence had to work closely together in order to fulfil their tasks, which were:

- to give protection to all German shipping moving both between the Islands and between the Islands and the French mainland. They also had to give protection to naval vessels using the core route between Cherbourg and Brest.

- to protect the Gulf of St Malo from any invasion by Allied forces.

- to prevent landings on the Channel Islands.

Divisional artillery

AR 319 was, as has been explained, reinforced in order to be able to cope with all three islands. Battle HQ (*Kernwerk*) was located at L'Aleval on Jersey and CO AR 319 was ARKO Jersey. His four battalions were located thus: [10]

Jersey

I./AR 319   HQ at St Brelade, with batteries as follows:

Derflinger (unnumbered) — at Mont de la Rocque, St Brelade (2 x 8cm FK 30[t])

Fritsch (No 1 Bty) — at Mont Cambrai (4 x 10cm le FH14/19[t])

Seydlitz (No 2 Bty) — at Mont du Coin (4 x 8cm FK 30[t])

Ziethen (No 3 Bty) — L'Oeillere, St Brelade (4 x 10cm FH14/19[t])

II./AR 319   HQ at Mont Mallet (Victoria Tower) Geory, with batteries as follows:

Seeckt (No 4 Bty) — Rue de Blancq, St Clement (4 x 10cm FH14/19[t])

Dietl (No 5 Bty) — Maufant Road, St Saviour (4 x 10cm FH14/19[t])

Brauchitsch (No 6 Bty) — Daisy Hill, Gorey (4 x 10cm FH14/19[t])

Guernsey and Alderney (all on Guernsey except where shown)

III./AR 319   HQ at Les Vardes, St Peter Port, with batteries as follows:

Georgfeste (No 7 Bty) — Fort George (4 x 10cm FH14/19[t])

Sperber (No 8 Bty) — Delancey Park (4 x 10cm FH14/19[t])

Tiger (No 9 Bty) — Best's Brickyard (4 x 10cm FH14/19[t])

IV./AR 319   HQ Les Eturs House, with batteries as follows:

Wolf (No 10 Bty) — Talbot Valley (4 x 10cm FH14/19[t])

Falke (No 11 Bty] — St Anne, Alderney (4 x 10cm FH14/19[t])

Lux (No 12 Bty) — Mont Saint (4 x 10cm FH14/19[t])

(Source *CIOS Review [Jersey]* of May 1975)

Fire Direction control of these batteries was co-ordinated and run via the various naval direction and rangefinding positions (*Marinenpeilstände* [MP]) as explained in a later chapter.

Table 6: **Artillery Guns of AR 319**

Type and calibre	FK 30(t) 8cm	leFH 14/19(t) 10cm
Country of origin	Czech	Czech
Weight (kg)	1,816	1,505
Weight of shell (kg)	8	14
Range (m)	13,500	9,970
Remarks	originally Skoda M30	originally Skoda M14/19

Opposite top:
Cars and even buses were also taken over and used as troop transports. This party is on a tour of the island.
Hans-Gerhard Sandmann

Opposite:
One of the heavier military vehicles used on the Islands was this Tractor Semi-Track Medium, 8-ton SdKfz 7, which was used as an artillery tractor for weapons like the 88mm gun. Some 12,000 were built, all under Krauss-Maffei guidance. *IWM* — HU 29052

Above:
Men of 319. ID carry out
practice gun drill on a 3.7cm
Pak 35 anti-tank gun. An
excellent little gun,
it was considered too light to be
effective against most Allied
armour and was phased out in
many places, but not on the
Channel Islands.
IWM — HU 29018

Left:
A 5cm Pak 38 anti-tank gun in
a camouflaged emplacement,
thought to be on the high
ground south of Perelle Bay,
Guernsey, at Widerstandsnest
Perleberg. The gun, which is
just being loaded by its crew,
was considered good enough
to penetrate most Allied tanks
when it was introduced in 1940.
IWM — HU 29025

Above:
A gun crew manhandling a 7.5cm Pak 40 in a steep street near Havelet Bay, St Peter Port. Note the soldier hanging onto the gun barrel — he is not just 'having a free ride' but rather helping to balance the anti-tank gun as they reach the steepest part of the hill.
IWM — HU 29022

Above: The most feared anti-tank gun was the 8.8cm Pak 43 L71 (there were none on Jersey). The dreaded '88' was actually an AA gun, so it was used in both AA/Atk roles. It could penetrate 226mm of armour at 500yd in its ground role. *IWM* — HU 29050

Above: This French Canon de 105mle 1913 Schneider was pressed into German service and used for coastal defence work, and was known as the K 331(f). It was used on all three islands to block harbours. *IWM — HU 29033*

Opposite above: In 1941, a few 4.7cm Pak 36(t) auf GW Renault R35(f) appeared on the Islands and by the end of 1942 there were approximately nine of these SPs in Jersey, ten in Guernsey, two in Sark and one in Alderney, but it may have been that the last three came from the Guernsey ten. The anti-tank gun was a Czech weapon mounted on a French tank chassis — the Renault turrets being replaced by a box-like fixed armoured shield. *IWM — HU 29031*

Opposite: The main tank on the Islands was the ex-French Char B1*bis*, known by the Germans as the PzKpfw Char B1*bis* (f). Tank Battalion 213 was equipped with a total of 36 of these 32-ton heavy tanks, of which two were the command version and ten were equipped with flamethrowers. *IWM — HU 29037*

Above: Before the 'Hunger Winter' and supply lines were cut, the Occupation forces ate reasonably well. Here butchers of 216. ID cut up a carcass and distribute pieces. Is the soldier pouring a drink for the butcher in the hope of getting a nice cut? *Hans-Gerhard Sandmann*

Above: 'Are you receiving me?' A signals commander (*Nachrichten-Kommandeur*) watches two of his men at work. Military author Frank Kurowski reckoned that every fifth man in the German Army was in the signals arm of service. While I do not think this applied in the Islands, there was, nevertheless, a large amount of communications equipment used there by all three Services, although most of them used line rather than W/T and the Kriegsmarine provided the long-distance communications (see Chapter 6). *IWM* — HU 29041

Left:
The gunlayer of this 7.5cm FK 231(f) infantry gun checks his lay carefully during a practice shoot. The old French 75 was one of a number of foreign guns used to help provide close protection for coastal batteries.
IWM — HU 29030

Below:
A battery of 15cm guns at La Coupe to the north of Fliquet Bay, Jersey. Note the removable wire and scrim netting arrangement in order to camouflage the tell-tale circular gun pit from the air.
Société Jersiaise

An artillery battery on Guernsey

In one of the opening features I included drawings from *Festung Guernsey* which showed the layout of 7./HKAR 1265 (HKAR 1265's 7th Battery). This battery was part of III. Bataillon and was known as *Elefant Batterie*. I was fortunate enough to contact, via the good offices of Brian Owen, the Social History Officer of the Guernsey Museum, the son of one of the members of the battery, Herr Ludwig Späth. He has also kindly supplied some details about his father, the late Georg Späth, who served with the battery nonstop from 1 December 1940 until the surrender.

The map shows an enlargement of part of the layout of the battery area, which helps to fix the locations of some of the photographs and I must thank Richard Heaume, Pierre Renier and other members of CIOS (Guernsey) for positively identifying the locations around the Bailiff's Cross Road, La Mannie, in the parish of St Andrew's. The photographs show the arrival in Guernsey, the preparation of the gun positions, etc, and some of the living accommodation.

Above: The large 16,700kg howitzers needed a lot of muscle power in order to be manhandled off the lighters and onto the jetty at the docks when they arrived at Guernsey. The 21cm *Mörser* M18 was a medium howitzer manufactured by Krupp and dated from 1939.
Ludwig Späth via the Guernsey Museums and Galleries

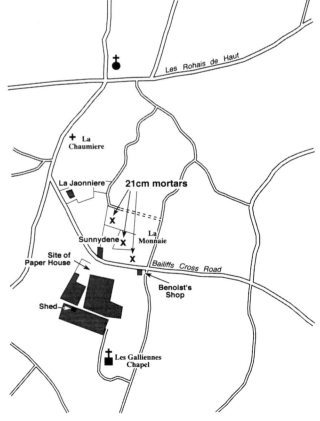

e: The battery commander poses against
f his howitzers. He is wearing the ribbon
1914 Iron Cross, 2nd Class in his
d buttonhole, which he won in World
. It has on it the added 'bar' indicating
ubsequent award of the 1939 Iron Cross,
Class. *Ludwig Späth
e Guernsey Museums and Galleries*

Right: A great deal of excavation was
then needed around the gun pit for
ammunition storage, crew shelters, etc.
*Ludwig Späth via the Guernsey
Museums and Galleries*

ove: Then the howitzers had to be 'tried for size', before the main excavation work
an on the gun pits. *Ludwig Späth via the Guernsey Museums and Galleries*

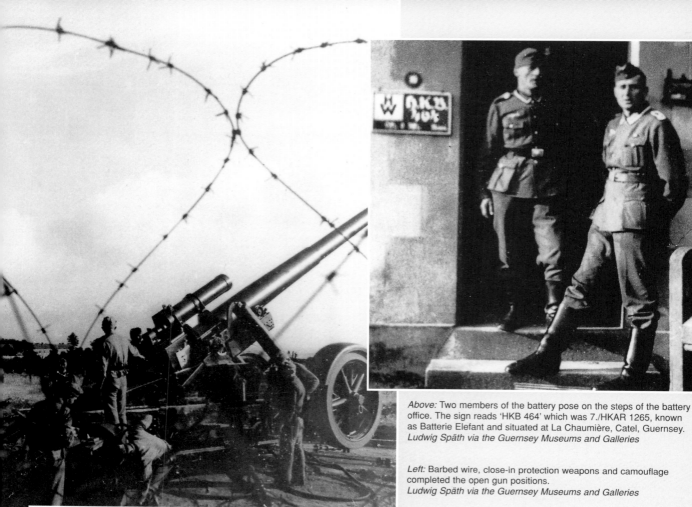

Above: Two members of the battery pose on the steps of the battery office. The sign reads 'HKB 464' which was 7./HKAR 1265, known as Batterie Elefant and situated at La Chaumière, Catel, Guernsey.
Ludwig Späth via the Guernsey Museums and Galleries

Left: Barbed wire, close-in protection weapons and camouflage completed the open gun positions.
Ludwig Späth via the Guernsey Museums and Galleries

Below: La Jaonnière, Bailiff's Cross Road. This appears to have been on of the billets for the battery senior ranks, possibly the officers. The hous still looks much the same, except that it has lost its ivy and flower bed
Ludwig Späth via the Guernsey Museums and Gallerie

Above: At his desk, the battery commander is hard at work. His battery sergeant-major beside him is wearing a 1936 service uniform with the double rings of 0.9cm braiding worn on both cuffs to indicate '*der Spiess*'. Note the field telephone on the desk; also the stereoscope for looking at aerial photographs.
Ludwig Späth via the Guernsey Museums and Galleries

ove: Part of the battery on parade outside
ds on The Vinery behind the 'Paper House'.
 sheds are still standing but somewhat
nged. *Ludwig Späth*
 the Guernsey Museums and Galleries

ow: 'Sunnydene', Bailiff's Cross Road. Another
 t for battery personnel. The main changes
 t have been made here are a new porch and a
 galow built next door. *Ludwig Späth*
 the Guernsey Museums and Galleries

Right: This striking black and
white building was known as
the 'Paper House'. It was
clearly an important part of the
battery fire co-ordination set-up
and its observation tower was
subsequently draped with a
camouflage net. It was
demolished postwar.
*Ludwig Späth via the Guernsey
Museums and Galleries*

Above: Battery personnel relax outside Benoist's Stores at the corner of
the crossroads of Bailiff's Cross Road. The building is still there but is no
longer a shop. *Ludwig Späth via the Guernsey Museums and Galleries*

Above: Manhandling the howitzer shells onto a handcart to take them to the guns. Each shell weighed 133kg. *Ludwig Späth via the Guernsey Museums and Galleries*

Below: Battery personnel on parade outside some of the vinery glasshouses, many of which have now been cleared.
Ludwig Späth via the Guernsey Museums and Galleries

Above: Presumably these are members of the battery marching past the houses on Bailiff's Cross Road. They wear a mixture of uniforms, including the unbleached denims — jacket and trousers — worn with the normal leather belt, and jackboots. *Ludwig Späth via the Guernsey Museums and Galleries*

Left: Gun control and range-taking staff at work in the observation tower of the 'Paper House'. The range-taker is nearest the camera. *Ludwig Späth via the Guernsey Museums and Galleries*

Left & below: Inside some of the vinery glasshouses construction work also went on, but on a much smaller scale than at the gun positions. *Ludwig Späth via the Guernsey Museums and Galleries*

Left: The result of this building work was a 'sand table' model of the battery area. *Ludwig Späth via the Guernsey Museums and Galleries*

Right: The end product. Firing one of the 21cm howitzers. The Mörser 18 had a range of some 16,700m. *Ludwig Späth via the Guernsey Museums and Galleries*

Chapter 5
The Sailor

NAVAL ORGANISATION

As we have seen, the basic Kriegsmarine organisation ran down from the OKM, Grossadmiral Erich Raeder's supreme naval command, through Admiral Theodor Krancke's (1) Naval Group West HQ in Paris, to the Admiral in Charge of the Channel Coast and thence to the Naval C-in-C, Channel Islands — SEEKO-KI — Kapitän sur Zee Julius Steinbach (July 1942–July 1944, then Vizeadmiral Friedrich Hüffmeier), whose HQ was on a par with the other SEEKOs at Le Havre, Cherbourg, etc. Before a SEEKO-KI was appointed, the senior post had been *Hafenkommandant Kanalinseln* (Harbour Commander Channel Islands) created in July 1940, and filled by Korvettenkapitän Freiherr von Nostig, whose HQ was at the Terminus Hotel, Weighbridge St Helier, Jersey, but soon moved to the Pomme d'Or Hotel. SEEKO-KI's HQ was initially located, from the summer of 1942, in two large houses (La Porte and La Collinette) on Guernsey, the latter being adjacent to the naval signal bunker, and the other just across the road. From February 1944 a bunker at St Jacques, on the outskirts of St Peter Port, was built for *Marinenachrichtenoffizier Kanalinseln* (Naval Signals Officer Channel Islands) and, later, another connecting bunker was added for SEEKO-KI.

NAVAL RESPONSIBILITIES

SEEKO-KI's responsibilities covered all usual naval activities via the three *Hafenkommandanten* (Harbour Commanders) of St Peter Port, St Helier and St Anne, on Guernsey, Jersey and Alderney respectively. However, perhaps his most important function as far as the actual close defence of the Islands was concerned was the command of all the naval and coastal artillery. There was from the outset considerable sea traffic between the Islands and mainland France concerned with routine island garrison administration (eg troop movements, supplies, leave parties, mail, etc), but this traffic increased dramatically after Hitler's decision to fortify the Islands led Organization Todt to begin its work. There was a certain amount of disruption caused by Allied activity — both naval and air — with ships being lost, until a total ban on all day convoys had to be imposed. In addition, existing cargo handling facilities on the Islands simply could not cope with the massive increase in traffic and new machinery had to be brought in — one outstanding example being a large French-built, Dutch-owned floating derrick, the *Antee,* which arrived in Guernsey in 1941. Its first job was the unloading of the massive 30.5cm gun barrels for the *Mirus* Battery.

Above: 'The pledge of the German Navy'. A propaganda poster issued in 1939. *Author's collection*

NAVAL ARTILLERY

In view of their importance to Island defence, we will look at these responsibilities first. Under one of the many orders issued by Hitler's headquarters, Directive No 40 of 23 March 1942, it became one of the primary tasks of the Kriegsmarine to prevent an enemy landing on the Channel Islands. Only if and when they had landed, did it become the business of the Heer. SEEKO-KI was thus responsible for the firing of a wide range of coastal artillery weapons.

Marine Artillerie Abteilung (MAA) 604 and 605

These two Naval Artillery Battalions operated coastal artillery batteries, MAA 604 on Jersey and Guernsey and MAA 605 on Alderney. MAA 604 had originally been formed in 1940 as a result of a directive from Hitler to neutralise the British strongholds in the western Mediterranean, including occupying Gibraltar. MAA 604 had been formed from various naval artillery units at Wilhelmshaven where, by the end of November 1940, it had been rearmed and fully kitted out. The appropriate ships to carry them had been refitted and vehicle transport assembled at the embarkation port of Hamburg, where the soldiers of MAA 604 were allocated the turbo-electric ship *Potsdam* as their floating barracks.

The western Mediterranean project (Operation 'Felix') was cancelled on 21 December 1940, after the Spanish dictator, Gen Franco, had made strong objections; this left MAA 604 fully operational, stationed at Hamburg, but with 'no place to go'! The fortunate artillerymen, therefore, were given leave — half over Christmas (mainly the married ones) and then the rest early in the New Year. In January 1941, they were transferred to the Hook of Holland and later carried out practice firing using old captured French railways guns (19.4 cm K(E)486(f)), which were identical to the weapons emplaced on the islet of Cezembre, outside St Malo.

By March 1941, Hitler had decided to boost the Channel Islands' defence, fortifying them and equipping them with naval coastal batteries. Thus, MAA 604 was the ideal unit to send. They began to arrive in May 1941, to be located as follows:

HQ and Staff (*HQ und Stab*) — St Martin's, Guernsey.

No 1 Battery — *Strassburg Batterie* — Jerbourg Point, Guernsey (4 x 22cm K 532[f] guns).

No 2 Battery — *Steinbruch Batterie* — Les Vardes, Guernsey (4 x 15cm SK c/28 guns).

No 3 Battery — *Lothringen Batterie* — Noirmont Point, Jersey (4 x 15cm SK L/45 guns).

Mirus Batterie — Le Frie Baton, Guernsey (4 x 30.5cm K 626[r]).

Mirus was the largest coastal battery, with the longest range. Named 'Mirus' after a Kriegsmarine captain who had been killed during an air attack, the battery was 'ready for action' in mid-1942.

Sark Batterie. In October 1944 a battery of 3 x 8.8cm SK guns was established on Little Sark, with guns taken from a laid-up naval vessel.

Marine Artillerie Abteilung 605 first made its appearance in the Islands around mid-1942. It was connected with the establishment of the Channel Islands as a Sea Defence Area in its own right.

Close protection weapons
Each of the batteries' guns had first to operate from temporary positions, but later concrete platforms were added, as were bunkers and ammunition shelters. In order to provide close protection for these large coastal guns, a range of smaller weapons and searchlights were supplied. As an example, these details are of the allocation to Batterie Lothringen:

2 x 7.5cm FK 231(f) field guns

6 x 2cm Flak Oerlikon AA guns

1 x 2.5cm Pak 113(f) light anti-tank gun

2 x 5cm GrW 36 mortars

2 x MG 311(f) machine guns in tank turrets

11 x MG34 machine guns

16 x flamethrowers

1 x 60cm searchlight

1 x 110cm searchlight

1 x 150cm searchlight

Initially MAA 604 also had to provide coastal artillery defence on Alderney. However, there was a considerable lack of recreational facilities on the island, so the batteries were rotated there every three months or so. They still did not like the upheaval and in any case it was soon discovered that, whilst the changeovers were taking place, neither of the two batteries concerned was fully operational. This was rectified in June 1942, when MAA 605 arrived and took over Alderney completely, with the CO MAA 605 becoming ARKO Alderney. MAA 605 had three batteries:

No 1 Battery — *Elsass Batterie* — Fort Albert (3 x 17cm SK L/40)

No 2 Battery — *Annes Batterie* — West coast (4 x 15cm SK c/28)

No 3 Battery — *Marcks Batterie* — Western slopes of Fort Albert (4 x 10.5cm K 331[f]) — from June 1944 onwards.

Fire control and command
All these naval coastal batteries had their command posts (*Leitstande*) within well-constructed bunkers which contained the sort of fire control equipment which could have been found on an up-to-date German warship. Probably the most complex was the one for Batterie Mirus, but most were of two or more storeys and all incorporated crew quarters on the lower level. One such command post remains virtually intact at Noirmont Point, Jersey.

Heeres Küsten Artillerie Regiment 1265
I have already described the layout of this Army Coastal Artillery Regiment, which had batteries on all three islands. It will be remembered that the weapons operated ranged in calibre mainly from 15cm up to 22cm, forming a considerable slice of SEEKO-KI's potential firepower. Guns of the 12th battery on Alderney (four K18s) were able to reach out to the edge of the Cotentin Peninsula, but not as far as Cherbourg. As we will describe later, this battery was heavily engaged by the British battleship HMS *Rodney* and one of the guns was put out of action. It was only

Above: The office of the *Hafenkommandant der Kanalinseln* was at the Pomme d'Or Hotel, St Helier, Jersey. *Société Jersiaise*

temporarily silenced, however, as the Germans were able to improvise replacement shock absorbers and thus get the weapon back into action quite quickly. Identical guns were transferred between the Islands by a ship called *Robert Mueller 8,* which was often attacked by Allied destroyers, but survived all of their assaults. HKAR 1265 also operated six batteries of three 21cm medium howitzers — three on Jersey and three on Guernsey. Accurate but slow in action, because they had to be hand elevated/depressed after every firing, they would have been extremely useful had the enemy landed.

Artillerie Regiment 319

This was the artillery regiment that was normally an integral part of 319. ID, so SEEKO-KI's responsibility was only for those elements which manned the coastal guns and beach bunkers. As we have already seen, the regiment also manned numerous Czech-built 10cm leFH 14/19(t) field guns, which provided normal artillery support all over the Channel Islands.

Flak Batteries

These were manned by the Luftwaffe, so once again control was not absolute and the AA guns could fire at enemy aircraft without having to get approval from SEEKO-KI.

GENERAL NAVAL RESPONSIBILITIES

SEEKO-KI was thus responsible for the fire of a wide range of weaponry and in his absence permission to fire requests went to the CO of 1265 Coastal Artillery Regiment, Oberstlt Pedell. SEEKO-KI was also responsible for a range of general, but none the less important, naval responsibilities such as:

Hafenschutzflotillen

The Harbour Defence Flotillas in St Peter Port and St Helier. These comprised small armed boats, primarily for harbour defence duties; however, as we shall see later, they did take part in other activities, especially after D-Day.

Matrosenkompanien 'König' und 'Hilger'

These special companies of naval infantry were based in Jersey and Guernsey. The former took over the manning of most of the infantry strongpoints in the St Aubin's Bay area, whilst the latter looked after the strongpoints from St Peter Port to St Sampson.

E-Boats *(Schnellboote)*

There were no E-Boats permanently stationed in the Islands for long periods; instead they normally operated out of Cherbourg, where in 1943 both the 5th and 6th Flotillas were based. However, from time to time they would be temporarily located in Guernsey in order to carry out raids (as below) or would call in on their way from/to their main base. They had their usual docking spaces in St Peter Port harbour. Other E-Boats were based at Ostend (2nd Flotilla) and Boulogne (4th Flotilla), but later in the year all returned to their normal bases in Holland, leaving just the 5th Flotilla resident in Cherbourg for operations against Allied shipping.

The following year, they would score a major success in the Lyme Bay area, while the Allies were in the middle of training for the D-Day landings. On the night of 27/28 April 1944, six E-Boats of the 5th Flotilla and three of the 9th sailed from Cherbourg and attacked a convoy during Exercise 'Tiger', while it was on its way across Lyme Bay to land troops and equipment on Slapton Sands. Two heavily-laden LSTs were sunk and another badly damaged. Allied losses were 197 sailors and 441 soldiers — more than would be killed on 'Utah' Beach on D-Day.

Above: An E-Boat travelling at speed. This was the design of the normal E-Boat, which had two torpedo tubes and space for a crew of 14 men. Later, with the increasing danger of air attack, a new style bridge (known as the 'Skullcap' *Kalottenbrücke)* was introduced and armour progressively fitted. *Author's collection*

Below: This was the type of small coastal trawler on which Helmut Lucke served. Note the various armaments which could be used both for AA defence and for engaging naval targets. *IWM — HU 29101*

Above: Helmut Lucke and the rest of the crew of the small wooden trawler pose somewhere on Alderney. They wear the standard blue pullover shirts (*Bluse*) and matching trousers and sailor's caps. *Helmut Lucke*

Left: In this portrait shot of Helmut Lucke he is wearing his pea jacket with his Leading Seaman (*Matrosen-Obergefreiter*) chevrons and Signaller (*Signal*) crossed flags above. *Helmut Lucke*

Right: This white, summer-only uniform, is on show in the Occupation Museum, Guernsey. Note the various badges on the sleeve which are: flag at the top denoting admiral's staff, next the Petty Officer/deck rating anchor (in silver metal), *Flak* artillery specialist badge (in red embroidery), mine laying/boom defence specialist badge (also in red embroidery), whilst on the pocket is a silver wound badge denoting several wounds. *Brian Matthews*

E-Boat operations

Dr Hardy Hoogh was serving in the 5th Flotilla and has recalled some of his adventures on an E-Boat:

'The "Jockels" (auxiliary motors) of the 5th Flotilla E-Boats begin to roar in the bulky air-raid shelter at Cherbourg's west harbour, as the machines are pre-heated. Tonight we plan to lay mines near Eddystone Rocks.

'After dark the six E-Boats slowly pass the breakwaters. Once outside: "All Aller!" (Aller = French: "Go"). We wind up to 6,000hp. The boats plough at high speed through the Channel. Course true 2800. Wakes gleam fluorescent behind the boats, so do the white crests at wind speed 4. No stars. No moon. The sky is completely overcast — so conditions are ideal. The engines roar along steady and soothing. We're crossing Hurd Deep, and check our position by comparing our chart position with the sonic depth-finder. The difference is less than three fathoms.

'Long after midnight, starboard ahead the tall needle of Start Point Lighthouse emerges. The flotilla turns west. After a while, Eddystone Rocks Lighthouse rises out of the gloom with a faint light, which is surprising, as usually the lights are switched off. Anyway there is no time to speculate. The boats form line abreast as we arrive at the target area. Tension among crews rises and the commanders confer briefly. Binoculars watch the Chief-of-Flotilla's boat.

"Speed all slow!"
At the stern sailors stand by. The shackle of the first mine is opened.

"Ready?"
"Ready!"

"Let go!" A push and the first of the "Devil's eggs" rushes down the leading rails into the depths. A stopwatch punctuates the work as mine after mine now disappears with a splash into the water. The deck-crew works hard.

"Here she goes!" — "Pop 'er down!" — "Get ye gone!" After a time the work is done and a new minefield blocks the entrance to Plymouth Harbour.

'The Flotilla turns for home. Cornwall's silent silhouette falls behind. We haven't been discovered — at least not so far. Relief from strain. A "Backschafter" (a cook's galley rating) enters the bridge with fresh hot coffee and sandwiches. If the Limeys stay away and nothing unexpected happens, the Flotilla might pass beyond Cap de la Hague before dawn. At that instant our radio-operator mounts the bridge. Headquarters have announced an enemy convoy SSW off the Lizard, heading on an easterly course. The night promises to become interesting — but that's another story!'

His next reminiscence is about an attack on a British convoy off Torquay, which he called 'Raid in a row' as that was the formation in which the E-Boats went into the attack. He recalled:

'It was one of those gentle nights in the spring of 1942. In the silky air you might forget the damned bloody war. However, roaring engines remind everyone that the flotilla's E-Boats are on their way to raid an incoming enemy convoy off Torquay. Some time later we lie in wait, with silence pervading the smooth waters. Binoculars try to penetrate the darkness. The boat sways in the swell. Something rattles on deck. S81 drifts from her position.

"All Ahead Dead Slow."
"Going Dead Slow."
"Port Ten."
"Going Port Ten"
"Stop!"

'S81 is once again with five other E-Boats in a row, which stretches over about half a sea mile. Where is the convoy? On the bridge the strain is almost tangible. Then all at once silhouettes emerge from the darkness — six, seven, eight shadows. There follows a short burst of communication among the commanders. The fourth ship, a cargo-liner of some 10,000 tons, is selected as our target.

"Position 40 — Speed 12". The "Mixer" (torpedo-mechanic) adjusts the "eels", preparing the pressure valves.

"Starboard Ready?"
"Ready!"
"Port Ready?"
"Ready!"

'One last correction — "Position 50," then: "GO!"

'Push on the button and two shocks rock the boat. The "eels" leave bubble-tracks in their wake. Stop-watches tick — 10 seconds . . . 15. At both sides of the boat the sailors hurry to prepare the next two torpedoes . . . 40 - 50 seconds . . . the new "eels" are put into the tubes . . . 80 . . . 90 . . . Worried, waiting, then at 108 seconds there is a huge flash. One torpedo has hit the target just behind the bridge. The other one missed. Suddenly all is brightness as parachute flares illuminate the night. Guns bark. Fountains of water splash up rather too close for comfort.

"Hard to port!"
"Full throttle."
"All EK (Erste Kraft = highest possible speed)!"

'Now we are no longer all in a row. I have no idea how long we grappled with British naval units, the flotilla is scattered over a wide area. Dawn creeps up and we cross Hurd Deep (the deepest part of the English Channel — 565ft) returning to Cherbourg. Two E-Boats have sustained casualties — seamen wounded by shell fragments. Two ships of the convoy have been sunk by our torpedoes, and we discover later that a third ship had to be towed into Torquay harbour. No boat of the flotilla is lost — good luck indeed!

'Did we think about what we were doing? At the time certainly not — we had a job to do and we tried to do it to the best of our abilities. In 1942, we thought of it almost as a game.

'I remember another night mission in the Channel when we tangled with the enemy south of Beachy Head — even aircraft were involved on that occasion. *Afterwards, as we made our way back to base, we heard a faint shouting. Engines were stopped, but we could not turn on our searchlights as the English fighter aircraft were still around and it was pretty dangerous. The rest of the flotilla was already long gone. Cautiously we manoeuvred in the direction of the cries and rescued a ditched pilot in his tiny rubber raft from out of the waves. The lad turned out to be a young Polish pilot. For more than an hour he had paddled in the rough sea. He didn't dare fire his emergency flares, because he was afraid of being caught by the Germans, who — so he had been told — would brutalise their prisoners. He was brought down into the crew mess. The shivering guy was given some hot coffee and sausage sandwiches. Offering him a cigarette, one of our sailors tried to cheer him up a bit: "Look, you lost the game" he commiserated, "but you gained your life!" As I remarked earlier, at that time we looked at the war more from a sporting angle.'*

Minesweeping flotillas

From D-Day onwards, Minesweeping Flotillas (*Minensuchflottillen*) 24 and 46 were virtually trapped on the Channel Islands. The former comprised nine vessels (*M343, M402, M412, M422, M432, M442, M452, M475* and *M483*), whilst the latter consisted of a variety of fishing vessels.

Submarines

As with E-Boats, there were no U-Boats permanently stationed in the Channel Islands, although they did visit from time to time to berth up and refuel. For example, on 14 June 1944, *U275* entered St Peter Port harbour during the early hours and berthed there. That evening, at about 17.15hrs, the submarine was attacked by American P-47 Thunderbolts, but they missed with their rockets, which struck the Dutch-registered MV *Karel* berthed opposite causing it to catch fire, killing two crew members and wounding two others. The MV *Karel* was being used to run supplies from France to the islands for the German garrison and the OT.

Below: A tug towing protective anti-submarine nets at St Peter Port harbour, Guernsey. IWM — HU 29098

There was a plan to build an underground fuel store near the harbour of St Peter Port for the refuelling of U-Boats, because the Germans were experiencing problems with the RAF bombing the fuel tanks adjacent to Castle Cornet. U-Boats were to be refuelled in the bay behind the Aquarium tunnel and fuel pumped through to the vessel's mooring. However, the complex was never completed. The site now houses La Valette Underground Military Museum.

Merchant shipping

A fair number of assorted merchant ships originating in Germany, France, Holland and other European locations were used to bring supplies of war materials, food, clothing, etc for both the German garrison and the civilian population, from the French mainland to the Islands. They also carried service personnel, OT and slave labour and other passengers, both to and from the Islands. Indeed, without the sea convoys throughout 1940–44, the Islands could never have become or been maintained as a fortress. If one considers that at the peak of activity, when the building of fortifications was in full swing and work at its height, the Islands contained over 60,000 people, then the enormity of the task to supply food alone can be appreciated. This dependence was shown dramatically when the cutting of the sea supply line imposed the 'Hunger Winter' of 1944/45, bringing everyone to near starvation level.

Some of these merchant vessels were crewed by German merchant seamen, others still by their original French or Dutch crews. However, all invariably had German anti-aircraft gun crews and their weapons added for protection purposes, while the convoys would be further protected by both E-Boats and *Artillerieträger* (artillery carriers). These ships would be attacked by the Allies from the sea and air, when it was impossible to discover beforehand what cargo was being carried. Consequently, as might have been expected, many of the lives lost in such encounters were civilians, some being forced labourers and other such innocent victims. Some examples of losses of these vessels is shown in Table 7. This list is not exhaustive, but will give some idea of the range of activities on both sides.

Table 7: **Examples of Ship Losses around the Channel Islands**

SS *Staffa* (motor sailing boat) German (Guernsey origin) 12 Mar 41	Taken over as a 'prize of war' and used for a regular trading service between the Islands of Guernsey, Alderney, Sark, Herm, Jethou and Brechou, taking passengers as well as cargo, provided they could get the necessary travel permits. Eventually the condition of the small motor sailing boat deteriorated so badly that she needed continual maintenance. After a delayed departure on 12 March from Alderney, she broke her stern moorings and was driven onto the rocks and badly holed.
SS *Batavier V* (cargo/passenger ship) German (Dutch origin) 3 Nov 41	A Dutch cargo/passenger vessel, seized by the Germans in May 1940 and used for supplying the Channel Islands until she was sunk by a British MTB west of Cap Griz Nez.
SS *Lafcomo* (bulk carrier) German (USA origin) 6 Jan 42	French owned, she was seized by the Germans in Bordeaux in August 1940, then used for irregular visits to the Islands. Bombed in Guernsey by Beaufort fighter-bombers whilst discharging a cargo of cement. Refloated in February 1942, but thereafter not used in Channel Islands waters.
MV *Henca* (coaster) German (Dutch origin) 9 Sep 42	Dutch registered, she was sunk north of Alderney by RAF aircraft whilst with another coaster MV *Tinda* and being escorted by two armed trawlers, one of which was also badly straffed (two dead and 17 wounded), whilst the *Henca* was hit by a bomb.
MS *Helma* (motor schooner) German 27 Apr 43	Sunk by Whirlwind fighter-bombers off Jersey, she had been built as a sailing ship in 1914, but converted to a motor schooner in 1936. Used for supply running between Granville, St Malo and the Channel Islands. Bombed whilst carrying a cargo of potatoes.
MV *Oost Vlaanderen* Dutch 23 May 43	Dutch registered, she arrived with a convoy of some seven other ships at St Peter Port with a cargo of cement. However, before she was able to berth, she was sunk by the RAF.
SS *Livadia* German 4 Oct 43	One of the largest ships used on the supply run, she had been ordered for OP Sea Lion. She carried some of the tanks of Pz Abt 213 to the Islands. She was sunk by British coastal batteries whilst near Calais.
SS *Bizon* German (Belgian built) 8 May 44	Taken over by the Kriegsmarine from a Danish firm and used for supply running along the French coast and the Islands. Sunk by French MTBs off Guernsey.
SS *Maas* Dutch 14 Jun 44	Badly damaged off Jersey in April 1943, then sunk in June 1944 at Le Havre.
MV *Hydra* German (Dutch origin) 22 Jun 44	Used mainly by Organization Todt, but also made two journeys with French Red Cross medical supplies in April and May 1944. Sunk by Canadian MTBs near St Helier.
SS *Normand* German (French origin) 2 Jul 44	Another prize of war, sailed by a German master and crew in the St Malo area, then by a Jersey master and crew on the Islands supply route, until the Jersey master was arrested for refusing to ship munitions for the Germans. Later, she was scuttled by her German crew in order to attempt to block Cherbourg harbour.
MV *Rheinland* German 7 Aug 44	Another vessel requisitioned for Op Sea Lion, then used to transport supplies to the Islands. Bombed in St Malo harbour and later salvaged and returned postwar to its original owners.

Source: All these examples are taken from CIOS (Jersey) Branch Archives Book No 5: *Channel Islands Merchant Shipping 1940-1945* by Capt John Wallbridge and David Hocquard, edited by Peter J. Bryans and published by CIOS (Jersey Branch).

'Floating artillery'

This was the Artillerieträger which was used in the Kriegsmarine for a number of tasks which included escort duties, minelaying, troop transportation and even as landing barges. However, in the Channel Islands they were used as artillery carriers.

Four such vessels had operated out of Cherbourg prior to D-Day, being used to lay mines, then they had fallen back to St Malo, one being sunk by British MTBs on the night of 23/24 June 1944. From St Malo, the three remaining artillery carriers — AF65, AF68 and AF71 — were sent to the Channel Islands to become part of the sea defence under 2. *Vorpostenflottille* (2nd Patrol Boat flotilla), based at St Helier Harbour, Jersey. In an article which appeared in the 1983 edition of the *CIOS Review*, Capt John Wallbridge tells how their main job became escort work for the many small convoys which had to run the gauntlet between the Islands:

'They sailed day or night with their convoys under the protection of the shore-batteries on each island. At one stage, after the British and her Allies had tightened their grip on the Islands sea ways, they had two boats stationed in Guernsey and one in Jersey which then only required them to run out half-way to meet or deliver the convoy into the other's charge and then return to their original bases.'

He also talks about the atrocious weather in which they had to operate, which caused convoys to be cancelled. On one occasion, the CI Commander, GenOb von Schmettow had to put up with a stomach-wrenching six-hour journey on board an Artillerieträger, in order to get to Jersey from his HQ at Guernsey.

Above: Artillerieträger 65 which was used for a variety of tasks, including the protection of local convoys between the Islands. They were built mainly in Belgium and converted in Holland and had a displacement of some 200-280 tons. *IWM — HU 29097*

Left: Good close-up of an Artillerieträger. Note the insignia of crossed shells on the side of the bridgehouse. One can see a bicycle parked against the breech of one of the guns! The officer wears the ribbon of the Iron Cross, 2nd Class and the Iron Cross, 1st Class on his pocket, while his naval artillerymen wear a mixture of uniforms. *RAF Museum*

Right: An excellent photograph of an operational Artillerieträger, showing two sets of armament forward of the bridge, plus life rafts, etc and some members of the 50-man crew. *Société Jersiaise*

The Naval Signals Bunker

One of the most important officers in SEEKO-KI's headquarters was Oblt Willi Hagedorn who held the post of Naval Signals Officer, having been specially asked for by Steinbach. An enthusiastic postwar radio ham and a visitor to the Islands, Hagedorn's phenomenal memory of the war years was used to considerable effect by the CIOS during his visits. For his part he was somewhat shattered to discover that all his radio signals, over which he had lavished so much care and attention, had been intercepted and decoded by the enemy. It was he who had also supervised the construction of the signals bunker at St Jacques, which was completed in February 1944. The bunker was his pride and joy and after the war he kept a large blown-up copy of an RAF aerial reconnaissance photograph of the bunker whilst it was under construction, in his cellar radio room in his house in Hoxter, from where he would contact other radio hams all over the world. 'I used to think that my bunker was a closely guarded secret,' he once said with a rueful grin, 'but all the time the British knew exactly where it was!'

Over a period of some 12 months in 1996–97, the CIOS (Guernsey) had been renovating the signals bunker at St Jacques and had hoped to ask Willi Hagedorn to perform the opening. Sadly, however, he died on 4 July 1997. To quote from his obituary which appeared in *CIOS Review* No 25:

'He was an impressive man, larger than life and his many reminiscences will be greatly missed: eg he never stinted in his praise for the activities of the Royal Navy, and when relating the circumstances of the German commando raid on Granville, he emphasised that the raid would never have been attempted had the British been in charge at the French port that night. "Because," Willi said, "whenever we carried out operations against the British Navy they always responded correctly and fiercely!"

BASIC DRESS AND PERSONAL EQUIPMENT

Headgear

This was mainly traditional, being the sailor's cap with tally ribbon for the lower ranks and peaked cap for the officers. The former was gradually replaced by a blue woollen forage cap, while the latter had gilt wire embroidery on the peak to indicate rank. Hat bands (for ratings, caps only) had the name of their ship or just '*Kriegsmarine*' embroidered onto them. On the front of the various headgear was the national cockade with the eagle and swastika above it.

The pullover shirt (*Bluse*)

One of the most widely used items of naval uniform was the *Bluse*. The winter version was made of navy blue melton cloth, with cuffs that fastened with a button, and a cornflower blue collar edged with three white bands and a black silk. The national emblem was worn on the right breast (in yellow silk/cotton embroidery), and badges of rank/trade were worn on the left sleeve. There was a summer version which was worn in tropical waters or between April and September in temperate climes. Its cuffs were cornflower blue, trimmed with white and fastened by gilt anchor buttons; insignia was also cornflower blue on a white backing. The *Bluse* was worn with navy blue trousers of similar material to the winter shirt. Finally, there was a very strong working version of the *Bluse* made out of white woollen cloth, with a simple plain collar.

The uniform jacket (*Dienstjackett* or *Paradejackett*)

Considerably more elaborate was the uniform jacket which could be worn over the Bluse (with the pullover collar outside). The jacket fastened with a small chain link and was worn by sailors and petty officers only as service dress. Badges were worn as per the Bluse, and the cuffs of PO/CPOs' jackets were decorated with gilt wire braid. Two other types of jacket were worn: the pea jacket (*Uberzieher*) and the reefer jacket (*Jackett*).

The pea jacket was designed to be worn in lieu of a greatcoat over the Bluse or the Dienst/Paradejackett, by all grades of seamen and POs. It was thick, warm and double-breasted, being fastened with five anchor buttons. In addition to the national emblem and normal rank/trade badges, collar patches were also worn.

The reefer jacket was worn by all ranks above CPO as parade dress/service dress, or as walking out uniform. The material was similar to that of the pea jacket (thick blue melton cloth), but it was better cut and was normally worn with the top button undone. The national emblem in yellow thread (for warrant officers) and gilt wire (commissioned officers) was worn on the right breast.

Standard uniform for officers and WOs in the summer was the white summer jacket (*Weisses Jackett*) which was single-breasted and fastened with four gilt buttons, with an open collar (a collar and tie was worn below) and four pleated patch pockets. Shoulder-straps indicated the wearer's rank and the national emblem was worn as normal in gilt wire. All buttons and insignia could be removed for cleaning. It was worn with white trousers, white shirt and black tie.

Exclusive wear for officers was the mess jacket (*Messejackett*), made of fine blue material with four buttons on each side in front and fastened by a small chain. Sleeve rings indicated rank and it was normally worn with a matching waistcoat, stiff white shirt and black bow tie. There was also a white version of the mess jacket for summer wear, on which rank was indicated by shoulder-straps instead of sleeve rings.

The greatcoat (*Mantel*)

Only worn by WOs and above, it was double-breasted, had a double row of seven buttons and a half-belt at the rear, deep turned back cuffs and was normally worn buttoned up to the neck (unless the wearer had a neck decoration — such as the Knight's Cross to display). The coat had cornflower blue lapels for admirals, while ranks were indicated on the shoulder-straps.

There was also a three-quarter length coat — the *Gehrock* (frock coat) sometimes worn by officers for official functions and an 'opera-type' cloak, secured at the neck by a chain and lined with silver-grey silk.

War badges

A large number of war badges were created during the war, designed to reflect bravery/combat experience/special duties, etc. The design reflected the type of unit in which the sailors were serving; so, for example, there were special badges for U-Boat service (awarded after two operational cruises or being wounded); for service on minesweepers and escort vessels (three operational tours, or six months' active service, or wounded in action, etc); and a motor-torpedo boat badge (there were even special gilted solid silver editions of this badge, with nine diamonds on the swastika, but only eight were ever awarded).

Naval artillery and other land-based personnel

A field grey-green tunic, with stand-up collar and four patch pockets was worn by all land naval artillery units (coastal defence or AA) and other land-based units (eg Matrosenkompanie König in Jersey), which closely resembled the normal army uniform.[2] It was also worn by sailors during their initial training and by some sailors towards the end of the war, when crews of obsolete vessels were drafted into land units. An army-style cap was also worn or the regulation steel helmet (possibly camouflage-painted in grey-green and dark yellow blurred patches). On the blueish-green wool cloth shoulder tabs (pointed and with no piping) of the jacket was the artillery insignia — an anchor overlaid with a bomb — in bright yellow thread. The tunic chest eagle was also in yellow thread, whilst the collar patches were woven in grey thread with thin yellow piping down the middle. Straight grey-green trousers were worn with the tunic, tucked into black leather jackboots. The field-grey tunic buttons were adorned with the Kriegsmarine anchor. Naval personnel who served with these units could earn the Naval Artillery Badge (*Kriegsabzeichen für Marineartillerie)* by earning a total of eight 'points' — for example two were given for shooting down an enemy aircraft, one point if another gun was assisting and half a point for detecting an enemy plane, etc.

Personal weapons

The standard small arms, as already described, were normally used by naval personnel; daggers (including a highly ornate honour dagger) and swords were worn, but only on special occasions.

A SAILOR'S LIFE

Helmut Lucke — also known as 'Fred', sailed on one of the boats of the Harbour Defence Flotillas as a signaller, using both semaphore (with flags) and Morse code — with the German equivalent of an Aldis lamp. Born near Berlin in 1924, Helmut had volunteered in July 1941 at 17 to join the Kriegsmarine —

'for the uniform!' he recalled later — as it helped to attract the girls (much to his mother's disgust!). He had wanted to be a wireless operator, but didn't manage to make the grade, so was selected as a signal man instead.

Posted to Guernsey in early 1942, he had arrived from Cherbourg in March, and recalled how peaceful everything had seemed — the 'Bobby on his bike' had amused them most of all and made a lasting impression. Fred went out as a crew member on board one of the small German fishing vessels which made up Hafenschutzflottille. The fishing boats — theirs was a small wooden trawler — normally belonged to the skipper who volunteered or was called up for the naval service, together with his boat! They were fitted with some armament — a 2cm cannon and some heavy machine guns was normal. The task of the 4/5-man crew was local patrolling around the coastline, dealing, for example, with unexploded, drifting mines, which had broken loose of their moorings in the minefields and presented a hazard to shipping in the supposedly 'safe' lanes. Fred recalled that he had destroyed at least 20 by rifle-fire. Sometimes the trips lasted for 24 hours, others were just all night. After a while they were posted to Alderney to do much the same job. He liked this better as the discipline was more lax and the crews were billeted in houses in Braye Road, near the Harbour Master's office — everyone that was except for the skippers, who invariably slept on board their boats. He was present on Alderney on 14 August 1944, when HMS *Rodney* bombarded the German batteries there, severely damaging No 3 gun of Batterie Blücher, killing two of its gun crew. Fred later recalled, on a tape he made for the IWM Sound Archive,[3] that he had been in the shower when the shelling started and had hastily taken cover in a foxhole in the hillside near his billet.

Fred Lucke had also been lucky enough to be allowed leave to go home for four days during his tour on Alderney. He had also served four days 'jankers' in the Alderney prison, soon after his leave, for sending money home under another sailor's name (they were only allowed to send 30 Marks home and he had sent his 30, plus a further 30 in someone else's name and been found out, hence the punishment).

One of the few Alderney men to remain on the island when it was evacuated was the Casquets lighthouse pilot George Pope, who had sailed into Alderney on his yacht with his family a day or so after the Germans had arrived on the island. Pope worked for the Germans throughout the Occupation, then mysteriously sailed away again after the Liberation. Was he a secret agent? Until all the Closed files in the PRO are opened to public view we will never know for certain (see also the photograph of Pope's children in Chapter 9). Helmut grew quite friendly with 'Mr Pope' as he called him, which led on to another interesting anecdote on his tape, about the result of the British commando raid on the Casquets, discussed in a later chapter. After this raid, the Germans put a garrison of 30-plus marines there plus a naval signaller, a job which Fred did on a month-long tour.

Life was also not without its moments of high drama, such as in early July 1944, shortly after D-Day, when Helmut and the rest of the crew of his trawler volunteered to sail to the French coast in order to try to rescue some isolated senior German officers. Admiral Hüffmeier had personally asked for volunteers. The plan was for them to sail to the French coast and to wait some few yards away from the beach for a rubber dinghy to bring the officers out to their little boat. The mission went according to plan, except that no one ever came!

Fred Lucke tells that one of the senior officers who was to have been rescued had a wooden leg — presumably this was the brave and energetic General der Artillerie Erich Marcks, commander of LXXXIV Armeekorps. Marcks had lost his leg on the Eastern Front and wore an artificial one, but did not let this impediment get him down. He was a capable and well-liked commander who was killed en route to Carentan on 12 June 1944 — well before the rescue attempt took place — when fire from a strafing Allied fighter aircraft struck his vehicle.

Fred Lucke's trawler had remained close to the French coast until daylight, then they had 'sneaked off, avoiding Allied ships and planes and reached the Islands safely'. All the crew of the trawler were decorated, the skipper receiving the Iron Cross, First Class, and the rest, including Fred Lucke, the Iron Cross, Second Class.

E-Boats in gun action

The following appeared in the *Guernsey Evening Press* on Monday, 1 March 1943:

'The German Supreme Command announces that during the night 26/27 February, a formation of German Motor Torpedo Boats attacked a strongly escorted convoy in the immediate vicinity of the English coast and sank two steamers and a tanker of together 65,000 gross registered tons as well as two patrol boats. In the course of the engagement the armed British supply ship T381 was torpedoed. As the ship did not sink immediately, she was boarded by the crew of the MTB, whereby 11 prisoners were taken. The boat was then sunk by a torpedo. The formation of German MTBs returned to its base undamaged and without losses.'

In an article in the *CIOS Review* of 1980, David Kreckler examined this report and looked closely into the action, coming to the conclusion that, although the action did take place, the claims are somewhat exaggerated. However, English vessels were undoubtedly sunk and 11 British prisoners, including four wounded, were brought to Guernsey after the battle, most going almost immediately on to Germany, the wounded sailors first getting two weeks' hospital treatment before following the others to POW camp. In the War Diary of SEEKO-KI for 27 February 1943, the entry reads, 'At 08.30 Schnellboote *S65* and *S85* entered St Peter Port after a successful enterprise against the enemy bringing with them 11 prisoners.'

The War Diary of 5. E-Boat Flotilla which carried out the attack records the action in detail. Four boats of the flotilla were in the action — *S68*, *S81*, *S85* and *S65* — which was under the command of Kapitänleutnant Klug, CO of the flotilla. They left St Peter Port at 20.45hrs on the 26th, making for Lyme Bay, off the Dorset coast, where they expected to find convoy traffic: this was not guesswork, but based upon Luftwaffe reconnaissance reports of shipping movements along the English coast earlier that day. Two convoys were due to pass each other that night in the vicinity of Start Point, so all the German calculations proved to be correct and the convoys were intercepted.

The E-Boats concentrated their attentions on the southern eastbound convoy and claimed to have sunk six ships, including the armed supply ship *T381*, which was torpedoed by *S85* and a hit confirmed. However, the vessel did not sink, and later it was decided to board her, although whether the object was to rescue the crew or to take prisoners is not clear. At 02.45hrs, two British officers and nine ratings were transferred to the German ship, undoubtedly in doing so saving their lives. The rest of the crew (six men) were all dead in the flooded radio and chart rooms. *T381* was finally sunk at 03.08hrs and the E-Boats then broke off the action, probably so that they could get back to port before daylight.

South of Alderney, *S81* and *S68* left the formation and headed for Cherbourg, leaving *S85* and *S65* to return to the Islands. They both entered St Peter Port at 06.15hrs on the 27th bringing with them the 11 prisoners. The E-Boat claims were: *S85* — sank one steamer (2,000 tons), one tanker (2,000 tons) and armed supply ship *T381*; *S65* — sank one escort vessel; *S68* — sank one steamer (2,500 tons) and one escort ship. These figures make up the six ships claimed to have been sunk.

The War Diary of Plymouth Command records the attack taking place in much the same manner, describing the approach of the E-Boats on the two convoys (PW300 and WP300) which were due to pass one another in Lyme Bay at about 02.00hrs on the 27th. It was the southern convoy (WP300) that was attacked and it consisted of nine merchant ships, escorted by HNorMS (Naval Minesweeper) *Eskdale*, HM Trawlers *Mousa* and *Lord Stanhope*, LCT381 (it was this landing craft that the Germans called *T381*) and HNMT *Harstad*. The losses were recorded as being four vessels: a merchant ship of 4,858 tons called the *Modavia*, HMT *Lord Hailsham*, HNMT *Harstad* and *LCT381*.

In his report to the C-in-C about the attack on the convoy, the naval officer in charge of Dartmouth says, 'from the enemy point of view the attack was very successful as of the British forces four ships were sunk, and the E-Boats would not appear to have suffered any serious damage'. He goes on to bemoan the fact that the *Modavia,* which was carrying an important cargo of foodstuffs from Canada, had already called at two British ports but had not been unloaded. The report closes with the words, 'Fortunately all her crew was saved but casualties among the trawler crews were heavy.'

Thus there is a discrepancy of two ships — a tanker and one other merchant vessel, claimed by the E-Boats but not substantiated by the RN report. Following the night's action, further convoy movements from 20.00hrs to dawn were strongly supported by both Swordfish and Sunderland aircraft in order to intercept any E-Boats — none were seen. The same applied to a strong force of destroyers which was sent to patrol the PW and WP convoy routes. Two months later, the E-Boats of the 5th Flotilla struck again, sinking the escort destroyer HNorMS *Eskdale* (convoy WP300's escort destroyer) and the merchant vessel *Stanlake*, some 12 miles off the Lizard. The six E-Boats which had taken part in the action entered St Peter Port the following morning at 06.30hrs.

The E-Boats clearly had their successes in the Channel as they did in other theatres, but on the whole their history was one bedevilled by lack of resources. As one naval historian (M. J. Whitley) commented in his *German Coastal Forces of World War Two*:

> 'Like the rest of the surface units, their history is one of isolated successes: of a valiant force overwhelmed by a quantitatively superior enemy and subjected to inter-service competition for resources and high level command incompetence.'

Action against Granville

On the night of 8 March 1945, a force of four E-Boats, three Artillerieträger and six other vessels, under the overall command of Kapitänleutnant Mohr, who had been a U-Boat commander earlier in the war (*U124*), set out from the Islands to raid the small port of Granville, which the Americans were using as a supply base. The assault force managed to get on shore, blow up several ships and destroy the port installations and lock gates. In addition, they brought down heavy fire on a French barracks (occupied by the Americans) and freed a number of prisoners. They also brought back an empty collier and badly damaged an American patrol boat (*PC564*) which was beached near Cancale. Losses were surprisingly small — just one minesweeper (*Minenraumboot*) that ran aground at Granville in the unexpectedly low tide, which then had to be blown up.

And a raid that failed

This naval success would lead to the army trying their luck to 'show their teeth' with a commando raid on the Cotentin peninsula the following month. Approved personally by the C-in-C (Hüffmeier), the raid was aimed at an important railway bridge south of Cherbourg. If knocked out, it would seriously hamper one of the major American supply lines. The raiding party would consist of 22 men: the commander — Lt Maltzahn (adjutant of the infantry regiment based on Guernsey) — two NCOs, 17 engineers and two naval ratings (a radio operator and an assistant to carry the wireless set and batteries). The operator was Funkobergefreiter Bernd Westoff, one of the best operators in the Islands' Naval Signals Department. In an article published in the CIOS Review in 1986, he explained how they had gone into hard physical training for four weeks prior to the operation, but had received good extra rations (despite the 'Hunger Winter'). He had to wear army uniform and his job was to maintain the radio link back to Guernsey. On 4 April 1945, they had embarked on minesweeper M4613 *Kanalblitz* and, as he recalled:

Above: 'If you want to know the way — ask a Jersey Policeman!' *IWM* — HU 25959

Below: Naval billets on Alderney, on Braye Road near the Harbour Master's office. *Helmut Lucke*

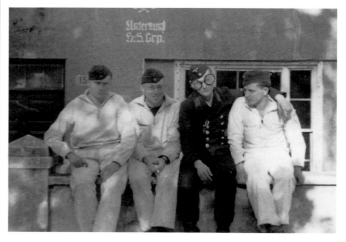

'In order to conceal our destination we sailed first to Sark and then on to the landing site on the Cotentin Peninsula. With the aid of a couple of rubber boats we landed apparently unnoticed. Each man had to carry his personal arms and ammunition, food rations and 16kg of explosives. During the landing one man fell overboard; he was rescued but he lost all his equipment. I was astonished that the boats were left unconcealed on the shore; had they been taken back to the minesweeper we might not have been discovered so quickly!'

They set off, crossing an old German minefield and heading in the direction of Cherbourg, passing an American billet, where they heard the GIs 'singing and joking loudly — apparently celebrating; to them the war seemed far away'. The party then hid in undergrowth near a busy road and waited for dark as they watched a seemingly endless stream of American trucks passing by.

At dusk, Bernd set up his radio and sent a short signal to say that they had landed undetected, which was immediately acknowledged by Guernsey radio. So far so good, but then things started to go wrong. The engineers decided that their explosives were not powerful enough to demolish the well-built railway bridge, so Lt Maltzahn decided to attack Cherbourg railway station instead, and to blow up engines and rolling stock. They marched along quite openly in the dark — answering in French when addressed in English and vice versa! Just before they reached their target, the two sailors hid near the roadside at an agreed RV. Almost at the same moment as they reached Cherbourg station the raiding party was detected and, illuminated by searchlights, it came under heavy small-arms fire: clearly the Americans had learned from the Granville raid! The two sailors heard the shooting as they waited anxiously at the RV, but only Maltzahn returned. After waiting for the others in vain, the three of them hurried back to the coast:

'Here French Maquis opened fire and Maltzahn disappeared. Earlier when hurrying to the coast we had managed to hide in a wood which was combed by GIs apparently searching for us. Maltzahn raised his sub-machine gun to fire at them, but we prevented his foolish reaction.'

The two sailors had no idea what to do when Maltzahn disappeared; no one had told them where or when to re-embark. They moved on down towards the beach and found an old deserted barn. Bernd then enciphered a final signal to say that the raid had failed and the commando had dispersed. Then, with Guernsey's agreement, he burnt all the codes and confidential documents and destroyed the wireless set as best as he could, throwing what was left into a nearby stream:

'At dawn four jeeps mounting heavy machine guns approached the barn. We were told to come out and surrender and shots were fired into the roof. We climbed down the ladder from the loft to surrender. As we were about to walk out, a GI came in, saw us and was as terrified as we were; we faced each other all

with our hands up! My mate and I were ordered to sit on the bonnet of one of the jeeps and they drove us in triumph through Cherbourg with French people shouting and spitting at us.'

Bernd was interrogated by the Americans, then taken to the Naval Prison at Cherbourg, where he was again repeatedly interrogated and told to repair the radio set, which had been recovered from the stream, so that Guernsey could be contacted and the garrison urged to surrender. He explained time and again that he was an operator not a wireless mechanic but to no avail, and this led to him being put in a special POW camp for troublemakers, where he met up with eight more survivors of the raiding party. From then on he worked as the camp blacksmith and, on 23 February 1946, was repatriated to Münster and released.

In fact Lt Maltzahn, although he had been wounded, was the only member of the party to re-embark. His report on what he had seen on the peninsula led to the 15cm guns of Batterie Blücher on Alderney engaging the area of American supply dumps, ammunition depots and tank/vehicle parks where 'large clouds of smoke suggested success'. That last quote was from a covering article to Bernd Westhoff's narrative, written by his CO, Willi Hagedorn, in which he says that Bernd was 'one of my best radio operators'. He also explains how Kapitänleutnant Armin Zimmermann changed the order of the codewords/phrases which Hagedorn had drawn up, so instead of the first one reading: 'raid failed, embarkation tomorrow night according to plan' it now read: 'raid successful' — because he thought it was better psychology to start off with the best message instead of the worst. A good idea, but he neglected to alter the three letter groups in which the messages were sent. So Hagedorn received the codeword which he thought meant 'raid successful' instead of 'raid failed' and only just managed to stop the wrong message going up to the German High Command!

No surrender!

Vizeadmiral Friedrich Hüffmeier, who had at an earlier stage in his career commanded the battleship *Scharnhorst*, was a ruthless Nazi — despite his somewhat benign appearance and manner. There was a constant battle for supremacy between the Heer and Kriegsmarine on the Islands, and this reached boiling point after the February 1944 declaration that they were a fortress of no surrender, like the Channel ports of Brest, Dunkirk, Boulogne and Cherbourg. Hüffmeier led the campaign to oust GenOb von Schmettow, whom he considered to be far too soft on the Islanders, and this became easier for him to achieve once he had been appointed to replace von Schmettow's Chief of Staff, Oberst Graf von Helldorf, in late June 1944. When he eventually succeeded in getting rid of the top army general, replacing him in February 1945, his first order of the day stated: 'I have only one aim and that is to hold out until final victory.' So obsessed was he with this aim that he is said to have stated that he would let his men eat grass before he allowed them to surrender! Fortunately, when the time came, commonsense prevailed and he chose to follow orders from higher authority and thus saved the inevitable bloodbath which would have ensued.

Above: St Peter Port harbour, Guernsey, looking from the North Jetty towards Castle Cornet. *IWM — HU 29083*

Below: The French motor barge *Saigon* arriving at St Peter Port from Jersey. The barge was one of a number used on the Rhine at Strasbourg, which had been sailed down the coast to prevent them falling into enemy hands, but was captured at St Malo. They agreed to work for the Occupation forces and were invaluable to the Islands. *IWM — HU 29102*

Above:
Motor Vessel *Spinel* and the SS *Staffa* were both British vessels, taken over as war prizes by the Germans (the former at Dunkirk, the latter in Guernsey). Here they are seen at Braye Harbour, Alderney.
Hans-Gerhard Sandmann

Above: This partly submerged German patrol boat was photographed in St Peter Port harbour, where it was sunk by the RAF. *IWM — HU 25955*

Above:
A German minesweeper tied up at Victoria Pier, St Peter Port, with Castle Cornet in the background.
IWM — HU 29081

Above: Kriegsmarine sailors provided the Honour Guard at the funeral of British sailors from the cruiser HMS *Charybdis*, sunk off the Channel Islands by E-Boats, 23 October 1943 at Foulon Cemetery, Guernsey. Many of the Island's civil population attended. *IWM* — HU 25921

Right: 'Goodbye Jersey!' This was the most colourful drawing in the Guest Book of the Soldatenheim at the St Brelade's Bay Hotel, Jersey, from the officers of Minesweeping Flotilla 46, when they left on 28 September 1944.
Robert Colley

Chapter 6

The Airman

GUERNSEY

We have already covered the arrival of the first Luftwaffe personnel at Guernsey airport on 1 July 1940. Within a month of this, the Luftwaffe was using the airport as a forward fighter base as it fought the Battle of Britain. JG27 and JG53 operated from the grass airfield which had been known prewar as La Villiaze airport. The first German station commander was named Fehr. The two fighter groups were equipped with Messerschmitt Bf109 single-seater fighters. [1] The ground staff had to use commandeered civilian cars and trucks to help in running the airport, for example, J. H. Miller's Commer truck being loaded with petrol drums and used as an aircraft refueller. Sandbag defences were placed around the airport buildings and extra hangars erected.

Working off the grass strip did have its problems — for example, on 9 August an aircraft of 1./JG53 made an emergency landing following an engine failure and collided with a Flak emplacement, killing three men and injuring a further three more. Writing in *Air-Britain Digest* in January 1951, Mr M. Le Page recalled those days:

'Although it is now over ten years since the Battle of Britain, we in the Channel Islands still remember how, on bright sunny afternoons, the Luftwaffe gathered overhead, preparing to fly northwards over England. In Guernsey, the Bf109Es gathered on the aerodrome, their ground crews busy rearming and refuelling them for the next sortie. I wish it were possible to describe the terrible feeling of helplessness and despair as we watched them take off to join the Dorniers, the Bf110s, and Heinkels flying from France.'

Below: Guernsey airport. The swastika flies over the terminal building at La Villiaze airport, whilst the protective wall of sandbags which the islanders had begun before the Occupation still remains unfinished. *Michael Payne*

Göring set the date of *Adler Tag* (Eagle Day), the start of the Battle of Britain, for 10 August 1940. (It was actually postponed for three days because of bad weather.) In the Luftwaffe Order of Battle for that day, the two Guernsey-based Fighter Groups are shown as being in the following Air Corps of Sperrle's Luftflotte 3:

JG27 — part of Richthofen's VII Air Corps
JG53 — part of Junck's 3rd Fighter Command

After the Luftwaffe had lost the Battle of Britain, the air activity at Guernsey decreased, as Mr Le Page recalls:

'Air activity declined as the Battle of Britain ended until the only aircraft left were a Henschel Hs126 and a few Dornier Do17s. A Fieseler Storch replaced the Hs126 in 1941 and was a source of interest to all — particularly when flying in strong winds with slots and flaps down. I don't believe any of us had seen an aircraft flying backwards before!

'Bf109Fs were often seen about at that time and one was shot down by the local anti-aircraft guns during a "flap". The "tip and run" raids brought us more activity with Fw190 using Guernsey as their base. They would come tearing back at low level to land under protection of the island's Flak. Several were towed through the town to be transported to repair depots by sea. Gradually the Luftwaffe faded from the scene as the RAF began to take more interest in the local scenery, but at least two interesting types were still seen occasionally. One was, in fact, a very rare bird on the Western Front — the Fw58 Weihe (military communications and light transport plane) which only landed once or twice and the other was the Fw189 reconnaissance aircraft which stayed for some time and was unusually quiet in the air.'

The Fw189 was not actually used for reconnaissance as it belonged to the Organization Todt, who used it as a courier plane, shuttling between Guernsey and Dinard. By 1943 it was the only aeroplane to be permanently based in the Channel Islands.

JERSEY

Over in Jersey the airport at St Peter's had not long been in existence, having been opened in March 1937 to replace the beach strip in St Aubin's Bay where landing had been dependent upon the state of the tide! The new grass aerodrome had four runways, ranging from 530yd to just under 1,000yd in length, plus a modern terminal building, complete with control tower, which had state-of-the-art direction-finding equipment, plus floodlights to assist in night landings. 'The most completely equipped of any in the British Isles apart from Croydon' — that was the proud boast of Jersey airport at the time!

It was the Messerschmit Bf110Cs of ZG76 and the Dornier Do217s of Fernaufklärungsgruppe 123 (a long-distance reconnaissance group) that operated from Jersey airport during the Battle of Britain. The small airfield rapidly became congested, to such an extent that the Germans finally had to extend it by adding further grassed areas which allowed for a 930m NW to SE runway, in addition to the others. Its main use then was for communication runs between the Island garrison and France.

Table 8: **Main Types of German Aircraft Using Channel Islands Aerodromes During World War 2**

TYPE	NAME	ARMAMENT	RANGE	CREW	MAX SPEED	DETAILS
Fighter	Messerschmitt Bf109	2 x MG17 (fuselage mted) 1 x Mauser cannon (firing thro' propeller shaft)	600km 1,000km (with 300litre drop tank)	one	620km/h	The main model in service at the start of the war was the Bf109E-1 and the Luftwaffe had over 1,000 in service and a production rate of some 140 per month.
Fighter/ fighter-bomber	Focke-Wulf Fw190D	2 x MG 2 x cannon 1 x 500kg bomb	835km	one	685km/h	First operational unit in Aug 1941, a most impressive aircraft, some 20,000 were built in many versions. Superior performance to the Spitfire.
Fighter-bomber	Messerschmitt Bf110D	2 x MG17 (rearward firing fixed MGs)	2,100km (with drop tanks)	three	550km/h	Designed in the mid-1930s, it proved its ability in Poland and the Low Countries but was really no match for the RAF Spitfires and Hurricanes it then met in the Battle of Britain.
Bomber	Dornier Do17	up to 7 x MG15s and 1,000kg of bombs	1,160km	four	410km/h	Known as the 'Flying Pencil' it was used for both recce and as a bomber, being used extensively in France 1940 and against Channel convoys. Withdrawn from frontline service in late 1941.
Command & Recce	Focke-Wulf 58 Weihe (Kite)	1 or 2 x MG15	800km	up to six	270km/h	Used extensively as a crew trainer, light transport and communications aircraft. One version was a six seat transport, another had two MGs — one in the nose, the other behind the cockpit.
Recce	FW189 Uhu (Eagle Owl)	4 x MGs (2 x MG15 and 2 x MG17) plus 4 x 50kg bombs	670km	two	335km/h	A two-seat, short-range reconnaissance aircraft, the Luftwaffe 'eye in the sky'.
Recce	Henschel Hs126	2 x MGs, plus 1 x 50kg or 5 x 10kg bombs	720km	two	310km/h	Another two-seat reconnaissance aircraft, over 600 of which were built.
Army co-operation	Fieseler Fi156 Storch (Stork)	1 x MG on pivotal mount	385 km	two/ three	175km/h	The versatile two-seat army co-operation/recce aircraft with remarkable STOL (short take-off and landing) abilities — with just a light breeze blowing it could take off in 60m and land in about 20m!
Transport (also used as a medium bomber)	Junkers Ju52/3m	1 x MG15 plus up to 500kg of bombs	1,300km with aux fuel tanks	three +13 paras or 18 inf	275km/h	Over 5,000 'Tante Jus', as they were nicknamed, were built in Germany and France by the end of the war. Widely used in numerous versions (both float and wheel for example).

Other Aircraft
Other German aircraft 'used' the Channel Islands aerodromes from time to time — even if it were just for a crash landing! These included the Junkers Ju87 dive bomber, the Ju88 bomber, the Heinkel He111 bomber and the Heinkel He177 long-range bomber.

AIRCRAFT TYPES AND AIRCRAFT LOSSES

Table 8 on the previous page shows the various types of German aircraft that were operational in the Channel Islands during the Occupation. Appendix 2 contains details of aircraft losses — both Allied and German — in the Channel Islands area, between July 1940 and May 1945. These details are taken from a list compiled by Mr John Goodwin which appeared in the Channel Islands Occupation Review of 1974 and I am much indebted to him and the CIOS (Guernsey) Branch for allowing me to repeat it in this book.

ANTI-AIRCRAFT ARTILLERY

When war began almost a million men — nearly two-thirds of the total Luftwaffe manpower — were serving in the Flak arm (Flak being the abbreviation for *Fliegerabwehrkanonen*, or anti-aircraft guns). The size of the Flak arm grew even larger as the war progressed, to a staggering total of 1.25 million men and women by the autumn of 1944! Whilst the anti-aircraft units on the Channel Islands were just a tiny fraction of this total, they did form a significant part of the garrison — once it was up to its reinforced strength there was a complete Flakbrigade on the Islands. Initially this was Flakbrigade XII which had its headquarters at 'Bon Air', Saumarez Road, Guernsey and was comprised of two Flak regiments: Flakregiment 39 in Guernsey and Flakregiment 40 in Jersey. In April 1943, there was a change of brigades when Flakbrigade XI serving in Brittany replaced Flakbrigade XII.

Weapons

There were both heavy Flak weapons, such as the 8.8cm Flak 41, and lighter weapons, such as the 2cm Flak 38 and the 3.7cm Flak 18 in service on the Islands. While the latter were more numerous, there were still more 8.8cm Flak guns on the Islands than on any other part of the Atlantic Wall. There were six batteries of 8.8cm guns in both Guernsey and Jersey and three more batteries in Alderney, making a total of 15 batteries containing ninety guns in all.

Table 9 Main Types of Flak Guns Used

CALIBRE AND WEAPON	DATE IN SERVICE	RATE OF FIRE (IN RPM)	WT IN ACTION (KG)	WT OF SHELL (KG)	MAX EFFECTIVE CEILING (M)
8.8cm Flak 18	1933	15	6,861*	9.24	8,000
8.8cm Flak 36/37	1936/1939	15	6,861*	9.24	8,000
8.8cm Flak 41	1943	20	784	9.4	15,000
3.7cm Flak 18	1935	80	1,750	0.64	3,523
3.7cm Flak 36/37	1936/37	80	1,550	0.64	4,800
2cm Flak 30	1935	120	450	0.119	2,200
2cm Flak 38	1940	180-220	420	0.119	2,200

Notes: *5,150kg on self-propelled carriage

Heavy guns

The 8.8cm heavy Flak weapon had a firing crew of ten (later reduced to seven) and was fitted with a semi-automatic breech mechanism, whilst the upgraded version, the Flak 37, had an improved mounting and an electrical date transmission system which carried fire control data directly from the predictor. The Flak 41 was an entirely redesigned gun with a longer, stronger barrel and a powered ramming system. The guns fired time-fused HE shells. First used in action in the Spanish Civil War, the Flak 18 gained notoriety in the Western Desert in the ground anti-tank role (firing AP40 armour-piercing shot) and self-propelled mountings were produced.

Light and medium guns

The principal automatic weapon used by the Luftwaffe light Flak units was the 2cm gun, there being two models: the –30 and the –38. The two weapons were virtually identical ballistically, and the ammunition for both was fed through 20-round box magazines. There were various mountings, some of which are illustrated. The standard medium Flak gun was the 3.7cm, which was fed by six-round clips of ammunition that was normally HE with a percussion fuse. A self-destruct mechanism detonated the shells when they had reached their maximum effective range, so as to prevent them causing damage when they fell to earth. Clips contained both tracer and non-tracer ammunition. Both the 2cm and 3.7cm weapons were fired using open sights and corrections made from following the flight of the tracers. The standard fire unit was a section of three guns, whilst a battery of 2cm guns had four or five sections and a 3.7cm battery three or four.

BASIC DRESS AND PERSONAL EQUIPMENT

National Emblems

The Luftwaffe versions of the National Emblem and the Reichskokade were worn generally as for the other two services, but their design was slightly different. For example, the emblem of the Luftwaffe consisted of an eagle with outstretched wings in the attitude of flight (compare with the attitude of both the army and navy eagles) and clutching a swastika in its left talon. By law this had to be worn on the right breast of all air force tunics and jackets, while a smaller version adorned all types of headdress. The national cockade (worn on all types of cloth headgear) had a red centre, encircled by a band of white or silver, with an outer band of black, then a further narrow silver/gold outline (depending on rank) around the black band.

Headdress

Both officers and other ranks wore similar headdress: uniform peaked caps (*Schirmmütze*) with a blue-grey top and crown, and a black peak, the officers' version being of a much better quality and shape. The Luftwaffe version of the national emblem had an

Das Photographieren auf dem Horst ist streng verboten. Der Horstkommandant.

oak-leaf wreath and stylised wings made of pressed aluminium around the white aluminium cockade, and on the front of the hat above it was the eagle and swastika motif. This was also repeated on the left side of the M35 steel helmet (universally issued to all the armed forces) which was coloured blue-grey for all airforce issues. The most usual form of headgear worn, again by all ranks, was either the blue-grey version of the replacement field cap (*Einheitsfeldmütze*) which came in during 1943, or the very similar but better made flying cap (*Fliegermütze*) which it partly replaced. Both were similar to the British forage cap and were designed to be worn when a flying helmet was not required and there was no call to wear either a steel helmet or peaked cap. Officers' caps had piping, whilst all had the national emblems (cockade and Luftwaffe version of the eagle and swastika).

Uniform

The service tunic (*Tuchrock*) worn by all ranks was single-breasted, four-button, open-necked and had four pleated patch pockets, with single-button flaps. NCOs and other ranks' garments were made from a blue-grey wool-rayon mix, whilst officers had tunics of superior quality blue-grey gabardine (purchased from their uniform allowance). It was worn with a light blue (collar attached) shirt and black tie. Normal straight long trousers were made of blue-grey cloth and worn by all ranks; however, riding breeches (*Stiefelhose*) could be worn by officers. Footwear was either black leather jackboots or black lace-up shoes. Officers wearing riding breeches would naturally wear black riding boots.

Other types of uniform included the flying blouse (*Fliegerbluse*) which was available to all ranks, being designed to be worn for flying. Both the Tuchrock and the Fliegerbluse were going to be replaced by the uniform tunic (*Waffenrock*), which would combine the smartness of the service tunic with the practicality of the flying blouse. However, the introduction of the new uniform was never entirely completed. It closely resembled the service tunic, but it was designed to be worn closed to the neck and had five buttons down its single-breasted front. There was also, as with the other services, a lighter weight summer-only uniform, the jacket being of unlined white gabardine, which strongly resembled the Tuchrock. On all tunics, badges of rank were shown both on collar patches and shoulder-straps, the winglike motif which was used in many rank badges being one of the most instantly recognisable features of Luftwaffe uniform in black and white photographs.

Left:
A Messerschmitt Bf109E-3
prepares to take off from
Guernsey. The white bar near
the tail denotes 4./JG53.
The pointed spinner was an
unusual fitting in August 1940.
Michael Payne

Right:
This aircraft at La Villiaze,
Guernsey, bears the markings
of the Kommandeur of II./JG53,
Major von Maltzahn. The pilot with
it is Lt Gerd Michalski, the Group
Adjutant. The red cowling band
replaced the 'Ace of Spades' emblem
during the summer of 1940.
Michael Payne

Left:
J. H. Miller's Commer truck was
commandeered for use as an
aircraft refueller for Bf109s for their
sorties across the Channel. Hptm
Wilhelm Meyerweissflog force-
landed in this Messerschmitt near
Ramsgate on 5 September 1940.
At 51, he was one of the oldest
pilots to become a POW.
Michael Payne

Above: Waiting for take-off. Luftwaffe personnel enjoy the lovely summer weather at La Villiaze. The aircraft were dispersed and partly camouflaged with foliage, because RAF Blenheim fighter-bombers frequently shot up their airfields during August 1940. *M. and J. Payne*

LIFE ON A FLAK BATTERY

One of the postwar visitors to the Islands in 1996 was Dieter Hankel, who 53 years earlier had been posted with his unit — 8./ *Gemischt Flakabteilung* 292 (the 8th Mixed Battery of the 292 AA Battalion) of which he was first a platoon commander, then the battery commander — to Guernsey, to take over a position on the west side of Perelle Bay. Each of the four platoons in the battery comprised three 2cm Flak 38, two machine guns and various small arms. Herr Hankel recalled those days thus:

'In autumn 1943 my unit was posted to Guernsey, where I had to take over the position on the west side of Perelle Bay. The site was regarded as particularly vulnerable and therefore I had a larger detachment than normal. We had three AA guns (2cm Flak 38), two machine guns and small arms. When my platoon and I arrived there I was astonished because the term "defensive position" was a misnomer. That slight elevation overlooking the bay consisted of thin soil over solid rock and the simple emplacements were cemented and made safe by sandbags — that was all, no more. The soldiers' quarters and my office were in two small houses about 50m apart from each other.'

Hankel had been given this as his mission: to repulse air attacks — especially from low-flying aircraft — and also attacks from the sea. That sounded both simple and straightforward, but what if he were faced with both attacks at the same time? He was also immediately worried by the fact that he had no safe shelter for ammunition, equipment and spare parts, except for the two very obvious small houses. 'We were there on show and a single heavy naval shell or a small bomb could have blown us into the air and would have put a quick end to our defence position at Perelle Bay.' As if to add to his fears, he then heard a rumour that a British commando raid had just wiped out an infantry position on the north coast of the Island. The British commandos had come in at low tide, wearing dark overalls and with blackened faces, and had not been detected. 'Now I got a funny feeling in the pit of my stomach,' commented Dieter Hankel, so he discussed matters with his second in command, battery chief and NCOs and hastily put in a demand for additional weapons and fortifications, which included an anti-tank gun, two big bunkers (one as a shelter for the gun crews, the other to hold ammunition and vital spares), steel obstacles, barbed wire, etc, together with an OT labour squad complete with the necessary tools to help his soldiers to build the defensive system of trenches which he had planned.

Above:
Photographed clandestinely at Jersey aerodrome was this Dornier Do217, known as the 'flying pencil', partly camouflaged with foliage.
IWM — HU 5784

Above:
Photographed at Guernsey was this Junkers Ju88 undergoing repairs to one of its 1,340hp Jumo engines.
Hans-Gerhard Sandmann

Right:
Beyond the Bf109 is one of the remarkable Fieseler Fi156 Storch aircraft which could take-off in 60m and land in 20m!
Hans-Gerhard Sandmann

Left: A very young-looking Obergefreiter (Leading Corporal) Josef Gerhaher wearing his Luftwaffe Replacement Flight Cap (*Einheitsfliegermütze*) which came in from September 1943. The photograph was taken in November 1944. *J. H. Gerhaher*

Top: Josef Gerhaher walking in Guernsey with some other Flak NCOs. They all wear the Fliegerbluse, open at the neck, with their straight long trousers not tucked into their jackboots (except for one) and the Fliegermütze flying cap. *J. H. Gerhaher*

Above: This friendly donkey appears to have joined a Luftwaffe Flak unit as he is wearing the Gefreiter's (Corporal's) cap! The AA gunner is wearing the normal Fliegerbluse open at the neck, together with straight trousers and leather belt. Note the breast eagle is in the attitude of flight instead of static like those worn by the army and navy. *Richard Heaume*

Above: This Luftwaffe Flak officer Leutnant Avierdieck, who was on the staff of HQ 292 mixed AA Battalion, is photographed with two German Red Cross nurses at St Martin's, 1944. *J. H. Gerhaher*

Left: A senior Luftwaffe officer photographed in St Peter Port, Guernsey. He is wearing a Schirmmütze (peaked cap) and Tuchrock (Service Tunic). Note the Iron Cross, 1st Class on his tunic pocket. *La Valette Museum*

Having put up his report through 'official channels', he waited for a couple of weeks but heard nothing, so he contacted the relevant staff officers at the Island HQ, who told him that everything would be looked into. After another fortnight of inactivity he approached his battalion commander, who supported him completely. Then at last, some staff officers came to his position and wanted to see everything:

'I used all my powers of persuasion, but they were only willing to grant a part of my demands. Most of all they denied the need for a bunker with an anti-tank gun and one of them said that it should be possible for me to get one of my AA guns and anti-tank ammunition transported down to the roadside in time to meet a sea-borne attack. That was enough! In correct military posture I said: "Sir, I could do so if the English announced an intended attack beforehand." The officers seemed to be offended and left my base without a word of goodbye. I immediately informed my CO and he gave me a severe dressing down because of my answer.'

Despite giving Dieter a rocket, his CO personally went to see the regimental commander and Island commander on his behalf:

'One day a general, my superiors . . . and a small number of staff officers came to inspect my base. After only an hour everything was granted and within one week work began. Together with the construction workers and thanks to good equipment and tools we all worked hard including myself and all ranks of my unit. After three months my position was finished to a sufficient extent to enable us to defend it to the best of our ability.' [2]

Fortunately for everyone Dieter Hankel and his gun crews did not have to put their guns or their much-improved gun positions to the ultimate test.

Another Flak gunner was Feldwebel Josef H. Gerhaher, who was in the same battalion as Dieter Hankel, but in a different battery. He told me that 292 was a very strong mixed battalion, which had arrived in Guernsey by ship (the *Bordeaux*) from St Malo on 11 November 1943:

'Each of Batteries 1 to 6 had six 8.8cm Flak 36 and three 2cm Flak 38; 7 Battery had twelve 3.7cm Flak 37 (in four platoons each of three guns); Batteries 8 to 14 had twelve 2cm Flak 38 (also in four platoons of three guns).'

When one considers that the normal Flak battalion had only three to four batteries, one can tell how much larger this one was. His CO was Oberstlt Otto Kraiger, whom he described as:

'A World War 1 officer, a practising Roman Catholic and anti-Nazi. He regularly attended the Sunday Services for German soldiers at St Joseph's Church. He was very helpful to men of the battalion in trouble politically and was the good father of his men of all ranks.'

Josef was first stationed at Castle Cornet with the 1st Battery, then at the battalion HQ at St Martin's and finally with the 9th Battery at Fort George:

'The daily life was normally fairly quiet, but from time to time there were air raid alarms, mostly without attacks. However, in my diary I found the following listed:

31 Dec 43	two planes shot down.
7 Jan 44	one Thunderbolt shot down.
27 May 44	two Thunderbolts shot down during an air raid on Fort George Freya Würzburg Riese Goldfisch radar. No damage.
28 May 44	Ditto. No damage.
5 Jun 44	three planes shot down.
18 Jun 44	one plane shot down during a raid on St Peter Port harbour.
24 Feb 45	two planes shot down during a raid on Fort George radar.

[It is difficult to compare these figures with the actual day-to-day casualties as given in the official RAF records — but then all Ack-Ack gunners are invariably optimists!]

'An average day comprised normal military duties such as watch, training, lessons, instruction of various kinds, all carried out under the continual pressure of everlasting readiness, being ready to fight with the enemy at any time. Also, our gun crews were smaller than normal, so free time was rare. There was a German bookshop in Guernsey and also libraries in the Soldatenheim (see Chapter 8), so reading was for me one of the best ways of spending free moments. The Soldatenheim was also a good meeting place, to see friends, have refreshments and listen to interesting talks. The Soldatenheim near the airport became, after April 1944, a meeting place for Christian, anti-Nazi soldiers of all ranks on the island.

'Special classes for young law students were started in September 1944 by 319. ID and the lessons were given by Dr Benjamin Rillings, a captain in administration, also an anti-Nazi judge from Stuttgart. The lessons were given on two or three afternoons every week until February 1945, when Dr Rillings was transferred to Alderney for disciplinary reasons (political). There was also a German choir which I joined in November 1944.'

One can imagine that the classes and other non-military activities made a welcome change from the boredom of daily life on the gunsite. Clearly the Luftwaffe Flak gunners had a similar 'maintenance of morale' problem to the soldiers of 319. ID.

Left: This was the transport ship *Bordeaux* on which Josef Gerhaher and his battery travelled to the Channel Islands from St Malo. *J. H. Gerhaher*

Right: Dieter Hankel is seen here in the centre of an informal group photograph of the officers, warrant officers and NCOs of his battery, taken in the summer of 1944. On his knee is his white-topped summer peaked cap (*Sommermütze*). *Dieter Hankel*

Left: Dieter Hankel with two of the gun detachments from his platoon, standing in front of a prewar hut, December 1943. *Dieter Hankel*

Left:
Target practice for some of Dieter Hankel's Flak gunners, but with a rifle instead of a Flak gun! The gunner on the table wears a set of one-piece off-white fatigues.
Dieter Hankel

Below:
On watch. This Flak sentry observes out to sea from his cliff-top position. Note the twin MG34s on their AA mounting, complete with ring sight.
IWM — HU 29168

Right:
This quadruple 2cm Flakvierling 38 was in a position at Fort George, Guernsey. It needed a crew of eight: detachment Commander, No 1 — gun layer, No 2 — range setter, Nos 3 and 4 — loaders, No 5 — rangetaker, Nos 6 and 7 — ammunition numbers. In extremis the gun could be manned by three men.
IWM — HU 29088

Below:
This photograph shows clearly three 3.7cm Flak emplacements at Les Tarres Point, Clarence Battery, Fort George. This gun also required a crew of a detachment commander and seven men. *IWM* — 29086

Left:
A dual-purpose 8.8cm
AA/AT gun firing in an open
emplacement. In the Flak
role the weapon had a crew
of 10 (detachment
commander and nine).
IWM — HU 29048

Below:
A *Freya* lattice radar array
and a single MG34 on its
Flak mounting. *Freya* had a
range of some 75 miles,
360-degree coverage, but
no height-finding capability.
Hans-Gerhard Sandmann

Right:
A member of 5./Anti-Aircraft
Battery 292 at Les Huriaux,
Guernsey, demonstrating the
plotting of an aircraft and its
bearing (in mils) in relation to the
battery location.
The bearings are superimposed
on a grid, called *Jägermeldemetz*
(the fighter-message grid).
Guernsey Museum

Below:
Funeral of two RAF men at
Mont-à-L'Abbé Cemetery,
St Helier, Jersey, 6 June 1943.
They were Sgts Butlin and
Holden, and this was the first
burial of Allied servicemen on
Jersey during World War 2. The
Luftwaffe provided both the pall
bearers and the graveside firing
party. When a new Allied
cemetery was opened in
Howard Davis Park, they were
exhumed and reinterred there.
IWM — HU 25909

Chapter 7
German Civil Organisations

ORGANIZATION TODT (OT)

The SS apart (and we will get to them in due course), the most brutal treatment to any individuals on the Islands was that meted out to some of the workforce of the Organization Todt, a quasi-military group of construction engineers and workers who were responsible for capital construction projects of high strategic value, like the Siegfried Line, the Atlantic Wall and the railways in rear of the German armies in Russia. On the positive side, it was estimated in a British Intelligence report of 1945 that the 1.4 million members of OT had carried out in just under five years the most impressive construction programme since the days of the Roman Empire. However, as the *Oxford Companion to the Second World War* comments:

'They were technicians, slave-drivers and in some cases murderers. Their technical ability was doubtless greater than their discipline . . . and after the German defeat the OT itself was broken up and banned . . . While the buildings left by the Romans can still be seen and marvelled at today, most of the buildings erected by the OT for Adolf Hitler's "Thousand Year Reich" have long since disappeared in the dust of history.'

Some parts of their Atlantic Wall have survived, especially in the Channel Islands.

Despite being civilians, the German OT personnel wore uniform (normally captured Czech khaki rather than German army uniform) and filled the posts of foremen, camp administrators and officials. They were subject to military law, enjoyed paramilitary status and thus were allowed access to military facilities. Their chain of command was similar to that in the armed forces but with their own nomenclature, for example: *Einsatzgruppe* equated to an army group, the *Einsatz* to an army, the *Oberbauleitung* was the Chief Construction Office, the *Bauleitung* or *Abschnitt* was a Sector, then finally down to the *Baustelle*, which was a single construction site. The chain of command of the OT on the Channel Islands is shown on Table 10.

Below:
Dr Fritz Todt, wearing Luftwaffe uniform (facing camera, right foreground) inspecting a proposed gun position at South Hill, St Helier, Jersey, November 1941. He held the honorary rank of General in the German Air Force. *CIOS Collection*

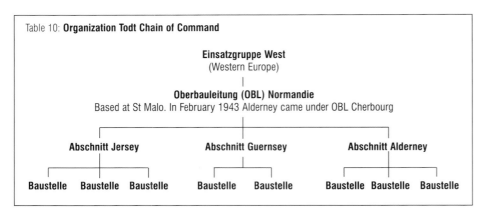

Table 10: **Organization Todt Chain of Command**

Einsatzgruppe West
(Western Europe)

Oberbauleitung (OBL) Normandie
Based at St Malo. In February 1943 Alderney came under OBL Cherbourg

Abschnitt Jersey	**Abschnitt Guernsey**	**Abschnitt Alderney**
Baustelle Baustelle Baustelle	Baustelle Baustelle	Baustelle Baustelle Baustelle

Thus the OT operated on all the main islands and the workers were housed in requisitioned accommodation of varying standards, although most of it was in a reasonable state. In Jersey, for example, the HQ was in a house in St Helier, the OT hospital in the Jersey College for Girls, the 'OT Cafe' — which was a brothel staffed by imported French girls — was at the Abergeldie Hotel (later at the Norman House Hotel at First Tower), the lorry repair workshops, the laundry, ration store, bakery, command post, etc were all suitably located.

The labour force

Many unfortunate people were swept up into the German labour force and used by the OT, some clearly affected by the paragraph in Hitler's Fortification Order where he states that: 'Foreign labour, especially Russians and Spaniards but also Frenchmen, may be used for the building works.' One such Spaniard was John Dalmau, who later wrote a pamphlet entitled *Slave Worker*, which was published privately after the war. In the little book's Foreword, the then Lieutenant-Governor of Guernsey, HE Air Marshal Sir Thomas Elmhirst, points out that John Dalmau's story was not a nice story: 'In places it is so horrible that it is hard to believe that the conduct of human beings could sink so low. But it is a true story and one that should be told.' Having said this, some of what John Dalmau says happened is not supported directly by the evidence which has been collected by a number of Island historians who have made a careful and detailed study of these activities — for example, Bob Le Sueur, who deliberately cultivated friendships with the Spaniards in order to improve his Spanish. Bob Le Sueur mingled with the Spaniards, visited them in their camps and met them socially. He felt that the main problem was caused by the fact that, having fought against Fascism for four years during the Spanish Civil War, they now found themselves having to exert all their energies building fortifications to keep Fascism in power! So it was no wonder that, once the Liberation had arrived 'five years of pent up frustration were released. The boiling saucepan of emotion, internecine hatred and suspicion, or circulating rumours, had suddenly had its lid removed and it is not surprising if some of what boiled over should have been less than accurate.'

Michael Ginns MBE, another respected historian, who was living in Jersey during the Occupation, remembers seeing Spanish and French conscripted workers on Grouville Common in Jersey during 1941–42:

'They were not well clad at the time, but they were fed after a fashion and did not seem to exert themselves too much; and of the OT overseers, only one was a miserable character on a par with a miserable foreman on, say, a British building site. As teenagers, we used to stand and watch the trains at work on the beach, and speak to the workers (well, the French ones at any rate to try out our school French), and nobody chased us away apart from, as I say, the miserable overseer who would say the German equivalent of: "Bloody kids! Clear off!"'

So, the upshot is that sources such as Dalmau need to be treated with caution — but most of what they say is based on what happened. Clearly there was brutal treatment meted out by the OT, in particular to the Russian prisoners (the term 'Russian' was used to cover people from many different countries in Eastern Europe) and to the French prisoners of North African extraction. Dalmau had fought against Franco — and thus also against the German Condor Legion [1] — in the Spanish Civil War, had escaped over the French frontier at the end of the fighting, joined the French Army, and, in 1940, was taken prisoner by the victorious German Army, ending up in a camp outside Cologne. Here all the Spaniards were separated from the French and later they were told that they would became part of a 'great army of workers' who would begin the construction of the Atlantic Wall. Next he found himself on the west coast of France, constructing U-Boat pens, one of a mixed bag of Poles, Czechs, Spaniards, French, Dutch and Belgians. 'There was a common language employed by our German guards: kicks and sticks. But far, far worse was to come.' From France they were shipped to Jersey, arriving at St Helier and then were taken to Lager Udet, where a few days later they were joined by the rest of the 2,000 workers and their OT guards. Their first job was the construction of a sea wall at St Brelade's Bay, which was intended to stop British landings. Unfortunately, he was soon in trouble and given three months' special treatment at Elizabeth Castle. He later wrote:

'I was sent to the castle, where I worked all day with a pint of clear soup a day as the only food and slept standing all night, due to the fact that I was allowed about two square feet of floor space in the cell — shared with others condemned for similar offences. At any time of the day or night we were taken out into the yard and there made to run round and round. If any man went down he was soon helped to his feet with a few cracks of the whip. Amid the laughter of German guards, every night men died. Others were found dead when the cell doors were opened next morning. A young Frenchman, almost a boy, died standing next to me. His last words were: "Maman! Maman!"'

'By the end of three months at Elizabeth I was little more than a crawling skeleton, full of sores and weals. I was taken back to Lager Udet and dumped from the top of a lorry and left on the ground. The giant Chepka (he was a 6ft 5in tall Pole with whom Dalmau had teamed up) slung me across his shoulders and carried me back to the barracks, where I devoured all the food that came within my reach. I had to work the following day with all the others. Chepka carried me most of the time and did most of my work.'

Having completed the wall at St Brelade's Bay in the middle of the summer of 1942, John Dalmau and his comrades were put to work on tunnels which were to run underneath Fort Regent (see Chapter 9). That summer more slave labourers arrived, '. . . a long column of crawling humanity came into the camp. They were Russians, men, women and children — 2,000 of them, the remains of 150,000 who had walked all across Europe, a trophy of the German war machine'.[2] Again Dalmau is being less than precise. Most certainly had not walked all the way across Europe — although their journey in crowded cattle trucks, with minimal if any sanitation and the occasional bucket of swede/cabbage soup to eat must have been horrific.

After weighing the evidence of this controversial subject, the only sensible conclusion that one can reach is that the OT workers were, indeed, treated dreadfully. The very worst excesses have probably been overstated in order to drive the point home — namely that numbers were undoubtedly worked to death — but perhaps not as many as some books may report. However, what is inescapable is that the vast majority of OT workers were working for a regime which they hated and which did not care whether they lived or died, that they were forced into this work without any freedom of choice and that when times got hard, they were at the bottom of the food chain. Also, that those who 'kicked hardest against the pricks' were dealt with in a most violent manner.

Opposite:
The Russian Cemetery on Longis Common, Alderney. This photograph was taken in 1945, when it still contained burials which were later exhumed and reburied in 1963 in Normandy. The burials were haphazard, unkempt and inaccurate — even Hans Spann who took over the outstation of FK515 on Alderney in April commented about graves not being marked and the conditions being 'repulsive'. *Alderney Museum and Mrs Pantcheff*

Opposite below:
Entrance gates to Lager Sylt are all that remains of the infamous SS camp. *Brian Matthews*

Above: This suitably decorated locomotive is a Corpet et Louvet 0-6-0T, built in France in 1906 and used on the metre-gauge OT railway, opened on 15 July 1942. *CIOS Collection*

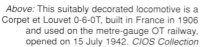

Right:
Platzkommandant Hans Max von und zu Aufsess held the key position of Head of Civil Affairs in FK515, in Jersey. He kept a diary whilst serving in the Channel Islands, which was published in English in 1985. *IWM — HU 25912*

Above: French colonial troops such as these were among the worst treated of all the forced labourers used by the OT in the Islands. *Hans-Gerhard Sandmann*

Alderney — fortress island

The late Major 'Bunny' Pantcheff also spent time on Alderney, both before and after the war. He first went there in 1931, to visit his uncle, then the war intervened and he became a military intelligence officer. In May 1945, he was asked by the War Office to go back in order to conduct a detailed inquiry into what had happened there during the German occupation. Subsequently he retired to the island in 1977 and a few years later wrote his book *Alderney — Fortress Island*. Pantcheff chronicles everything that went on and verifies the brutality and inhumanity that was the way of life for the slave workers. Between 26 February 1942 and 22 June 1944, when they were all withdrawn to the mainland, he lists 389 confirmed deaths among the slave workers on Alderney.

The workforce on Alderney was put into four camps, each named after an island in the North Sea. The camps were wooden-hutted, surrounded by a wire fence and had been built by a force of volunteer, paid, Belgian workers between January and June 1942. The camps were:

Helgoland or No 1 Camp
Built on the south side of a new concrete road constructed by the Germans in the Platte Saline beach area. It housed slave labour, principally Russians, and had a capacity of some 1,500.

Norderney or No 2 Camp
Built on the low ground between Saye Farm and Château à L'Etoc. It housed a mixture of Russian and European slave labour, plus some German volunteers, and had a capacity of about 1,500. It was taken over by the SS in February 1944.

Borkum or No 3 Camp
Built behind Longis House and used to house German and voluntary specialist craftsmen, with numbers fluctuating between 500 and 1,000.

Sylt or No 4 Camp
Built to the south of the airfield and although it was initially used by the OT for Russians and other slave labour, it was handed over to the SS in March 1943. It could hold up to 1,000.

Although it is difficult to work out an accurate figure of workers on Alderney at any one time, Maj Pantcheff does attempt to do so for May 1943, giving a grand total of some 4,000 workers of which 2,200 were OT workers only and broken down as follows:

700   Russians at Helgoland Camp

400   volunteer workers of various European nationalities

100   women, mostly French

300   French Jews in Norderney Camp

700   German OT workers — 400 in Borkum, 150 in Helgoland and 150 in Norderney

Treatment

Some examples of the way that the OT workers were treated are given by Maj Pantcheff as told to him by survivors:

'Every day the Camp Commander made a habit of beating any man he found not standing properly to attention or who had not made his bed properly or did not execute a drill movement properly. The beatings were carried out on the head, face or body with a stick about 2.5cm in diameter. The Camp Commander's assistant also beat workers daily with a stick of the same thickness on all parts of the body until their faces were covered with blood and they could not rise from the ground, when he would call on the prisoner's mates to carry the prostrate body away.'

And again:

'In October 1942, there was an occasion when a carrot was thrown from a window by one of the cooks and was picked up outside by a Russian who was beaten mercilessly with a stick … The Truppführer gave an order to cut ten sticks on which they fitted rubber tubes. Then we were beaten with them. Very often we were beaten out of hatred. They called us "Communist swine" and "Bloody Poles" etc. Often the men were beaten so long that they fell down from sheer weakness… We were beaten every day. My friend Antoni Onuchowski died that way. He was from my native village and of course I knew him very well. He had stayed behind in Sylt Camp for a few days because of illness. He had swollen feet. Afterwards they got a bit better, but he was still very weak and could not walk properly. One day, after work, when our squad was marching back to camp he could not keep up and fell behind. I saw the Truppführer remain with him and get to work with his truncheon. Later we lost sight of him. All the evening we kept waiting for him, but he never returned. The next morning after reveille, when I went to the latrine, Onuchowski lay on the other side of the barbed wire at the side of the camp. His face was covered with red weals and when we later brought his body into the camp and undressed it, we could distinctly see the weals and blotches on his body.'

Stealing their meagre rations
Not only did the OT staff beat their workers, they also misappropriated their meagre rations, those being responsible for receiving the rations in bulk did so, as did the army quartermasters who supplied the rations. However, they were extremely careless in their endeavours to hide their misdemeanours and 'Bunny' Pantcheff records the fates of two army Oberzahlmeisters, Frank and Kruger, who were accused of diverting supplies for their own ends. It took some years for cases to be brought against them; nevertheless, Kruger was eventually reduced to the rank of private soldier, whilst Frank committed suicide. OT Hauptmanntruppführer Helling and Standorp, who were in charge of the OT Central Supply Depot on

Alderney, were accused of misappropriating rations, by indenting by some 600 over the top of the actual ration strength, then selling the surplus for their own personal profit. They also were brought to book, Helling receiving two years' penal servitude from a 319. ID court martial, which he served in Aschendorfer Moor Penal Camp in Emsland, where he is reported to have committed suicide. Despite such examples being made, the practice still continued and the workers were seriously undernourished, as one explained: 'Within a month of my arrival at Norderney Camp the average death rate was 2-3 per day. At the time of our arrival we had all been in normal health, but constant beatings and starvation diet had reduced us to an extremely feeble condition.'[3]

There is evidence that some soldiers working on Alderney felt compassion towards the OT slave workers; however, from the beginning, the garrison was forbidden to give them any food. A standing order, by Oblt Zuske, the Island Commandant, was regularly read out on parade to all units: 'I hereby forbid the employment of any Russians except those especially designated, and further forbid the giving of bread or any other foodstuffs to them. Unit commanders are responsible to me for compliance.'

Maj Pantcheff comments that those who did not comply with this order were indeed punished. However, he goes on the explain that there were still some officers and men who did not comply, and COs who gave 'token' punishments when a case was brought up before them. A German NCO sums up the bewilderment of many of those who witnessed the deliberate starvation of the workforce thus: 'I could never understand why the Russians were fed as they were, because at the time we had as much as we wanted to eat. I used to give them bread myself because I felt sorry for them. I have a large family and I know what hunger means.' Clearly, however, he was in a minority in a regime which had cynically written off the Russian prisoners as sub-human creatures who no longer counted and who could always be replaced.

Another victim of the OT

Although Hitler's order specifically mentioned Russians, Spaniards and Frenchmen, many other nationalities found themselves working for OT, one such victim of the tide of events being a young Dutchman, Gilbert Van Grieken, who would also find himself transported to the Islands. In his book *Destination 'Gustav'*, (the OT called the three main islands by the codewords 'Jakob' for Jersey, 'Abel' for Alderney and 'Gustav' for Guernsey), he tells how he was required to register for employment and then found himself reporting to Amsterdam railway station for transport to Germany where he would be given employment. At the same time his food ration card was taken away from him, so 'with no job, no money and the prospect of no food without a ration card', he had little choice but to comply.

This was the start of five years of conscript labour, and whilst he was not treated as badly as John Dalmau, he was no longer able to work in Holland because the Germans dictated where and when the labour would be performed. He began in Berlin,

then moved to La Rochelle and finally to Guernsey. It was at La Rochelle that he first came under the OT, which, as he recalled in his book was 'mustered on military lines, and . . . became notorious for the brutal treatment handed out by the German officers and NCOs of the Korps to the workers under their command.' Gilbert explains how most of the OT workers were slave labourers, who were 'given only the barest of necessities in the shape of clothing, the minimum of food rations and housed in the most appalling conditions. The Germans regarded them as subhuman, to be treated as harshly as possible and worked them until they dropped. They were given no dignity. They were regarded as expendable.'

He then goes on to explain that, although the conscript labour force was treated far less harshly than the slave labourers and allowed a degree of freedom, the impact of such sights on the mind of an 18-year-old should not be difficult to imagine. Van Grieken found himself in a group of some 50 workers, some of whom were conscript forced labourers like himself, and others were slave labourers. As he later recalled in his book:

'The slave workers, Moroccans, Algerians and Greeks who had been living in occupied France, were rounded up by the Germans and, together with petty criminals found in French prisons, drafted into the Organization Todt for construction work. Their condition was pitiful. Clothed in little more than rags, underfed and denied any proper sanitary facilities, they were accommodated in what was, to all intents and purposes, miniature prison units and given the minimum of subsistence rations. The conditions under which the slave workers were housed were so bad that a German doctor, after an outbreak of typhus in one of the camps, warned the German authorities of the danger to their own troops if the sanitary conditions of the slave workers camps was not improved.

'The work the men were given was backbreaking. Only hand tools — pickaxes and shovels — were provided for the men to prepare the site located on a granite outcrop. Each swing of the pickaxe might loosen half a shovel load of granite, if that, so progress of the work was slow. If the OT guards thought the slave workers were not working fast enough they were ready to urge them to greater efforts with the aid of the pickaxe handle or a whip.

'The Germans had laid down a light mineral railway at the site and the spoil from the workings had to be loaded into rail trucks and taken to the cliff edge where it was tipped.

'Each midday the conscript workers were lined up and given a ration of thin watery soup fit only for drinking, there was nothing in it to spoon up. This "meal" had to be taken while working. There was no lunch break. The slave workers were also given soup which they had to drink out of any receptacle they could find, old food tins, a disused saucepan, anything that would hold liquid. The OT slaves were so ravenous they would battle to reach the food lorry but it has to be said that the old hands held back and waited as they knew the soup at the bottom of the container was thicker. The

OT guards went off elsewhere for their food, which was undoubtedly more substantial and sustaining than that given to the workers.'

At the end of each day the slave workers would be taken back to their camps, given their usual meagre ration and left to sleep on the floor of whatever building they were billeted in. The conscript workers undoubtedly fared better. Van Grieken and his group were taken back to their billets and lined up in the kitchen which had been set up in the garage of the bungalow in which they lived. There they were given a ration of warm food, vegetable, lentil or macaroni soup or sometimes boiled potatoes and vegetables and a tiny piece of meat. At the same time they were given half a pound of bread with some butter and jam and, occasionally, a piece of meat. This was to be their breakfast for the next morning. They would take the warm food back to their rooms to eat. After that they were free to do as they liked but since there was little attraction to be found at L'Ancresse, particularly in wintertime, and the strenuous nature of the day's work they had done, most of the workers simply went to bed to prepare for another day of picking and shovelling on the battery site.

Van Grieken goes on to explain how massive concrete structures, which were the results of their hard work, soon began to appear around the island. The most impressive he considered to be the Mirus Battery at St Saviour's which is explained in some detail in a future chapter, as are the maze of underground tunnels for use as ammunition stores, command posts, etc, and even a 600-bed hospital. As the work increased, more and more slave labourers were brought to the Islands, requiring in turn extra workmen at the docks and he was lucky enough to be transferred to work in the harbour at St Peter Port. This resulted in him getting, as he explained, 'an opportunity to get away from the oppressive regime of the OT guards . . . and to be placed under the day-to-day control of the German army'.

A worker from the Islands

G. Prigent was a teenager when the Germans arrived on Jersey, having been born in St Helier in 1924. He was learning his trade as a builder, working for a small firm in the town. He was employed by this firm until November 1943, when he was called up —to work for the Germans — his first job being the installation of 24,000gal fuel tanks in St Peter's Valley. He recalled those days on a tape he recorded for the IWM Sound Archive (Accession No 107/11/3):

'They were going to bury them under the ground and cover them with concrete. They were to refuel the aircraft at the airport. It happened to be a cold November day when I got out there . . . Three or four chaps were standing around a brazier warming their hands in a shed. A couple of Irish chaps were playing cards. The German soldier said to me: "You come, you have to paint the tanks." I knew I could paint them but there were already three painters in the shed so I said, "I'm no painter, there's one, two, three painters in the shed. Why should I paint them while they're sitting around the fire?" So an officer came, with red stripes. I said, "I couldn't care less, I'm no painter. I've been called up, I'm a builder, plasterer, concrete work, not painting." So we had a few words. I gave him back his paintbrush and the bucket of red oxide paint. I decided to walk home. At nine o'clock that evening I was arrested as an undesirable troublemaker.'

Mr Prigent soon found that he had got himself into more trouble than he had bargained for, being taken down to the harbour and sent with three or four other teenagers to Guernsey, then on to Alderney. The Germans had initially sought 24 volunteers and when these were not forthcoming, they detailed a requisite number of the Island's young men and sent them over to Alderney to work there for six months with German rations, plus pay which was twice as good as that to be earned in Jersey. He hoped that he was going to join them, but instead found himself sent to an OT farm, where he worked for a few weeks. Then, '. . . all of a sudden a German soldier came and said: "You come with me." So he took me down to the Soldatenheim, that was the German officers' canteen, an old convent. Soldier said I had to scrub floors. So I had to scrub floors.' Whilst working at the Soldatenheim he met some other 'Guernsey lads' who were also working there on kitchen chores. They discovered that there was a radio in the office and, when no one was looking, they sneaked in to listen to it. However, they were caught by one of the German nurses who lived there (a Sister Maria), who told the German officer when he returned and he said they must all go and work on the OT farm. They all refused to do so and 'the Rekensführer got a bit annoyed, then within ten minutes we had two guards from Lager Nordeney and an alsatian dog. They marched us three miles to this Lager Nordeney camp in which we spent the rest of the time in Alderney until three weeks after D-Day.' Asked about conditions in the camp, Mr Prigent replied:

'Morning was roll call, six o'clock. You queued for your hot ladleful of coffee, gave your number. Mine was 116. You had your ladleful of coffee and went back to the roll call. Then your Vorarbeiter, he was a chap like a foreman, he'd taken the orders from a German officer, he'd say: "You twenty, you get hoe." You went in the toolshed and you got a hoe and you marched to the fields, which was sometimes three and a half miles away. You'd hoe sugar beet, potatoes, cabbages, like farm work.
'At 12 o'clock two or three prisoners would come with like a water tank on back of a horse and cart. You all lined up. You all had a ladleful of hot water, cabbage leaf and one slice of bread. 12.30 the whistle would go and you'd go back to work. 6 o'clock you lined up and marched back, wherever you were, three miles or three and a half miles back to camp. Then you queued up again. You had another ladleful of hot water, cabbage leaf and slice of bread. Seven or half past seven roll call again.'

He was not only employed on the farm, but also breaking stones in the stone quarry, unloading ships in the harbour, and digging slit trenches. Once a fortnight they were given a Sunday afternoon off, but often as not, spent it hoeing around the camp barbed wire or the camp commandant's garden! The best job he did he said was undoubtedly working in the Soldatenheim — because of the chance of stealing food (sticking a finger in a tin of jam, or finding a piece of raw bacon or a bit of cheese in the larder) but he then suffered severe pains in the stomach because he was unused to such rich food. The worst job was undoubtedly breaking up rocks with a sledgehammer in the quarry.

Living conditions in the camp were Spartan: three-tier bunks with straw mattresses inside bare wooden huts. When asked if he slept properly, he replied:

'One was so exhausted . . . you were asleep in five minutes because you were working 12 hours a day and with no nourishment . . . some of the chaps died of starvation. The thing was they reckoned that once you lasted nine months on the island you weren't fit to be in the camps any more because you were so starved and you couldn't do a day's work. They used to ship you back to the main camp in Germany which had gas chambers, but there were no gas chambers where we were.'

Probably his nastiest moment came when he was getting out of his bunk and he lifted his arms to yawn and stretch:

'They thought I was going to hit the guard. He hit me in the face with the butt of his rifle and took my teeth out . . . After the war, I went to London for a while and had some false teeth done . . . I had to replace them every so often, every three or four years.'

Evacuation

There was still a considerable amount of work to be done to the fortifications, when other, more pressing work, required them to be evacuated. This concerned the building of the V1 and V2 rocket sites fortifications, so many of the OT workers were sent back to France to be relocated. This movement was normally carried out by sea in 'slave-ship' conditions, so that by the time the voyage ended, there were always emaciated corpses to be disposed of from the holds where they had been packed like sardines, with minimal food and no sanitation. The final withdrawal from Alderney of the OT labour force took place in July 1944 to St Malo. Mr Prigent thought that he was going to be deported to Germany, but instead was shipped to Guernsey and from there eventually got back home to Jersey.

THE SS CONCENTRATION CAMP

While the OT workers on all the islands had to work in bad conditions and were often subject to inhuman treatment, those on Alderney undoubtedly fared worst of all. And among all the workers on Alderney, those at the real bottom of the pile were the poor unfortunate 1,000 workers from *SS Baubrigade I* (SS Construction Brigade I). It was in March 1943 that the OT administration had handed over Sylt Camp to the SS.[4] The SS staff who acted as guards and administrators came from a concentration camp at Neuengamme near Hamburg, whilst the 'workforce' comprised about 1,000 inmates from the concentration camp at Sachshausen, near Berlin. About half of these were Russian POWs or partisans, 200 were German (classified as 'work-shy' (*arbeitsscheu*) including conscientious objectors, criminals or political prisoners, etc); the rest were a mixture of European political prisoners. The prisoners arrived by sea in two trips on 3 and 5 March 1943 — in battened-down holds without water or sanitation, despite protests from the ship's captain. Last to disembark were six bloodhounds.

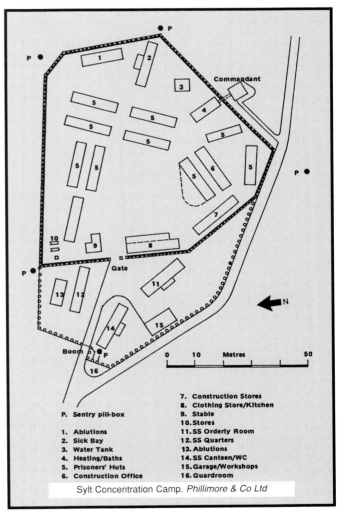

P. Sentry pill-box

1. Ablutions
2. Sick Bay
3. Water Tank
4. Heating/Baths
5. Prisoners' Huts
6. Construction Office
7. Construction Stores
8. Clothing Store/Kitchen
9. Stable
10. Stores
11. SS Orderly Room
12. SS Quarters
13. Ablutions
14. SS Canteen/WC
15. Garage/Workshops
16. Guardroom

Sylt Concentration Camp. *Phillimore & Co Ltd*

The security of Sylt Camp in which these poor unfortunates would be housed had been raised to a higher level than the other three, with a heavily wired inner compound for the prisoners and an outer compound for the guards and administrative staff. A number of concrete sentry posts were erected at strategic points around the perimeter (see drawing). The camp was commanded by SS Haupsturmführer Maximillian List, an experienced hand from Neuengamme. Having taken over in Alderney, List had a chalet built for himself just outside the perimeter, with an underground passage leading to the heating/bath house, so that he could come and go as he pleased. He had two deputies (SS Obersturmführer Klebeck and Braun), both experienced butchers like their commandant.

When List was posted to Oslo in the spring of 1944, Braun (a certified uncured syphilitic) became commandant in his place. Being SS, with his immediate superior in Germany, List did not come under local control and was thus his own master and his camp independent of any island control. This meant he could virtually do as he pleased, so they withheld the prisoners' meagre rations whenever they wished, confiscated their Red Cross parcels and sold them in France. The camp was run on the 'trusty' system, where a small number of prisoners were appointed to help with the administration — these 'Trusties' or 'Kapos' as they were called, were chosen from among the German prisoners and never from the foreigners. They maintained discipline amongst the other prisoners in the harshest possible way, receiving privileges for so doing — it is said that these included '. . . rooms to themselves, soft beds and white linen'.

Brutal treatment

There are many stories of the brutal way in which the prisoners suffered at the hands of the guards, but one will suffice. It concerned a demoted ex-Kapo called Ebert, who, in the summer of 1943, managed the impossible and escaped from the camp. The Island was thoroughly searched and eventually he was discovered hiding in a church. Another Kapo climbed up onto the roof, smashed a window, then got inside and opened the door, so that the SS guards could get inside. Ebert was brought outside and beaten with iron bars, so he decided to try to run away, hoping they wouldn't shoot for fear of hitting their own men. An NCO of 319. Divisional transport company was working in a nearby office and gave this eyewitness testimony:

'He ran through the graveyard towards New Street, but before he reached the street the SS fired and hit him three times. I came out of my office, which was immediately opposite, in time to see Hptm Söchtling arrive in his car. Ebert ran towards him, bleeding from the side of his head, his chest and his thigh and implored him to save him. He kept repeating "Herr Hauptmann, please help me, they are going to kill me." But Söchtling made a gesture with his hand to keep him away and said: "Go away, I do not want to have anything to do with you" and went into his house which was opposite the court house. Ebert tried to hold onto my side of the road by seizing the concrete pillars in front of our building and holding on to an iron gate, but the SS men kicked his hands away and trod into his stomach with their boots, so that he slumped forward and when he fell they shot him in the body. He was dying and asked for some water, whereupon one of the SS men kicked him on the head. He died then shortly afterwards.'

Departure

SS Baubrigade I initially left Alderney in mid-December 1943. However, following a strong protest from the commander of LXXXIV Armeekorps (GenOb Erich Marcks), they returned in February 1944. The unit finally left Alderney in June 1944, returning to the mainland with what was left of their prisoners, who were destined for other concentration camps, including Buchenwald. Sylt Camp itself was left to fall to pieces, although the materials were used for other construction work or burnt as firewood which was always in great demand.

THEIR PLACE IN HISTORY

Dr Fritz Todt, head of the Organization Todt, who was born in Pforzheim, Baden, in 1891, the son of a jewellery factory owner, had stressed the importance of keeping possession of the Channel Islands after the war, so as to preserve the 'great feats of German engineering', which as Charles Cruickshank comments '. . . he perhaps saw as a memorial to himself'. Unfortunately for Todt, he was killed in an aeroplane accident on the Eastern Front on 9 February 1942, so he never saw the surrender of the white elephants his forced labour had helped him create. His place was taken by the Führer's favourite architect Albert Speer (who had been scheduled for the same flight, but had cancelled at the last moment). Speer continued to run OT for the rest of the war. He was brought to book at the Nuremberg Trials and paid for some of his crimes with a sentence of 20 years' imprisonment for war crimes and crimes against humanity. He died in 1981.

Nothing more needs saying here about the place of the SS in world history. Some paid for their crimes, others unfortunately did not — in this world at least. Undoubtedly they were the most despicable instrument of the Nazi regime, and as Gerald Reitlinger says at the end of his book about the SS:

'The machinery of the SS as a state within a state will be forgotten because it never achieved its end. The successes of the SS in the field will be forgotten because the SS never fought as an army and its leaders never achieved more than local tactical control. The idealism of the SS will be forgotten because it meant nothing beyond loyalty to one man. But the racial transplantations, the concentration camps, the interrogation cells of the Gestapo, the medical experiments on the living, the mass reprisals, the manhunts for slave labour and the racial exterminations will be remembered for ever.'[5]

Opposite top: Gilbert Van Grieken at St Peter Port harbour, 1943. He is on the left-hand end of the 'workers row', whilst the German soldiers stand in the rear — Unteroffizier Wagner is at the end behind Gilbert. *Gilbert Van Grieken*

Opposite centre: Gilbert Van Grieken with the rest of his labour gang at White Rock Harbour, St Peter Port, in 1943. *Gilbert Van Grieken*

Opposite: Gilbert Van Grieken (centre) on the day of his arrival at L'Ancresse, Guernsey, 6 December 1941, with J. Van Velsen and J. Brand. *Gilbert Van Grieken*

Above: A memorial to the slave workers in the underground hospital in Guernsey. *Brian Matthews*

Below: One of the later constructions was this casemate for six loopholed machine guns in the grounds of 'la Rocque Onvoy', Mt Matthieu, St Ouen, Jersey, for Strongpoint *Doktorhaus. CIOS Collection*

Chapter 8
Daily Life on the Islands

LIVING WITH THE ENEMY

I have mentioned FK515 in an earlier chapter; now it is necessary to expand on how it carried out its work of organising military and civilian affairs.

FK515 was established when the Feldkommandant Oberst Schumacher arrived on 9 August 1940. As well as FK515 on Jersey he had set up three subordinate establishments:

- on Guernsey a *Nebenstelle* (Branch) which also administered Sark
- on Alderney an *Aussenstelle* (outpost)
- in France a *Zufuhrstelle* (a stores assembly point)

The basic split within FK515 was into two branches — a military branch (*Militarische Führung)* and a second branch responsible for the administration of the civil government (*Verwaltungsstab*). The military branch was headed by a major, based in Jersey, who kept in close contact with the military commander. His staff of three captains and two lieutenants were responsible for such matters as quartering, rations, leisure activities for the military, transport, weapons, air raid precautions (including gas attacks), complaints from servicemen, the secret military police (*Geheime Feldpolizei*), courts martial, discipline and other military matters. There was also on FK515 staff, a medical officer, a vet and a paymaster to assist the military branch. In the Guernsey Nebenstelle, there was a smaller but similar sub-branch. The Alderney Aussenstelle was too small to be divided, and in any case the very small number of civilians left on the island did not warrant it.

The civil administrative branch, which was run by a senior war administrator (*Oberkriegsverwaltungsrat*), had to supervise all aspects of the civil government to ensure that they were not only being run efficiently but also in the way in which the Germans wished them to be run. Within the branch there were four sub-branches, which between them were responsible for a wide variety of matters such as finance, including the fixing of the prices of all commodities; control of essential supplies and services such as gas and electricity; all aspects of health; education and propaganda; the police and the postal services; occupation costs and war damage and general administration. Initially there was a degree of harmony between FK515 staff and the local government officials, although from the outset it was clear that the Germans did not truly understand how fiercely independent the Islanders were, both as far as their prewar dealings with the UK had been concerned and now with an occupying foreign power.

The complex subject of what has by some been called a model occupation has already been dealt with by numerous respected historians and I can do no better than to quote from Peter King's excellent book *The Channel Islands War 1940-1945* in which he sums up the situation thus:

'German military government in the Channel Islands had been lenient in some respects: at first, when they thought the occupation would not last; later, because it suited them to build good relations for the benefit of the garrison; and most frequently when they were dealing with people in their own class among the Island rulers. But their occupation rule was in the end as destructive, futile and negative as Fascist and military rule was in the rest of Fortress Europe. The goodwill and work of those like von Aufsess and Knackfuss, were never more than icing on the cake. The real substance of occupation was a military machine maintaining itself in power by overwhelming force, threatening savage penalties, and using secret police informers and quislings. There was a change of personnel for the worse in 1944, but even the so-called moderates like von Schmettow were loyal to the orders of the Führer to stand firm.'

Mr King then quotes from a report made by Herbert Morrison, British Home Secretary, after he had visited the Islands, 14–15 May 1945, in which he wrote that, after talks with senior Island figures he had concluded that, 'on the whole the behaviour of the Germans had been correct, particularly in the early days . . . however, when Vice-Admiral Hüffmeier took over command from Gen Schmettow, there was a stiffening of the German attitude, but apparently without a great deal of difference to the practical outcome.'

Mr King clearly finds difficulty in agreeing with Morrison's findings, which must have been reached after only the most superficial investigation, and rightly comments that, 'To tens of thousands of starving Islanders and soldiers this would have seemed a strange conclusion about the five years of military rule they had just experienced.'

Negotiating

Raymond Falla, who was a member of the Guernsey Bulb Growers' Association prewar, was asked by the Bailiff, Ambrose Sherwill, if he would join the Controlling Committee in 1940. He then had the onerous task of establishing a purchasing commission, with both German and Channel Islands representation, which bought urgent supplies in France, both

THE CONTROLLING COMMITTEE OF THE STATES OF GUERNSEY

ORDER — REGISTER OF DWELLINGS

ALL persons in the occupation or otherwise having the care or charge of any house or other dwelling place in this Island of Guernsey, excluding premises in use under German authority, are hereby ordered to make a return of all such premises by giving correct and full answers to the questions contained in the form hereunder and to deliver or to send through the post (post free) such a form in respect of every such property in his or her care or charge addressed to The Controlling Committee, Dept. D., Hirzel House, Smith Street, Guernsey:—

FORM

FULL NAME OF PERSON MAKING THIS RETURN AND HIS OR HER ADDRESS:—

....

....

NAME (OR NUMBER) AND SITUATION OF PROPERTY:—

....

....

NUMBER OF PERSONS HABITUALLY SLEEPING THERE:—

BOYS UNDER 12: .... OTHER PERSONS: ....

GIRLS „ „ : ....

NUMBER OF BEDROOMS:—

FURNISHED: .... UNFURNISHED: ....

OTHER ROOMS:—

Sitting-Room(s) .... Dining-Room(s) .... Kitchen(s) ....

Bathroom(s) .... Lavatories ....

Any other apartment of floor area of 50 sq. feet or more:—

.... Area....................

.... Area....................

.... Area....................

MEANS OF COOKING:—

GAS? .... ELECTRICITY? .... OTHER MEANS? ....

HOW LIGHTED:—

GAS? .... ELECTRICITY? .... OTHER MEANS? ....

WATER SUPPLY:—

STATES? .... OTHER SUPPLY? ....

DRAINAGE:—

ON MAIN DRAIN? .... CESSPOOL? ....

State here if any of such services (lighting, water or drainage) is not ready for use and why:—

....

....

The required form(s) must reach The Controlling Committee not later than the third day of November, 1941.

Any failure to comply with this Order will render the delinquent liable to the penalties prescribed by Paragraph 92 of the Defence Regulations (Guernsey), 1939.

DATED this 28th day of October, 1941.

For and on behalf of The Controlling Committee of the States of Guernsey.
JOHN LEALE.

Genehmigt (Approved)
Nebenstelle Guernsey
der Feldkommandantur 515
FUERST VON OETTINGEN.
Rittmeister.
28. 10. 1941.

A selection of forms that the Channel Islanders had to fill in during the Occupation.
Guernsey Museum

FAHRERLAUBNIS
DRIVING PERMIT

Valid from
1st to 8th July.
1/7 - 8/7 40

Wagennummer
No. of Car

Der Deutsche
Commandant.

 "La Gazette Officielle"

The Controlling Committee of the States of Guernsey

ORDER RE CENSUS OF ALL-MAINS WIRELESS RECEIVING SETS

ALL those who own or are in charge of one or more All-Mains Wireless Receiving Sets must fill in the accompanying form and return same to the Labour Office, Hirzel House, St. Peter-Port, by the 29th August, 1941. Anyone who does not obey this Order renders himself or herself liable to the penalties prescribed by Regulation 92 of the Defence Regulations (Guernsey), 1939, as well as to the confiscation of his or her set or sets. Additional forms may be had at the Labour Office, Hirzel House.

DATED this 25th day of August, 1941.

R. H. JOHNS,
For and on behalf of the Controlling Committee of the States of Guernsey.

1. Name and address of owner or person in charge of set or sets ....

2. Address of building or buildings in which set or sets are: ....

3. Make of set or sets .... *Philips*

4. Whether A.C. or D.C. or Universal: .... D.C.

5. Description of building or buildings in which set or sets are
Example: whether dwelling, office, shop, etc. .... *Dwellings*

6. Does anyone sleep regularly on these premises .... *Yes*

7. Description of any other non-all-mains Receiving sets in your possession or charge: ....

8. Does any permanent invalid enjoy the use of the set:..................... *no.*

9. Any further remarks ....

Genehmigt (Approved)
Nebenstelle Guernsey
der Feldkommandantur 515
(Verw.)
DR. REFFLER
Kriegsverwaltungsrat
den 22.8.1941.

CERTIFICATE OF REGISTERY
— OF A —
GUERNSEY SEA FISHING BOAT.

Name of boat..................... Letters .... Number ....

Description of boat ....

Principal dimensions : Length .... feet .... inches

Beam .... feet .... inches

Depth .... feet .... inches

Skipper ....

Owner .... Address ....

Address ....

Date of Birth ....

Where Born ....

CREW LIST.

Name	Name
Address	Address
Date of Birth	Date of Birth
Where Born	Where Born

(ALL NAMES TO BE GIVEN IN FULL.)

Harbourmaster. Hafenuberwachungstelle, Guernsey.

BARES, BROWNSEY & CO., LTD., PRINTERS.

7

Above: Window shopping in King Street and Halkett Place, St Helier, Jersey. At the start of the Occupation the shops were full of luxury goods, at reasonable prices, for the German soldiers to buy and send home to their families. *Société Jersiaise*

officially and clandestinely via the black market. He routinely risked prosecution by the Germans for the black market side of his activities, but managed to hoodwink them throughout his time with the commission because of their studious regard of the sanctity of orders (remember his '*Befehl ist Befehl*' comment in an earlier chapter). He thus had to work with them for the good of the Islanders, but throughout his dealings managed to stay one jump ahead.

In a taped interview he made for the Imperial War Museum (Accession No 01000/4), he graphically describes his job with the purchasing commission. He also mentions other subjects; for example, when asked how tough he thought the Germans were on the local population, he replied that they were tough on certain matters — they were very, very worried about escapes and security generally, very tough on seeing that the curfew was maintained and very strict on rationing. As an example of the former he told of how, when visiting the Dame of Sark, for whom he had considerable admiration for the way in which she stood up to the Germans, he had been strip-searched to see if he was carrying any secret notes. They had found one from the Dame's grand-daughter, hidden in an old pair of shoes which he was taking to her — 'So they gave me a body search — starkers. It wasn't funny on a cold winter's day.' The Dame complained very strongly, but the Germans merely said that they were quite within their rights to search; having found one secreted note (albeit from a little girl to her granny) there might be more. As he was allowed a car to do his job, he also fell foul of the curfew restrictions, being caught out late at night and punished. As far as the food rationing was concerned, Raymond Falla found himself in trouble for complaining that German soldiers were stealing cattle, chickens and the like:

'Oh yes, I did complain and got severely reprimanded and threatened with deportation, because I told Commandant von Helldorf . . . that his troops were thieving. He was horrified that I should accuse the German armed forces of being thieves. He said it was an insult and if I repeated it he would deport me.'

It was clearly very difficult for honest men like Raymond Falla who was in constant daily contact with German officials to have to walk a tightrope between co-operation and non-co-operation, when the lives of so many depended upon them maintaining the delicate balance. I believe the same can be said of the vast majority of the Channel Islands wartime civil servants, who were decent, honourable people, and were on occasions forced to make unpalatable decisions adversely affecting the few on behalf of the many. It is very easy now, with hindsight, with the die already cast and the result known, to pontificate on what they should or should not have done about a particular issue. Some writers are only too willing to 'dish the dirt' and to exaggerate the degree of co-operation which did undoubtedly go on, but conveniently forget the simple heroism which the vast majority of the Islanders displayed in living their daily lives. Towards the end of his fascinating book *If Britain had Fallen*, Norman Longmate comments about the co-operation which had occurred in so many of the occupied countries and speculates whether it would have been the same in the UK, coming to the conclusion that:

'. . . however bitter the aftermath of a successful invasion, sooner or later some form of civil government would have had to be set up in the conquered British Isles, and some method of working with the Germans would have had to be evolved, however reluctantly and however much those old enough to remember a time when there were no Germans in the streets, longed for liberation.'

Later on, almost at the very end of his book, when writing about the actual Occupation of the Channel Islands, rather than the hypothetical Occupation of Great Britain, he says:

'During five years, when it must often have seemed that they had been forgotten and that the war would last for ever, the loyalty of the people of the Channel Islands to their own race and their own country, their pride in their past and their faith in its future never wavered.'

That, I believe, is a fair description of the way in which the vast majority of the Channel Islanders behaved in the wartime years. For example, when asked during a taped interview (IWM Dept of Sound Records Accession No 010066/2) about the attitude of the average civilian once the Occupation got under way, whether they would snub the Germans or be friendly and co-operative towards them, Jersey newspaperman Leslie Sinel replied:

'No, I won't say co-operate — but you had to work with them according to where you were, they took over places and you had to work with them, but that's not to say you were friendly. At the office there were some Germans there running their newspaper and in normal times you could have — they were quite likeable some of them — but obviously you did not entertain them. There were a few isolated cases but basically nobody entertained the Germans and got overfriendly except where they thought they could get something out of them. An empty belly had no conscience and when food got short if there was a chance of getting something it was obvious you forgot your scruples and you had something extra.'

'Absolutely correct'

Flak gunner Josef Gerhaher told me, 'We could not make any really good contacts with the inhabitants of Guernsey, but I know it was wartime and we the aggressors. So the only possible way to co-exist was to be absolutely correct, and if possible helpful, to the other side and I think that most people did so. After the war, as a prisoner in Yorkshire I had and still have, many friends in all walks of life, also now in Guernsey after six visits.'

That is all I intend to say about co-operation and the difficult business of working with the Occupation forces and vice versa. After all, this book is primarily about the way the Occupation forces went about their daily lives, so the following random examples should be treated in that context.

Below: The corner window of Burton's (compare with last photograph) became a prime site for Nazi propaganda — here books and pamphlets on such subjects as *The Decline and Fall of the British Empire* and *Famine in England* are displayed, together with a photograph of Hitler and numerous swastikas. *IWM* — HU 5189

Wacht am Kanal

Feldzeitung einer Armee an der Kanalküste

Nummer 1169   Herausgeber: Propaganda-Kompanie   Freitag, 5. Mai 1944

Jersey, Sonnabend, 7. Juni 1941.

Deutsche Inselzeitung

Druck: evening Post, Charles Str. Jersey.   Deutsch-englische Heereszeitung fuer die britischen Kanalinseln.   Jahrgang 1. Nr.
Verantw. fuer den Inhalt : Sdt. (Z) Kohl.

TO-DAY'S LESSON IN GERMAN

No. 29 OF OUR SERIES.

More useful phrases in English, with the German translation, approximate pronunciation in English spelling, and German pronunciation in English.

ENGLISH.	GERMAN.	PRONUNCIATION.
1 Has there been an accident?	Ist ein Unglück geschehen?	Ist ine Oonglück geshayn?
2 A car has run into a tree.	Ein Auto ist gegen einen Baum gefahren.	Ine owtoh ist gaygen inen Bown gefahren.
3 Has a doctor been called?	Hat man einen Arzt geholt?	Hat man inen Artst gehohlt?
4 Show me the way to the Hospital.	Zeigen Sie mir den Weg nach dem Lazarett.	Tsygen Zee meer den Vayg nach dem Lazarett.
5 Straight on, keep to the right.	Gerade aus, halten Sie rich rechts.	Gerahder ews, halten Zee sish rechts.
6 Is anybody hurt?	Ist jemand verletzt?	Ist yaymand ferletst?

AUSSPRACHE DES ENGLISCHEN.—1 Has zhär bien en achsident?   2 E kar has römm intu e trie.   3 Has e docter bien kold?   4 Schoh mi zhe uäi tu zhe Hospitl.   5 Strelt onn, kiep to zhe reit.   6 Is enibodi hört?

THE GERMANS OFF-DUTY

The daily news

Mr Sinel also explained how the Germans ran their own German language newspaper on Jersey, entitled *Deutsche Inselzeitung* (there was a similar paper for Guernsey — see photograph). They were produced on the presses of the Islands' newspapers, whilst the propaganda company also produced a newspaper *Wacht am Kanal*. In addition, they vetted everything that was produced in the normal Island English-language newspapers. He comments that their grammar wasn't very good and that they often made mistakes. However, they were keen for the Islanders to learn German and would have simple German lessons published in the normal daily newspapers under the heading: 'To-Day's Lesson In German'.

They had a special news service, getting news items off the *Deutschlands Sender* (Transmitter Germany). Sinel found it amusing because he and other Islanders would listen secretly to the news on the BBC on a 'tucked-away radio somewhere' then it would be given out by the Germans some two days later after it had been '. . . vetted and altered to suit their case'. *Der Fiend Hört Mit* (The enemy listens!). Sometimes, unbeknown to the authorities — or for that matter to most of the general population — some German soldiers as well as Islanders, did illegally listen to the BBC on the tiny crystal radio sets which the Islanders had made. Werner Wagenknecht, for example, told me that on D-Day he had gone to see his civilian friend 'B', but his wife had told him that he could not see him as he was occupied. 'I saw him in the corner of a back room with earphones on, so he did not hear me, but was choked when he saw me! He gave me the earphones and I heard a crackly voice saying, "we have invaded . . . landed at . . ." and so on. I kept this news to myself.'

Above:
Banners of German-language newspapers.
Oblt Dr Ernst-Heinrich Schmidt

Left:
Today's lesson in German.
Ms June Money from her book Aspects of War. *This appeared in the* Guernsey Evening Press *on 17 August 1940.*

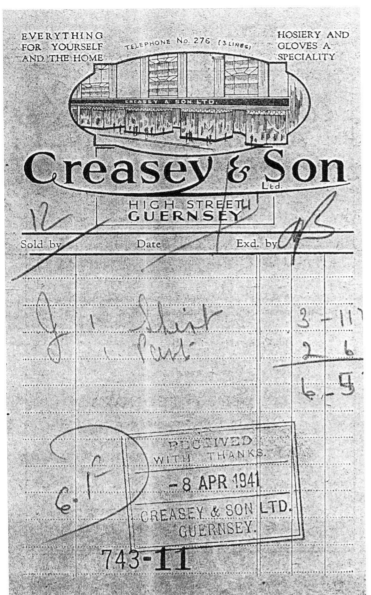

Above: 'V for Victory!' Other hastily-daubed signs put a different point of view, like this one in Jersey. However, being caught putting up such signs would have very serious consequences. *IWM* — HU 25934

Top: There were more sinister undertones to some of the notices appearing in shop windows — like this one in a Jewish-owned shop in Jersey. *IWM* — HU 25933

Left: Bill for a shirt purchased by Hans-Gerhard Sandmann's father on April 8 1941, from Creasey & Son of Guernsey.

Going to church and the cinema

The Islanders were permitted to go to church and to say prayers for the Royal Family. Leslie Sinel recalled that they did not sing the National Anthem out loud at church (although they did do at some private dances). Apart from that the churches were left more or less alone. The Germans of course had their own services, generally earlier, using their own Communion vessels. One of his abiding memories was of the smell of the German ersatz boot polish, which made the church smell! However, he had to admit that they were very well behaved in church and also at the cinema which they took over to show mostly propaganda films for audiences of about 1,500 strong. 'I would be supported by hundreds,' he said, 'who'd say when they came out at night any woman of any age could walk through the lot and feel safe, which I don't think applies today in certain places.'

Cinemas

Of the six cinemas in the wartime Channel Islands the Germans took over control of only two full time: the Regal in Guernsey and the Forum in Jersey. The others were compelled to show German films sometimes at weekly intervals and sometimes interspersed with British programmes, but the Regal was the only one under direct German supervision. They kept the manager, Eric Snelling, and his civilian staff and they began by giving two nights a week to German films. Troops were admitted free to these shows, but civilians paid. By the end of 1941, the programme was entirely German and no civilians were admitted, except on certain occasions. Programmes contained newsreels such as *Die Deutsche Wochenschau* which was similar to *Pathe Gazette*, but were mainly feature films, made by the highly successful German film industry, which in the 1930s rivalled

Hollywood. This situation lasted until November 1944, when dwindling power stocks forced the cutting off of electricity to all cinemas. In any case by then the British films must have been becoming a little tired and worn as no replacements were available. On 1 March 1945, performances at the Regal were resumed, with a block of 200 seats being allocated to civilians. On the whole the Germans were well-behaved audiences, seating being zoned by their Press Censor, who was also the Entertainments Officer, between officers, soldiers, marines and bearers of special passes, who were all segregated. On the plus side, smoking was forbidden. There was some vandalism as the rubber pads in the armrests were much sought after for boot-repairing! In her book *Aspects of War* , June Money tells of one secret which the Germans never discovered, which was the illegal all-mains radio set which Kennedy Bott had hidden inside the theatre's Compton organ. Thus twice daily, when he came up to play to the audience the illegal radio was in full view of about 700 Germans — and not one of them realised!

Werner Wagenknecht also remembers going to film shows and live entertainment at the Odeon cinema, near Elizabeth College, the performances being for everybody: 'At the end of the performances the Guernseyers sang their lovely songs like "Sarnia cherie" and "There'll be bluebirds over the white cliffs of Dover."'

Perhaps the strangest happening in the Regal took place during a live show by some German variety turns when a marks-man entertained the troops with his shooting prowess. After the war had ended, it was discovered that there were five bullet holes in the screen where he had missed his target. Fortunately, no one had been in the dressing room at the side of the stage at the time as one of the bullets had penetrated that too! [1]

Live entertainment

The islanders continued to put on amateur entertainments at, for example, Candie Gardens, which, as the photographs show, were attended by members of the Occupation forces. The German Press Censor would examine all scripts and programmes, cutting out anything he did not like. The difficulties of the curfew and lack of transport did, however, mean that attendance at such performances was restricted to townspeople. As has been mentioned already, live entertainers were brought over to the Islands by the German equivalent of ENSA, but this became more and more difficult as safe sea and air transport became more and more of a problem. The Germans also indulged their passion for military band music, putting on open air and indoor concerts, whenever and wherever they could.

Popular venues were, for example, Candie Gardens and the Candie Auditorium in Guernsey and the Royal Square in Jersey. Music by Jewish composers, such as Mendelssohn, was banned, but concerts took place regularly. June Money told me that she was a member of a children's dancing troupe which performed in concerts at Candie Gardens: 'Concerts were usually well supported by Occupation troops and civilians as there was a limited amount of entertainment available on the island.' She also explains that, unlike the cinemas, there was no segregation of audiences at these shows.

Above: As the inside of this soldier's locker confirms, 'pin-ups' were just as popular in the *Wehrmacht* !

Dances were initially banned by the German authorities, because they were worried that troops might give away military information whilst mixing with civilians. However, by 1942, both public and private dances were once again being arranged. Then in the summer of 1943, dances were banned in Jersey to prevent the spread of infectious diseases — diphtheria was one of the main problems and all parents were urged to have their children inoculated. In *Aspects of War*, June Money tells how one hotel advertised a ballroom dance as a dancing class, but unfortunately the Germans were not fooled and it had to be cancelled!

Sport

The civilian population and the Occupation forces tried to maintain their various sporting activities as best they could, despite a continuing shortage of equipment, which got steadily worse as the years went by and everything wore out and the islands became isolated. In *Aspects of War*, June Money tells how any form of footwear was used when the real thing wore out: 'Even bedroom slippers and rope-soled sandals were better than nothing, but later when these could not be replaced, some sports were played in bare feet.'

At times there were football matches arranged between the Occupation forces and civilian teams, but these were rare, especially after one was held between a Jersey side and the Luftwaffe, during the Battle of Britain, which was won by the Islanders 5-1. The main civilian football interest was strictly

Above:
Much of the soldiers' time was spent on such mundane matters as weapon cleaning, like this cheerful group from 216. ID, cleaning their rifles in their billet. *Hans-Gerhard Sandmann*

Above: 'Busy doing nothing!' As all soldiers know, much of one's time is spent waiting for something to happen. *Hans-Gerhard Sandmann*

Above:
Making the most of the
sunshine. Troops of
216. ID enjoy a picnic in
the summer of 1940.
*Hans-Gerhard
Sandmann*

Above: Rear view of Werner Wagenknecht's quarters, taken during a farewell
party given for '*der Spiess*' (at the end of the row). Werner stands next to him
and took over from him as sergeant-major of the medical unit.
Werner Wagenknecht

Right:
This was the inside of their dining room, decorated by unit soldiers, including the eagle and small lamps over the fireplace. In 1943, the walls were painted by an amateur landscape artist with views of home.
Werner Wagenknecht

Left:
And this was the result of all their hard work — they won the competition for the best accommodation in 1943–44 and were awarded this certificate in March 1944.
Werner Wagenknecht

between local sides (in 1944, the Jersey Occupation Cup was held and attracted a crowd of nearly 5,000). Among the servicemen swimming was popular in the summer, but the troops had to bathe in groups so that they could be more easily rounded up if there was an alarm and also could be policed by lifeguards and rescue boats, so this did detract somewhat from its popularity. The only swimming pool available on Jersey was the Havre des Pas pool on the front at St Helier, which was very popular. Games such as volleyball and table-tennis were encouraged, whilst such country sports as shooting game, riding horses and the like were permitted, always provided one had the necessary wherewithal to take part — there must have been a fair number of shotguns available which had been taken off the civilian population. During the 'Hunger Winter', game became less and less available.

Soldatenheime

In the main, most of the occupation forces kept themselves to themselves and used the German recreational facilities which were provided for them. Top of the list were the *Soldatenheime* (Soldiers' homes), which were not unlike some of the British voluntary clubs for servicemen — such as those run by the Church Army or Toc H, although they could also be likened to the British NAAFI and the American PX. In St Helier for example, there was an officers' club at Fort D'Auvergne and another ranks' club at the Mayfair Hotel, whilst at the St Brelade's Bay Hotel, there was one for all ranks. Here servicemen could relax during their off-duty hours. They were run by Red Cross sisters, who were themselves strictly controlled in dress and behaviour — no lipstick or nail varnish for example and hair had to be cut short. The only greeting allowed was 'Heil Hitler!' The regulations governing these clubs were drawn up by the OKH and very strictly adhered to. Officers had separate rooms in all ranks' clubs and codes of conduct were on formal military lines — officers, especially senior officers, being shown proper respect at all times. The clubs did serve food, but as supplies deteriorated, this was likely to be disappointing and unappetising. The alternative was to drink too much (in private that is, not in the *Soldatenheime*) and drunkenness became a continuing problem, especially as the troops' morale worsened.

Brothels

The Germans have always taken a different viewpoint to ourselves on the delicate subject of the establishing of official brothels — *Freudenhaus* (house of joy) where *die Prostituierte* were officially employed. They were set up on both islands as a matter of course, in St Helier and St Peter Port. Charles Cruickshank gives details of the first Guernsey brothel which had a staff of two men and thirteen women, all of whom were brought over from France. Later more brothels were opened, including an OT one in Alderney. The women were provided with civilian ration books on the orders of FK515, being classed as far as rations were concerned as 'heavy workers'!

'The queues of customers waiting in the gardens of the chosen houses afforded a certain amount of innocent amusement to the inhabitants of both towns, although in Guernsey the authorities were upset by the management of the institutions.' [2]

The Germans initially tried to make the local civilian doctors responsible for inspecting the brothels twice a week, but later they had to nominate their own MOs to do the job as the civilian doctors were always rushed off their feet attending to their civilian patients.

Soldatenkaufhäuser

In 1942, *Soldatenkaufhäuser* (soldiers' shops) were opened in both Jersey and Guernsey, where soldiers could buy two very different types of goods. On the one hand they could obtain personal necessities such as razor blades, shaving soap, shaving brushes, toothbrushes and toothpaste, whilst at the other end of the spectrum they could buy luxury goods such as perfume, silk underwear, stockings, etc, intended for the servicemen to purchase to send home to wives and girlfriends, or to take home on leave. They were extremely popular with the troops — they were open only to men of the Wehrmacht in uniform or to German members of the OT — just as long as the goods were there to purchase. In Guernsey, for example, the soldiers' shop had some 400 customers daily and there were grumbles from those stationed too far away from St Peter Port who couldn't get in to town to use the shop when it was open. Goods came mainly from France, so that supplies eventually dried up and by the end of 1944 they had all closed.

Hobbies

Photography was permitted (as is evidenced by the number of personal photographs in this book!). However, as the necessary supplies dwindled, the small number of photographic shops which were given permission to process the servicemen's films, could no longer do so. Michael Ginns told me that in Jersey the soldiers initially took their films to any photographer for developing, but after 1941 all troops films had to be processed at Scotts in Broad Street. Once developed, the photographs went across the road to the *Inselbildstelle* (the Island photographic interpretation post) where they were censored and any containing guns, fortifications, etc, were weeded out. Some troops, however, took their films home when they went on leave and had them developed and printed in Germany.

Even such a simple hobby as reading was restricted by the availability of books — which all had to be approved by the Feldkommandantur. Morale-boosting competitions were held on a variety of subjects which included painting, short story writing and even, so it is said, one to design the best model of a war grave!

Fraternisation

Human nature being what it is, there were inevitably some cases of German soldiers fraternising with local girls. For some it was a case of true love, as is evidenced by those who returned to the Islands after they had been released from prisoner of war camp, to marry their wartime sweethearts. As Leslie Sinel sensibly put it in his taped interview:

'You've got to remember that the girls were in their teens, they wanted things and they were attracted by the Germans — and some of the young Germans were quite likeable, especially those who worked on a farm and could get to know some girls in the district. They are to be condemned but it was a natural thing that happened in every place where there were occupying forces. That's the sort of thing you came to expect.'

'You scratch my back . . .'

Undoubtedly, but without the knowledge of higher authorities, a certain amount of bartering went on between soldiers and civilians. For example, Werner Wagenknecht recalls:

'Many knew the secret depots of petrol for the reconnaissance planes (the planes and the Luftwaffe maintenance staff were removed to other places on the Continent a few days before 6 June 1944). I asked a dairy farmer for some old milk churns and our "deal" was perfect. Old cans filled with petrol for the dairy, new cans with milk for us. The dairy was situated at the other end of the road where we lived. The dairy could work and we had milk and made curds. The filled cans were our wealth. Sometimes the churns were filled with sausages. No comment — the end justifies the means!'

As well as bartering with the locals, they were not averse to 'acquiring' goods 'damaged in transit':

'One of our lance-corporals who drove a motor lorry was ordered to transport newly-arriving rations from the harbour to the headquarters. He had also made good contact with Guernsey civilians and was befriended by a young Guernsey constable, whose wife helped us to clean our quarters. As the lorry was very old and not well suited to the transportation of delicate goods, there were many "damaged in transit" goods, which were just the ones we needed for cooking in our canteen!'

An E-Boat visits Guernsey

'After a raid on an Allied convoy south of Start Point, the 5th Flotilla experienced a heavy counter-attack by British naval units. Towards dawn only six E-Boats could leave the battle. *S81* had been driven so far off course to the southwest that returning to Cherbourg before daybreak was impossible. So *S81* was ordered to call at St Peter Port.' That is how Dr Hardy Hoogh begins a personal account of an unexpected wartime visit to Guernsey made by him and the rest of his crew. He continues:

'The crew looked forward very much to this unexpected short trip ashore on British territory. As we approach Guernsey speed slackens, white foam appears at both sides — there are rocks just below the surface and a strong current is evidence that the passage through the Great Russell is not child's play. Finally Castle breakwater lighthouse looms ahead. S81 goes alongside White Rock Pier. Ropes are fastened to wet rings on the lower gallery. We set foot on the slippery concrete as water drips from above, mussels and seaweed on the piles. This is the first impression of our visit at low tide early in 1942. Later the boat shifts a bit closer to St Julian's Pier for refuelling. There are not many ships in the harbour — a cargo coaster at the west side of the New Jetty, four fishing smacks high and dry in front of the impressive granite quay of the Old Harbour. Near the mouth two patrol boats sway at their moorings. This day we don't see much of the town and late in the evening we leave St Peter Port for Cherbourg.

'However, there were some occasions when we went to Guernsey for a couple of days. The crews were accommodated in requisitioned houses in Hauteville. Further up the same street there was the inevitable brothel. At least as possible as the red light location were the cafes of the South Esplanade and the Glatezney Esplanade. In peacetime they are not usually licensed, but during the early part of the occupation beer and spirits were served. For us mariners not permanently stationed on the island to walk through Pollett Street, Market Street and the High Street were especially interesting. Most shops and stores were open and we could pay with German Reichsmark notes and coins as well as Guernsey bank notes. Funny that there existed notes of two shillings and sixpence, one shilling and threepence and even sixpence. There were the same nominal values in English coins. It was not so easy to figure out prices using two currencies; however, I never experienced any difficulties. When buying souvenirs and things I occasionally saw a sailor holding out a handful of coins and notes and the shopkeeper selecting the correct amount or giving back change. I never heard anyone complain.

'Relations with the inhabitants were friendly — but distant, as far as we could communicate in normal English. I remember an excursion to Fermain Bay, there is a Martello Tower there, something unknown to me at that time. Two "oldies" were sitting nearby talking in an idiom I did not understand. Nevertheless I asked and in the course of the conversation I not only learnt about Martello Towers but also about the Patois English-spoken French. Fascinated by the island I was determined to return, but I could not make my wish come true until 1960. At that time Patois was fading out but I have made good friends in Guernsey since then.'

Die grosse Hungerzeit

Undoubtedly the most difficult time for everyone on the Channel Islands, both military and civilian, was the 'Time of Hunger'. One member of the garrison, Georg Brefka of MG Btl 16, wrote vividly about the problems which the soldiers faced after the islands were cut off.

'At the end of August our rations were reduced for the first time, and, at the end of September, a second time. This particularly affected the bread ration, and the soup from the Company kitchen became noticeably thinner and was less nourishing . . . It was in October that we first felt really hungry. We needed additional food; jam was running short — jam and artificial honey being the basis of breakfast in the German Army! We were sent into the hills to harvest the abundant quantity of blackberries, but the blackberry jam only lasted a short time and we ended up with sugar instead. In November the rations were again cut, and the hunger pangs worsened. The bread got worse as substitutes were mixed with the flour. We began to eat stinging nettles, and grew to like it. In spite of orders to the contrary, everybody tried to find something edible in his vicinity. There was hardly any farmland in our area. The few farms were small and the farmers could not give us much, although they were always ready to barter (by the end of the war most of us had lost our watches). Potatoes in the soup were replaced by turnips. Finally we got potatoes only on Sundays, otherwise only turnips, turnips!'

The soldiers had a hungry Christmas, but made the best of it with a box of dry biscuits instead of cake and cigarettes made out of locally-grown tobacco. [3] The standing joke was, 'Follow the Führer's example, he is a non-smoker.' They were also able to get a message of reassurance through to their families to say that they were still all right, having been out of touch with them since the previous August. Brefka continues:

'1945 began and the last four terrible months. The already small rations were reduced every four weeks. The whole day we talked about food, what we had eaten at home and what we would eat after the war. Some comrades came from poor areas but when they talked about their home cooking it seemed as if they were talking about food from the Waldorf-Astoria. During the harsh winter, discipline and morale broke down . . . Hunger controlled everything . . . Owing to the reduced rations, the daily duties changed. Drill and exercising disappeared almost completely. Before, we had got up at 6.00am — now it was 7.00am and on Sundays, 8.00am. Midday rest had been from 12.30 to 1.30, now it was 12.30 to 2.30. That was an order! By day we received a lot of instruction and theoretical training. In the evening the small rations were distributed (there was seldom any quarrelling) and gulped down ravenously. We then went straight to bed. You lay on your side, knees pulled up to the chin to try to subdue the hungry feeling.
'Breakfast was a problem. In the British Army rations were distributed three times a day, but in the German Army only twice — at noon and in the evening, which included breakfast for the following morning (in the morning you only got a dark liquid called "coffee"). In normal times with normal rations this was alright, but now in March 1945, the system no longer worked. Everything was eaten in the evening

and there was nothing for breakfast the following morning. This prompted a new order. Clever physicians had been busy watching the physical condition of the soldiers. An order was issued and we were told to cut off a slice of bread from the evening ration, put it into an envelope and hand it over to the corporal for storage until the next morning! The second part of the order stated that each morsel of the ration must be chewed 30-32 times to make maximum use of it. In future we were to eat together and the corporal was to ensure that every man chewed properly. We laughed at this order and called it a kindergarten joke. We had to observe the order to cut off the slice of bread, but everybody kept his own envelope; during the evening you opened it now and then and cut off a small piece, so that by the morning a piece the size of a postage stamp was all that remained.'

Georg Brefka and his comrades also turned to the seashore for sustenance — for example, they ate limpets, gathered off the rocks between La Corbière and La Rocco Tower. Initially these were cooked and the small intestine taken out, then they were merely scalded and nothing was taken out and finally, they were eaten raw! Netting fish at Petit Port Bay was also tried with minimal success, because, as the fishermen had already told them, where there were rocks and currents you don't get many fish. They even tried octopus, the arrival of which Brefka likened to a Biblical miracle, like the feeding of the five thousand or the manna from Heaven!

'Here and there on the beach at St Ouen we found an unknown sea creature which had a small body and big sucking discs. Some of our men who had been to the Mediterranean told us that they were octopuses. These "experts" got to work and slaughtered, cut up, cooked and ate the creatures. Most of us waited in spite of the hunger, but when the "experts" were still alive the next day there was no holding us back. At first there were only a few but every high tide brought more and more octopuses until the whole beach was covered with them. It was said that they had come with the Gulf Stream, and been stunned by the relatively cold water. For days there was only slaughtering, cooking and eating. I have always had an aversion to reptiles and even touching a worm is a great effort, but being so hungry I dealt with the octopuses like a butcher. The health authorities forbade consumption for three days until they had examined the meat, but we ignored them. There was a real public festival on the beach. Soldiers and civilians mingled and for a few days the prohibited area signs were disregarded. Hunger had taken possession of everybody without heeding nationality and we all felt that we were in the same boat.
'After nearly three weeks the last morsel had been eaten and everything returned to "normal". March and April were the worst months. A big disaster at the beginning of April — there were no more cigarettes! Hunger and nothing to smoke! We continued to go to the soldiers' club at St Brelade's Bay on Sundays. The Red Cross nurses always had some turnip soup.'

Above: The Gaumont Palace Cinema in Guernsey, showing 'Victory in the West'
IWM — HU 25980

Eventually of course the war ended and they all became prisoners of war. He recalls that they were given bottles of French brandy but that hardly anyone in his company drank it as their physical state was so bad that they were afraid to do so — instead they sprinkled it on the floor of the hut, 'to lay the dust' before they left for the last time!

> *'Our days spent at Grève de Lecq were few, but I shall remember them for the rest of my life. Everything that remained in the German food stores was issued. Almost everything was available, except for bread and cigarettes. By night you could see small fires everywhere, as food was cooked and roasted. By day we enjoyed the sea, the rocks, the sky, in short the whole landscape. The nightmare was behind us, we had survived.'* [4]

After all these privations it must have been somewhat incongruous for the soldiers to be ordered, after the surrender, to destroy their iron rations. Werner Wagenknecht, now an Unteroffizier, recalled the bonfire:

> *'Days later, another bonfire, our Iron-Rations — never touched by us (meat, bread, rice and conserves) were burnt under the watchful eyes of Allied soldiers.'*

Above: Unteroffizier Werner Wagenknecht and a *Gefreiter* read the German editions of the local newspapers. Werner wears his Marksmanship lanyard which was awarded to him whilst serving in the infantry from 1936–38. They are sitting on the roof of their underground bunker. *Werner Wagenknecht*

Left: One of the crystal radio sets as used by Channel Islanders to listen to the BBC. This one was given to Werner as a souvenir after the war. *Werner Wagenknecht*

Right:
'Let's go to the Movies!' The Forum Cinema, Jersey, plus a squad of patrons — did they volunteer or were they detailed to go to see 'Victory in the West'?
Société Jersiaise

Left:
This was the Island Cinema on Alderney for the Occupation forces, c1942.
Alderney Museum and Mrs Pantcheff

Right:
Notice placed in cinemas in Guernsey during the Occupation by the Germans.
IWM — HU 25941

NOTICE

FOR German films with English sub-titles the left-hand section of the stalls are reserved for Civilians only; the right-hand section and the Balcony for German troops only.

Left:
Both Islanders and Occupation forces were able to attend the live concert parties at Candie Gardens, St Peter Port, Guernsey.
Werner Wagenknecht

Below:
This band concert was being given in the Royal Connaught Square, St Anne, Alderney. On the left is the German island HQ, now the Royal Connaught Hotel. *IWM — HU 25903*

Bottom:
This German band had a good audience of both soldiers and civilians when it played in West Park, St Helier.
Société Jersiaise

Liebe Schwestern!

Ich glaube, wir Soldaten sind selten so gut betreut worden wie
hier im Soldatenheim II. Brelades. Gerade deshalb haben
wir auch unseren Abschiedsabend hier verleben wollen.

Wir danken Ihnen noch einmal vor unserem Scheiden für alles
Gute, das Sie uns durch Jahre hindurch erwiesen, und wünschen
Ihnen allzeit Freude an Ihrer schönen Arbeit und eine glückliche
Heimkehr in unser herrliches Großdeutschland nach gewonnenem
Kriege.

Heil unserem Führer!

Ihr

Kapolke

Hptm., Fest.Pi.Abschn.Gr.II/14

Opposite far left:
Good hunting! This rabbit will prove a welcome addition to the rations. No doubt the shotgun was one of those taken off the Islanders.
Hans-Gerhard Sandmann

Opposite left:
Entry from the Visitors' Book at the St Brelade's Bay Hotel Soldatenheim.
Robert Colley

Opposite below:
Riding would always prove to be an excellent means of relaxing — for those lucky members of the garrison for whom horses were available.
IWM — HU 25923

Above: Inside the Soldateneheim 3 at Grande Rocques (now better known as the Wayside Cheer Hotel). In May 1945, it was used as an internment camp for German officers and NCOs waiting to go to British POW camps.
Hans-Gerhard Sandmann (2)

Left:
Inside the officers' dining room of a Soldatenheim in Guernsey.
Hans-Gerhard Sandmann

Opposite far left: This interesting photograph of the children of Daphne and George Pope (pilot of the Casquets lighthouse) with two French women who were forced to work in a brothel on Alderney, was taken by Capt Helmuth Lang, Field Marshal Erwin Rommel's ADC when he commanded Army Group B. Lang spent some leave in the Channel Islands in 1944 and befriended the Pope family. *IWM — HU 67512*

Opposite left: Soldiers give local girls cigarettes at one of the bathing places in St Peter Port, Guernsey. *Richard Heaume*

Opposite below: German soldiers on the island of Sark, at Creux Harbour, during the summer of 1940. The tunnel entrance behind them leads to the Vallée du Creux and had been bored out of the solid rock. *IWM — 25907*

Above:
The Führer's birthday celebrations at St Peter Port, Guernsey, in 1942. *La Valette Museum*

Left:
A 'jolly' group of OT workers celebrate their Führer's Birthday. *IWM — 25962*

Right:
As one can see, the Germans had an addiction for signs! These were photographed at the bottom of St Julian's Avenue, St Peter Port, Guernsey. The civilian Morris car had been appropriated for use by the German Press Censor and is driving on the right-hand side of the road. *IWM — 25913*

Left:
Red Cross parcel distribution at Le Riches, St Peter Port, Guernsey, provided a lifeline for the civilian population as everyone was on starvation rations by the winter of 1944. *IWM* — HU 25920

Right:
The Swedish ship *Vega* was chartered by the International Red Cross, to bring Red Cross parcels to the Channel Islands. Here it is being unloaded alongside the jetty at St Peter Port, Guernsey. *IWM* — HU 25968

Left:
View of the hold of the *Vega* during the unloading of bags of flour. *Société Jersiaise*

Right:
The German cemetery at St Brelade's Bay, Jersey, as it was in 1945. In 1961, the bodies were all exhumed and reburied at Mont-des-Huisnes in Normandy. *IWM* — HU 5195

Chapter 9

Fortifications

Hitler had always taken a keen personal interest in the Channel Islands from the moment of their capture. In mid-1941, however, he made his mind up very firmly that they would be heavily garrisoned and heavily fortified and this was endorsed in October when the OKW issued, at the Führer's personal behest, an order for the 'build-up and defence of the English Channel Islands'. According to General Walter Warlimont, Deputy Chief of OKW Operations Staff, in his book *Inside Hitler's Headquarters,* as early as the opening phases of Operation 'Barbarossa' in June 1941, there had been worries that the Allies would be forced to mount some sort of retaliatory operation in the West to help the Soviet Union:

'The time had now arrived . . . when plans and prospects of German strategy had to be re-examined. Directive No 33 dated 19 July had contained an instruction of the type to which in those days we had become unaccustomed: in the West and North the possibility of British attacks on the Channel Islands and the Norwegian coast must be borne in mind.'

The direct result of this change of heart was the fortification of the Channel Islands, turning the garrison from an ordinary infantry division to the largest single infantry division in the German Army. At the same time it led to the Islands receiving far more than their fair share of coastal and other defences. Fortunately for the Allies, in the end all this worked to their advantage and as the defences were never put to the test, the Islands were spared from the sort of battle damage which devastated other parts of Europe.

Hitler's fortification order of 1941

The directive which was issued by the Führer's office on 20 October 1941 read as follows:

1. Operations on a large scale against the territories we occupy in the West are, as before, unlikely. Under pressure of the situation in the East, however, or for reasons of politics or propaganda, small scale operations at any moment may be anticipated, particularly an attempt to regain possession of the Channel Islands, which are important to us for the protection of sea communications.

2. Counter-measures in the Islands must ensure that any English attack fails before a landing is achieved, whether it is attempted by sea, by air or both together. The possibility of advantage being taken of bad visibility to effect a surprise landing must be borne in mind. Emergency measures for strengthening the defences have already been ordered, and all branches of the forces stationed in the

Islands, except for the Air Force, are placed under the orders of the Commandant of the Islands.

3. With regard to the permanent fortification of the Islands, to convert them into an impregnable fortress (which must be pressed forward with the utmost speed) I give the following orders:

a. The High Command of the Army is responsible for the fortifications as a whole and will, in the overall programme, incorporate the construction for the Air Force and the Navy. The strength of the fortifications and the order in which they are erected will be based on the principles and the practical knowledge gained from building the Western Wall. (a)

b. For the Army: it is important to provide a close network of emplacements, well concealed, and given flanking fields of fire. The emplacements must be sufficient for guns of a size capable of piercing armour plate 100cm thick, to defend against tanks which may attempt to land. There must be ample accommodation for stores and ammunition, for mobile diversion parties and for armoured cars.

c. For the Navy: one heavy battery (b) on the Islands and two on the French coast to safeguard the sea approaches.

d. For the Air Force: strongpoints must be created with searchlights and sufficient to accommodate such AA units as are needed to protect all important constructions.

e. Foreign labour, especially Russians and Spaniards but also Frenchmen, may be used for the building works.

4. Another order will follow for the deportation to the Continent of all Englishmen who are not natives of the Islands, ie not born there.

5. Progress reports to be sent to me on the first day of each month to the C-in-C of the Army and directed to the Supreme Command of the Armed Forces (OKW) — Staff of the Führer, Division L.

(signed) ADOLF HITLER

Notes
(a) This was referring to the Siegfried Line
(b) The heavy battery on Guernsey was Batterie Mirus. The two on the mainland were to be on the Jobourg Peninsula and near Paimpol on the Brittany coast, but they were never installed, two 20.3cm railway guns being put there instead — one in each location

Source: *Channel Islands Occupation Review 1973* and published here by kind permission of the Channel Islands Occupation Society (Jersey Branch).

As we have seen, this order was not the beginning of the fortification programme but rather 'dotted the i's and crossed the t's' of a whole series of high-level decisions which had been taken at numerous meetings in the corridors of power in Berlin since much earlier in the year. And of course, at the same time the expert engineers had been visiting the Islands. At their head was GenLt Rudolf Schmetzer, holder of the German Cross in Silver, who was in the 'Inspector of Fortifications' business for the entire war. Inspector *Landbefestig West* from 15 August 1940 until 1 April 1944, he was allocated two Fortress Engineer Staffs (*Festungs Pionier Stab*) — XIV for Jersey and XIX for Guernsey — which comprised teams of experts who made geological, geographical and strategic surveys of the Islands, then put forward recommendations regarding the siting of observation towers, gun positions, strongpoints, control towers, etc. As an article in the 1973 edition of the *Channel Islands Occupation Society Review* comments:

> *'They paid a great compliment to the military engineers of earlier days when they announced that not only were the granite fortifications of the Napoleonic Wars (and earlier) sited in the best possible strategic positions, but that they were so stoutly built that they only needed the addition of reinforced concrete ceilings to make them suitable for the needs of mid-twentieth century warfare.'*

Schmetzer left towards the end of 1941, to supervise the general construction of the entire Atlantic Wall, his place being taken by Oberstlt von Marnitz from the Jersey Fortress Engineer Staff. Another visitor was Dr Fritz Todt who came in November 1941, when the first of his workers arrived, to issue some construction orders.

Division of responsibilities
The OT did not of course simply come in and take on every single project which had to be done on the Islands. They were really just one of five elements concerned with the building programme:

Individual troops
Field fortifications, such as weapon pits, foxholes and trenches, etc remained the responsibility of the individual troops.

Divisional Engineers
All aspects of the distribution, recording and sowing of landmines, the location and use of flamethrowers.

Army Construction Battalions
The construction of reinforced field constructions, which were designed to give protection against small-arms fire, shell splinters, etc but not prolonged bombardment. Where concrete was used it did not exceed one metre in thickness.

Fortress Engineers and Fortress Construction Battalions
The supplying and mounting of fortress weapons, moving very heavy loads, some tunnelling, compiling construction progress reports and maps, ordering and supervising tasks undertaken by the OT.

Organization Todt
Quarrying, most tunnelling projects, constructing power stations, railways and roads, supplying building equipment and machinery, organising sea transport (in conjunction with Kriegsmarine), loading and unloading ships, supervising civilian construction firms, controlling non-military labour and building fortress-type constructions (built with reinforced concrete not less than two metres thick).
(Source: *CIOS Jersey Archive* Book No 8)

For the next two and a half years, until the late summer of 1944, the building work continued. Even then, not everything they wanted to build had been built, but the Islands were now almost completely isolated, so it was impossible to continue bringing in the raw materials needed to build and improve the vast network of observation towers, gun emplacements and underground tunnels which housed headquarters, storage areas, etc, even hospitals. A fair number of these structures still remain and details are given at the end of the book. The various volumes of *Festung Guernsey* and *Festung Jersey* prepared on the orders of GenOb Graf von Schmettow, give information on the Islands' defences in considerable detail in words, drawings and photographs. Whilst there were many amazing structures built, by way of example I will concentrate on just three types: firstly the observation towers, secondly, the tunnels and finally, the largest coastal battery position — that of the Mirus Battery on Guernsey.

OBSERVATION TOWERS
In all parts of the Atlantic Wall, the Germans built similar types of bunkers for obvious reasons, namely that the weapons and equipment to be installed was roughly similar; however, only on the Channel Islands did they design and build such an amazing array of tall, reinforced concrete observation towers. Alderney, Guernsey and Jersey all had these towers, immediately recognisable from the thousands of photographs since taken of them, with their futuristic-looking series of horizontal observation slots facing out to sea. Normally observation towers on the rest of the Atlantic Wall were much less complicated affairs, with just one, or at the most two, observation slots. This was all that was needed because the towers were themselves usually built upon the tops of high cliffs. The Channel Islands towers had on average at least five observation slots facing seawards. These observation towers were known as *Marinepeilstände* (naval direction and rangefinding towers) and were used to control the fire of the main coastal batteries on the islands. Of course the Nazis were not the first to have built observation towers on the Islands — there still being plenty of evidence of the large number of Round towers

built in the early 1800s as a defence against the threatened French invasion (some 35 still being in existence on Jersey and Guernsey). As explained in the footnote, these had the dual purpose of being both gun positions and watch towers, although additional gun positions were also built — remember how some of these elderly gunsites with their cannon were wrongly identified as modern gun positions by German reconnaissance aircraft before the Islands were invaded! Some of these towers were modernised and incorporated into the German defences.

Above: The German observation tower (MP2) and wireless station at La Corbière, Jersey. It is now used by Jersey Radio, monitoring all shipping in the southwest portion of the English Channel. *IWM — HU 5182*

Below: Pleinmont Tower (MP3), Guernsey. This *Marinepeilstand* for naval artillery direction-finding has been restored postwar. *Author's Collection*

Why so many observation slots?

The answer to this question is that each of the observation slots was meant to deal only with the fire control of one coastal battery, presumably for ease of control. Take, for example, the three-storeyed tower on Alderney *Marinepeilstand* 3 (naval direction-finding position), which stands on the rim of the Mannez Quarry in the north of the island. Each of its three storeys was there to deal with one of the three coastal batteries. Alderney was due, in the long term, to have no fewer than six of these towers!

Shown at Table 11 are details of the towers (both constructed and proposed) on the three main islands.

Table 11: *Marinepeilstände* on the Channel Islands

MP	LOCATION	REMARKS
Guernsey		
1	Chouet headland	Completed (now demolished due to subsidence)
2	Fort Saumerez	Completed (joined to Martello Tower)
3	Pleinmont	Completed (now restored)
4	L'Angle	Completed
5	La Prevote	Not built
5	Vale Mill	Completed as an Army coastal OP (now partly destroyed)
6	Icart Point	not built
7	Jerbourg Point	not built
Jersey		
1	Noirmont Point	Complete (open to public)
2	La Corbière	Completed (used by Jersey Radio, which monitors all shipping in the SW part of the Channel)
3	Les Landes	Completed (very impressive)
4	Plémont	not built
5	Sorel Point	not built
6	Belle Hougue Point	not built
7	La Coupe, St Martin	not built
8	Mont Mallet, St Martin	not built
9	Rue de la Hougette	foundations only built St Clement
Alderney		
1	Telegraph Bay	not built
2	SW of Essex Castle	not built
3	Mannez	Completed
4	Fort Albert headland	not built
5	Fort Tourgis	not built
6	La Giffoine	not built
TOTALS		
Proposed	22	
Built	9	
Still standing	7 (but Vale Mill is partly demolished)	

Above left:
Naval Tower MP2
in Stutzpunkt Langenberg, at
L'Eree, had its exterior painted
to resemble granite. Note the
camouflaged 3.7cm Pak gun in
a Renault R35 tank turret,
camouflaged in the foreground.
IWM — HU 29133

Above:
The Mouriaux Observation Tower
on Alderney. This postwar
photograph shows the addition of
a water tank on the top.
*Alderney Museum and Mrs
Pantcheff*

Left:
This is MP4, Guernsey, and was
built in 1942. It is located at
L'Angle, Pleinmont.
IWM — HU 29143

Opposite:
Entrance to the tunnel Höhlgang
12 below St Saviour's Church,
Guernsey. It was used for the
storage of ammunition and
vehicles. *IWM — HU 29075*

THE TUNNELS

Both the main islands had a network of tunnels dug out for a variety of uses, the favourable rock structure being ideal for deep shelter construction, although the work involved was dangerous. One of the largest single projects of this type undertaken by the Germans was the underground hospital and ammunition storage complex on Guernsey, where a staggering 40-plus tunnel complexes were planned, although only some 16 were constructed (and some of these were never completed). Another use of tunnels, this time near the coast, was for fuel oil storage by the Kriegsmarine. An example of this has already been mentioned, namely the U-Boat refuelling store which now houses La Valette Underground Military Museum at St Peter Port. It was never completed due to lack of materials, although some of the fuel tanks were installed. Built by Frank Werke of Bremen, they were transported to Guernsey in sections, then welded together on site. They each had a capacity of 30,000 gallons, weighed some 60 tonnes and held 120 tonnes of fuel, giving a combined weight of 180 tonnes! Four such tanks were installed and at the end of the Occupation were found to be full of coal oil. Some 50-80 forced labourers constructed the *Höhlgang,* as the complex was called, working up to two and a half days at a time without rest, whilst being fed on a meagre ration of cabbage and water. The tunnel bays were designed so that if any of the tanks sprang a leak, the whole contents would be contained within the pool beneath each tank or, alternatively, drain away through the drains — these drains were tested to the limit during the conversion of the complex into a museum and easily coped with 1,500 gallons of water pumped in by the local fire brigade!

Jersey had its share of tunnels, one of the largest housing an underground hospital at St Lawrence, which is described in more detail at the end of the book as it is still open to the public. Digging the tunnels was both difficult and dangerous, as John Dalmau explained in his book *Slave Worker*. His squad had been working on the wall in St Brelade's Bay in Jersey, then, when that project was completed, started working on the tunnels that were to run underneath Fort Regent. He wrote:

'Conditions of work were very dangerous. Innumerable lives were lost because of the loose quality of the granite into which the tunnels were bored. Almost every foot of those tunnels cost a human life. On one occasion while working on scaffolding against the face of the tunnel I felt a trickle of dust on my neck. Looking upwards, I saw the roof of the tunnel moving slowly. I shouted and jumped clear. Two others were not as lucky as I. One, a Czech, was killed outright and the other, a Spaniard, lost both legs.'

As with the other quotations from John Dalmau's pamphlet, this has to be taken with a pinch of salt — undoubtedly there were accidents during the tunnel building, involving both workers and OT overseers; but in Jersey the first tunnel was built with entirely voluntary labour, much of it local, and the only accident that one Jerseyman who worked there could recall was when two Belgians were drilling upwards to create an escape shaft and the ladder collapsed.

Left:
Sign above St Saviour's tunnel. *Brian Matthews*

Right:
No naked lights and no smoking in St Saviour's tunnel. *Brian Matthews*

Left:
One of the many tunnels on Guernsey. *La Valette Museum*

Right:
Another partly completed
tunnel in Guernsey.
Brian Matthews

Left:
One of the massive fuel tanks
which was fitted into the tunnels
which now house La Valette
Underground Military Museum,
Guernsey. Each tank had a
capacity of 30,000gal and
weighed (when full) 180 tonnes.
La Valette Museum

Right:
Underground
accommodation at
St Saviour's tunnel.
IWM — HU 29078

BATTERIE MIRUS

Heaviest of the coastal batteries were the four massive 30.5cm naval guns, located on the high ground at St Saviour's, Guernsey. The battery was not there with the primary role of defending Guernsey, but rather, together with the other heavy guns on the French coast and on Alderney, to provide protection for the entire Bay of St Malo. Named after a German naval officer who lost his life during an air attack while on a visit to Guernsey in 1941 [1], the battery comprised four reconditioned Russian guns which had once been part of the main armament of the Tsar's 22,600-ton Imperial Russian Navy battleship *Imperator Alexandr Troti* (later known as the *Volya* [Victory], when with the White Russian Fleet) which had been manufactured by the Russian Putilov Arsenal in 1914. The battleship was eventually broken up in a French Tunisian dockyard in 1935 and the 12 usable main guns put into storage. Winston Ramsey in his *The War in the Channel Islands then and now*, tells how, in the winter of 1939/40 when Great Britain and France had agreed to give Finland aid in its war against Soviet Russia, the guns were put on board three ships (four guns each) and shipped to Finland. However, one of the ships, the *Nina,* was delayed en route and

captured by the Germans when they invaded Norway in May 1940. When heavy coastal artillery was needed for the Channel Islands someone remembered the four guns (then in storage in Bergen, Norway), so they were taken to the Krupp's works in the Ruhr and reconditioned. Then began the next leg of their journey to St Malo and finally, again by sea, to Guernsey.

A special floating crane had to be brought to St Peter Port to unload each barrel, which was then taken from the Cambridge berth to St Saviour's on a 24-wheel trailer towed by four large half-tracks (probably the heavy 12-ton SdKfz8 as built by Mercedes-Benz). There is some excellent footage of this road journey on a Tomahawk Films video entitled *Channel Islands Occupied* (see the end of this book for more details). The road en route had to be widened in some places to enable them to negotiate all the corners! The enormous 12-inch guns had a maximum range of 26 miles — considerably less than their supposed maximum range of 32 miles, because firing trials had shown that reduced charges would have to be used on these

Below: Plan of one of the guns of Batterie Mirus. At 305mm, they were the largest guns in the Channel Islands. *IWM* — HU 25981

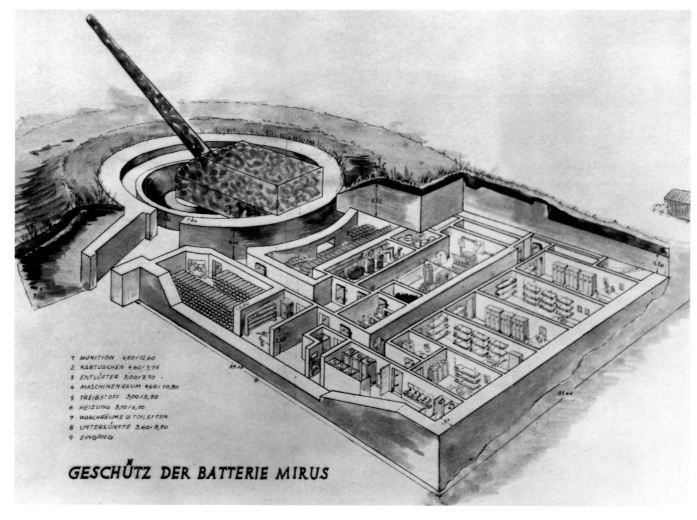

1 MUNITION 4,60/12,60
2 KARTUSCHEN 4,60/7,75
3 ENTLÜFTER 3,00/7,70
4 MASCHINENRAUM 4,60/10,80
5 TREIBSTOFF 3,00/3,50
6 HEIZUNG 3,10/4,40
7 WASCHRÄUME U TOILETTEN
8 UNTERKÜNFTE 3,60/8,50
9 EINGANG

GESCHÜTZ DER BATTERIE MIRUS

vintage guns. Indeed, the normal working range was reduced to 20 miles for this reason. In German parlance the Russian guns were known as the 30.5cm K(E)626(r) or just K14(r). The first gun was eventually test-fired on 13 April 1942 and by August of that year all four guns were operational, the event being celebrated by a report in the *Deutsche Guernsey Zeitung* for 12 August 1942.

Woe to the English!

The main part of the report was a eulogy to Kapitän zur See Mirus, a naval gunnery expert, after whom the battery was named (see note 1). Here all I will quote are the opening and closing paragraphs of the report which were full of confidence on the excellence of the new battery and read:

'The last gun of this heavy battery in the Channel Islands has now had its trial firing. The third trial salvo issued from the barrel with an enormous jet of fire, heading far out into the Atlantic. The giant barrel now points menacingly out to sea. Woe to the English should they ever dare to approach the Island! They will be met with a reception of firepower which they did not expect and which they would not have thought possible. The German defence of the Channel Islands is appreciably strengthened by the operational readiness of this battery . . .

'The Führer salute and the national anthem affirmed the words of the Naval Commander. The gunners then returned to their positions, always ready for action. The new heavy battery of the Channel Islands stands prepared to fire!'

War Correspondent: Herbert Ladda
(Source: *CIOS Review 9 May 1974*)

This newspaper report gives no indication of the immense amount of work that had gone into constructing *Batterie Mirus* which had taken over 18 months and had seriously delayed other construction work on Guernsey. In terms of concrete alone some 47,000cu m were needed to pour into the four gun emplacements, each with their associated ammunition stores, accommodation for a crew of 72 men for each gun (total battery strength was over 400!), then there was the fire direction centre (*Leitstand*) plus all the associated personnel shelters, radar mountings, anti-aircraft bunkers, etc — so the site covered a large area. The fire direction centre deserves special mention, consisting of three separate installations: a command centre and crew quarters; a radar location; and a rangefinder bunker. All were made of reinforced concrete and the rangefinder bunker was connected to the command centre by a long underground tunnel. The photographs show some of the gun positions, two of which were disguised as houses! It was estimated that each gun probably fired about 70 rounds, mostly on training or false alarms. One night, suspicious 'blips' on the radar were interpreted as a British landing force, and the rapidly panicking acting SEEKO-KI, Oberstlt Pedell (SEEKO-KI, the top Naval Commander, who was normally the only person who could authorise opening fire, was away visiting Alderney!) ordered the battery and other coastal artillery to open fire. In the morning the 'landing force' turned out to be two half-submerged British barrage balloons!

Left:
This small hut hid the entrance
to one of the deep concrete
shelters of one of the guns
of the Mirus Battery.
IWM — HU 29060

Right:
The large and the small. One of the
massive 305mm Russian guns of Batterie Mirus dwarfs
the AA machine gun beside it — an Austrian-
manufactured, Dutch Army *Schwarzlose*
7.9mm MG. *IWM* — HU — 29059

Below:
Looking down into the massive gun pit of one
of the Batterie Mirus guns. *IWM* — HU 29061

Opposite above:
The enormous shells for the 305mm
guns had to be raised by pulleys.
IWM — HU 29070

Opposite:
Inside the Battery Command Post
(*Leitstand*) for the Batterie Mirus,
which was underground.
IWM — HU 29069

THOSE WHO TOILED

Although I have recounted a few words of slave labourer John Dalmau in describing the work on the tunnels, it would also be useful here to delineate the 'working day' for the ordinary OT forced labourer — someone perhaps like Gilbert Van Grieken, whom we met in an earlier chapter.

Unless they were lucky enough to get onto a special job where conditions were easier, all worked a normal 12-hour day of heavy manual work, sometimes even longer, seven days a week. Their only break was in the middle of the day, when they supposedly stopped for 40 minutes to eat their meagre lunch meal (even this break was often shortened to only 10 minutes — barely time to eat the ridiculously small ration of watery soup). One Sunday in every month they received a half-day holiday. If there was need to work night shifts, then the day was free to sleep and the 'lunch-meal' was served during the night. Forced labourers had no right to complain about their conditions of work or the hours of work. In theory they were entitled to be paid for their labour at the rate of 55 Reichspfennig an hour; however, as one OT Frontführer explained: '55% of this was deducted at source as the so-called eastern levy (*Ostabgabe*), a compulsory contribution for the reconstruction of destroyed areas in Eastern Europe. Of the rest, 55 Pfennig per day was supposed to be paid out in cash; however, I never found that this had been done.' [2]

Clothing

No clothing whatsoever was issued to the forced labourers, so they wore what they had been wearing when 'impressed'. Many were impressed during the summer of 1941, and by the winter of 1942–43 they were freezing cold, dressed in rags and would jealously fight for the clothing of dead companions — meticulous German book-keeping noting that the man who had died was 'Possessed of no effects whatsoever'. When shoes wore out, feet were wrapped in rags, although sometimes wooden clogs were provided, in order to keep the workforce mobile — certainly not for any humanitarian reasons. Those volunteer labourers in Guernsey and Jersey who were paid were able to purchase such second-hand clothing as became available, but this was to the detriment of the civilian population. Undoubtedly the labourers who were in the most parlous state were the 'Russians' and the French North Africans.

Medical

No proper medical facilities existed for OT, although nominally they might be attended to by the local service MO. On Alderney this was nominally the Kriegsmarine MO, but there was no guarantee that being allowed to report sick would be granted. The decision to allow/not to allow a forced labourer to see the MO was, like everything else, at the whim of the camp commandant, who on occasions beat up the sick parade as he thought it was too large. Clearly if someone had a physical injury — for example a broken arm — they stood more chance of being allowed to report sick, than someone who was ill, unless his illness stopped him from working. 'There is no evidence,' reports 'Bunny' Pantcheff, 'that a constitutionally sick foreign forced labourer working for the OT ever received proper medical attention on Alderney or was sent from Alderney to receive it elsewhere.' As I have commented already elsewhere, the OT attitude was that the forced labourers could be replaced, so why bother to treat them or to waste time, effort and medicines on what the overseers regarded as expendables.

RESISTANCE POINTS

In addition to the large array of defensive structures erected/dug out by the OT, there were many other smaller types of defences. For example, at the very lowest level there were the many infantry positions which were situated in considerable numbers around the coastal areas of each island. If an attacker managed to get ashore, having overwhelmed the coastal artillery and the many anti-aircraft positions, then it would be the men in these infantry positions that would hold them up. There were basically three types of infantry position, which were known as:

- the strongpoint/base (*Stützpunkt* — STP) this was the largest.

- the pocket of resistance/defence post (*Widerstandsnest* — WN) which were by far the most numerous.

- the operational position (*Einsatzstellung* — EIN).

A description of manning a WN on Jersey was given in Chapter 4, by the late Georg Brefka of MG Btl 16. In a small number of cases these resistance points actually fired their guns at the enemy and these included:

- Prior to D-Day, when the radar array at Les Landes, St Ouen, was attacked by aircraft, an MG34 at EIN Hoehe 201, located at the south end of St Ouen's Bay, engaged them but didn't hit anything.

- On 14 June 1944, the MG34 located on the roof of Morville House, La Route de Trodez, St Ouen (WN Morville Haus) assisted in shooting down the Typhoon Ib which crashed at Grantez.

- On 19 June 1944, when a Mitchell bomber flew over the southern coastline of Jersey, the Flak-mounted twin MG34s of WN La Rocque A, situated on the top of the Round Tower at Platte Rocque Point, opened fire. The aircraft replied by dropping two bombs which straddled the target, causing extensive damage to some dozen or so houses, but no one was injured.

The garrison of Brefka's WN had strength of four NCOs and some 19 soldiers, all from 9. Kompanie III./Regiment 582, and it was part of the Island's eastern defence area. The firepower at the disposal of this WN was considerable — but by no means unique — for example, in addition to their own personal arms they had a 5cm Pak 38 (in an open concrete emplacement firing seawards, but with a ramp leading from the surface into a concrete shelter, where the gun would have been protected from any pre-invasion barrage); a 3.7cm KwK 144(f) with a coaxial MG 311(f) mounted in a turret from a French FT17 light tank (also set in a concrete emplacement); another MG 311(f) in an FT17 tank turret (again set into concrete); the Flak-mounted twin MG34s which had engaged the Marauder; a medium flamethrower (remotely-controlled); two searchlights (one 60cm and one 30cm).

The garrison could move between all their positions via concrete-lined zig-zag trenches, which also were connected to a concealed entrance to Platte Rocque House, where the garrison lived, via a tunnel. In addition, there were a number of small one-metre-thick concrete bunkers set into the sides of the slit trenches. The entire Widerstandsnest was surrounded by a belt of barbed wire, broken only by gates to allow movement down the coast road and a sallyport to the north which allowed access to more forward machine gun positions which were normally unmanned. Such a position, held by determined troops, would not have been an easy nut to crack and in the St Clement's Bay area alone there were four such positions, plus two EIN, then further inland to protect the coastal artillery positions, a further two WN and a single EIN.

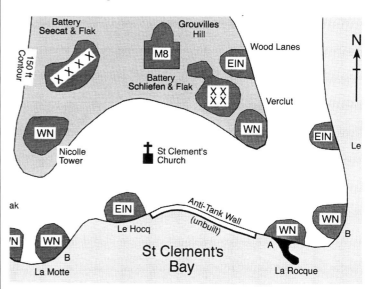

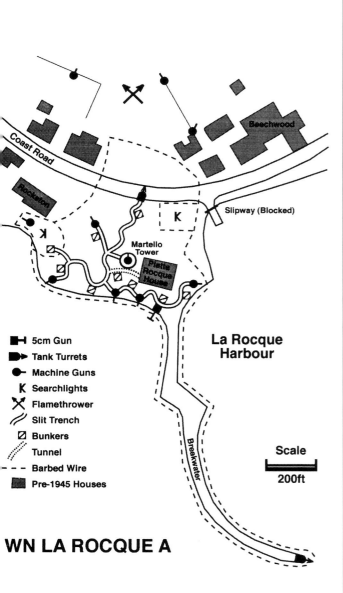

5cm Gun
Tank Turrets
Machine Guns
K Searchlights
Flamethrower
Slit Trench
Bunkers
Tunnel
Barbed Wire
Pre-1945 Houses

La Rocque Harbour

Scale
200ft

WN LA ROCQUE A

The drawings and information for this description of Resistance Point La Rocque A are taken from an article by Peter Bryans, which appeared in *CIOS Jersey Review 1977* and appear here with his kind permission.

Right:
This 220mm coastal gun
was at Jerbourg,
Guernsey.
La Valette Museum

Below:
Turrets from French
Renault R35 tanks were
often concreted into the
defences as gun positions.
IWM — HU 29012

Left:
Another beach to protect. German officers looking at yet another beach on which the enemy could land. *Hans-Gerhard Sandmann*

Below:
A gaggle of German staff officers surveying the islands. *IWM* — HU 29118

Right:
Inside the casemate of a 4.7cm Pak 36(t) which has been coaxially mounted with an MG 37(t), both weapons having been 'acquired' from the Czechs. *IWM* — HU 29046

Right:
Small but effective:
a one-man machine
gun post housing
an MG34.
IWM — HU 29108

·   *Right:*
Providing close-
range protection to
this coastal
casemate is an
MG34 on top and a
3.7cm Pak 35/36 at
the side in its own
sandbagged
emplacement.
IWM — HU 29107

Left:
This 8.8cm anti-aircraft/anti-tank was being used for coastal defence in an open position at La Mayne, Jersey. Note that its recuperator buffer (recoil) has been given protection from shell splinters by encasing it in thick wood.
IWM — HU 5798

Left:
A well-protected coastal artillery gun in its camouflaged casemate.
IWM — HU 29123

Right:
Good shot of an MG34 machine gun on a ground mounting inside a coastal casemate. *IWM* — HU 29011

Below:
In some cases the Occupation forces used dummy guns (*Schienstellung*) — this one was at Fort Le Marchant, Guernsey. *Guernsey Museum*

Above:
A small searchlight in its
coastal position.
IWM — HU 29149

Right:
A small coastal searchlight
on the ramparts.
IWM — HU 29040

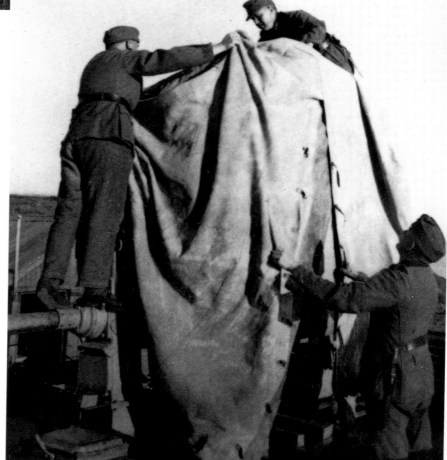

Above:
This rangefinder has
been concreted in to
give it better protection.
IWM — HU 29068

Right:
Sheeting up a
coastal searchlight.
IWM — HU 29038

Above:
Excellent shot of a *Würzburg* radar in Jersey, with trenches and bunkers for the crew. The *Würzburg* was an AA gun radar and was very accurate out to a range of 25 miles.
IWM — HU 5199

Left:
This *Grosse Würzburg* radar, festooned with live camouflage, was the radar installation at the Batterie Mirus. Its parabolic reflector was 25ft (compare with 10ft for the *Würzburg*). Note also its concrete mounting.
IWM — HU 29066

Above:
A fire direction control centre in operation. *IWM* — HU 29136

Right:
Anti-airborne assault devices which had explosives tied to their tops. The Island farmers did not like them at all, as they were worried that their cattle might blow themselves up!
IWM — HU 29117

Opposite:
Operating a *Würzburg Dora* radar dish. *Guernsey Museum*

Above:
These beach obstacles had Teller mines attached to their tops.
IWM — HU 29150

Left:
Note the line of infantry dugouts running parallel to the wall at the rear of this farmhouse.
IWM — HU 29137

Left:
A 'Roll bomb', suitably camouflaged at the top of the cliff. The bomb would be released and rolled down on top of anyone trying to climb up.
Guernsey Museum

Below:
Work in progress on a 10.5cm K 331(f) casemate on Guernsey, opposite the Imperial Hotel, at Pleinmont, Guernsey.
Guernsey Museum

Chapter 10

British Operations against the Islands

MAJOR OPERATIONS

We have already covered in some detail the original German assault on the Islands, plus their 'commando' operations against Allied forces in France. Therefore in this chapter we will concentrate on the British commando raids against the Channel Islands. None of these can be classified as a major raid, but they not only kept the Germans wondering when and where the British would strike next — and thus tied down German forces in static protection tasks — but also kept the newly-formed but ever-increasing Combined Operations organisation on its toes and in fighting trim.

These sabotage/reconnaissance/prisoner-taking raids were conducted by small parties of tough, determined men, some of whose actions had, as we shall see, far-reaching effects.

Operation 'Ambassador'

On 2 July 1940, just two days after Guernsey had been occupied, Prime Minister Winston Churchill sent a note to Maj-Gen Hastings Ismay, who was then his personal Chief of Staff and a member of the Chiefs of Staff Committee, commenting upon the way the Germans had carried out Operation 'Green Arrow' and recommending that plans should be formulated to land secretly by night on the Islands and kill or capture some of the invaders. [1] There should be, he said, a ready source of information about the Islands available from ex-inhabitants who had been evacuated or who were currently serving with British forces.

A few days later his memo was acted upon. 2-Lt Hubert Nicolle of the Hampshire Regiment, late Guernsey Militia, was the first ex-Islander to become involved in Operation 'Anger' — when he was landed on Le Jaonnet Bay on the south coast of Guernsey on 5 July. His expedition had a somewhat amateurish beginning, in that it is reputed that he had to buy his own

Below: Attack! Attack! Commandos under training in the UK. Here they are dashing up a beach under cover of a smokescreen after disembarking from their landing craft. *IWM* — H17485

Above: Storming the heights. Then it's up the 100ft cliffs with the aid of single ropes. *IWM — H17494*

folding canoe from Gamages before going down to Plymouth to board the submarine that would take him on his mission!

Despite this inauspicious start, Operation 'Anger' went extremely well. Nicolle was rowed ashore by a Sub-Lt Leitch, then met up with two old friends, who agreed to help him. His uncle Frank Nicolle was the assistant harbour master at St Peter Port, so he was able to pass on naval information, while from the local baker, who was supplying bread to the Germans, he obtained details of the garrison 'ration strength' (469 all ranks), together with information on their locations — namely that the main body was concentrated in St Peter Port and the rest were spread out manning machine gun strongpoints around the coast. His mission was purely reconnaissance, which included checking on the suitability of the intended landing site for the next operation. Once his mission had been completed, he would be replaced by two other ex-Guernsey Militia, who would then remain on the Island, ready to guide the raiding party of No 3 Commando, under Lt-Col John Durnford-Slater, when they landed to carry out Operation 'Ambassador'. Durnford-Slater (later Brigadier, DSO and Bar) had been serving as the Adjutant of the 23rd Medium and Heavy Training Regiment, Royal Artillery, at Plymouth in mid-June 1940, when they had received a letter calling for volunteers to raid the enemy coast. He had applied and shortly afterwards received a signal which not only appointed him to raise and command No 3 Commando, but also promoted him from captain to lieutenant-colonel! At that time neither No 1 nor No 2 Commando existed, so this made him the first commando soldier of the war. As he says in his autobiography:

'I had wanted action: I was going to get it. I should have been delighted to join in any rank, but was naturally pleased to get command. I was confident I could do the work and made up my mind to produce a really great unit.'

Back in Guernsey, initially all went well and the two new men — 2-Lt Philip Martel of the Hampshires and 2-Lt Desmond Mulholland of the DCLI arrived on the night of 9/10 July, via submarine and folding boat in the same manner as Nicolle, who met them at Le Jaonnet Bay, and, after briefing them, returned to the submarine, leaving them on shore. So far so good, but unfortunately, things then started to go wrong. The raiding party was supposed to arrive on the night of 12 July, meet the two guides, then assault the aerodrome, destroy fuel stocks, burn aircraft, etc. However, bad weather delayed the operation for 48 hours and it proved impossible to contact Martel and Mulholland to tell them. After hiding up for two days, they returned to the beach, found no one and nothing happening. They realised that something must have gone wrong, so decided to try to steal a boat and get away, rather than putting their innocent families, who still lived in Guernsey, at risk.

So while they hid — first in a barn, then in a house — near Vazon Bay, word was passed to Dame Sibyl Hathaway in Sark whose son-in-law and daughter owned the house in which the two officers were hiding, to ask for her assistance. In her memoirs she tells of how she '. . . took some tinned supplies and went across to Guernsey on the pretext of being in charge of my daughter's property'. They asked her if she could arrange for a fishing boat from Sark to pick them up and get them back to England. However, as she says:

'It was a miserable business having to explain that this proposition had no chance of success because our fishing boats were strictly guarded by the Germans and, apart from that, there was no possibility of getting sufficient petrol for such a venture.'

Nevertheless, they managed to steal a boat at Perelle Bay (just west of Vazon Bay) but it was broken up on the rocks and they were left stranded. They would give themselves up before they could be rescued.

Whilst this saga was unfolding the main operation, Operation 'Ambassador', was suffering a series of setbacks. After being delayed for 48 hours, the agreed plan then had to be amended. The original intention had been that 40 men of 3 Commando, under Capt V. de Crespigny, would land first and create a diversion, while No 11 Independent Company attacked the aerodrome. This company would be split into two groups, the larger (68 men) under Maj Todd would come ashore at Moye Point (directly south of the aerodrome), whilst the rest (20 men) under Capt Goodwin, landed a mile or so further west. Two destroyers, HMS *Scimitar* and HMS *Saladin*, would transport the commandos and escort the seven RAF sea rescue launches (they were just small motor boats, designed to pick up pilots who had to ditch in the sea) that would take the men from ship to shore. Port of embarkation would be Dartmouth.

On the morning of 14 July, Lt-Col Durnford-Slater discovered — via an officer from Combined Operations Staff who had been sent hotfoot from London — that the whole plan had been changed because the German garrison had been reinforced in just the places where his Commando was intending to land. A new plan was worked out on the spot: the force would now land at Petit Port on the south side of the island in Moulin Huet Bay. Departure was fixed for 18.00hrs that evening.

After completing their preparations — helped by cadets from the Royal Naval College at Dartmouth — they set off on a lovely summer evening. En route, they tied up the final small details, Lt-Col Durnford-Slater later writing:

'Lt Joe Smale's party was to establish a roadblock on the road leading from the Jerbourg Peninsula to the rest of the Island, so that we would not be interrupted by German reinforcements. My own party were to attack a machine gun post and put the telegraph cable hut out of action. Capt de Crespigny was to attack the barracks situated on the peninsula and 2-Lt Peter Young was to guard the beach. Peter did not relish this job as he wanted more action. "All right," I told him, "if it's quiet come forward and see what's going on."'[12]

The next problem came as the convoy began to leave harbour. Two of the crash boats were found not to be in a fit condition to make the voyage and had to be left behind. This meant quickly reorganising the loading plan for the three landing parties, transferring stores between boats, deciding that certain crash boats would have to make two ferrying trips and also making use of the whaler of HMS *Scimitar* to ferry others ashore. The convoy was a little late in starting (18.15hrs), and was further delayed by one of the crash boats which had to wait behind for stores, then didn't catch up with the rest until just about last light which all added to the delay.

It was a moonless night, but once they were about two miles from Guernsey, Durnford-Slater began to distinguish the cliffs on the south coast of the Island, 'dark, foreboding and very high'. At about 00.45hrs, as they crept along the coastline, he fortunately recognised the gap in the cliffs and the place where they would climb up them. He recalled later, 'Our two launches slid alongside the destroyer and we clambered down on rope nettings. The sea was calm. It was dead easy.'

Below: Operation 'Ambassador'. The other destroyer escort was HMS *Scimitar* (H21) and it is clear from this photograph how the RAF crash boats would have suffered from the wake behind the destroyer when it was moving at speed. *IWM* — FL 5424

Meanwhile the other party was not having such an easy time of it, missing Guernsey completely and having problems with leaking boats. One of the commandos in this group was Sir Roland Swayne MC, then a young officer in the Herfords, who had, like Durnford-Slater, been selected for commando training. In a taped interview to the IWM Dept of Sound Records in 1988 (Accession No 10231/3), he recalled how it had been the means of transport that had let them down:

'. . . it was a wonderful idea and could have been a very, very clever raid. But the means of transport were absolutely hopeless. They towed gigs and whalers and I think crash boats were towed — they may have gone under their own steam — but the gigs and whalers were towed by destroyers. Well, of course, it was much too fast for them and they got damaged going there. And when we got out from the destroyer into these boats they were all leaking. And one by one we were transferred and eventually I was in a, I think it was a crash boat, with two or three other officers and some men. And we were right down to the gunwales. All this had taken so long and we'd arrived at the rendezvous late, that it was near daylight. Fortunately, there was a bit of sea mist by this time. I think we had only one boat which was capable of carrying people. And we decided it was quite hopeless and we lost the destroyer.'

Swayne's group decided to put into Sark and drop off some of the party so that the rest would have a better chance of getting back to England in the leaking boat. However, as they were heading for Sark the destroyer spotted them and they were saved:

'Somebody on the destroyer — it was a soldier actually — spotted something in the water. He knew that there were people missing and he drew the attention of a ship's officer and he got the ship diverted to pick us up and we got home. It was very lucky we got home.'

Meanwhile things had also started to go wrong with Durnford-Slater's pair of launches. They had left the destroyer and set off on the agreed course, the naval officers in charge of the launches carefully watching their compasses rather than the coastline. Fortunately, he was watching the cliffs and was surprised to see that instead of heading for the shore, they were '. . . heading out to sea in the direction of Brittany.

"This is no bloody good", I said to the skipper of our launch, "we're going right away from Guernsey." He looked up from the compass for the first time. Then he looked back and saw the cliff. "You're right! We are indeed. It must be this damn de-gaussing arrangement that's knocked the compass out of true. I ought to have it checked."
"Don't worry about the compass: let's head straight for the beach."
"Right!"'

Thereafter they had navigated by eye and all went well until they were about 100 yards from the beach when a black silhouette came into view to their left. Some of the commandos thought it was a U-Boat, but fortunately it turned out to be a large half-submerged lump of rock in the shape of a conning tower! Durnford-Slater was just breathing a sigh of relief when: 'At that moment the launches, simultaneously and side by side, hit bottom.' The small craft did not have the flat bottoms of

Opposite:
Operation 'Ambassador'. This photograph shows an MTB with two RAF crash launches, which can be seen to be considerably smaller than the MTB, but were used for 'Ambassador'. IWM — A9921

Below: Operation 'Ambassador'. Not far from the top of the cliffs at Petit Port was the Doyle Monument. However, it was directly in the line of fire of Batterie Strassburg, if they needed to fire towards France. So the Germans blew it up — the rubble can be seen behind the gun position. This was not done, until after the raid took place. The monument has since been rebuilt. IWM — HU 29164

landing craft and, because of the 48-hour delay to the operation, the tide was not half-way out as had been expected, but full. Instead of smooth sand they grounded on rocks and had to jump into armpit-deep water!

Struggling ashore with not a dry weapon between them, they started to climb a long flight of concrete steps up the cliffs and safely reached the houses at the top, out of breath but otherwise without incident — then the local dogs started to bark! Fortunately, about that time an Avro Anson began to circle right above them — this was part of the agreed cover plan, to help deaden the noise they were making — and it worked. They reached the machine gun nest and cable hut but found them both unoccupied. De Crespigny's party also found the same at the German barracks — no one home! Somewhat disappointed, and realising they were well behind schedule, they started back towards the beach. Durnford-Slater was the last down the cliff steps and near the bottom he tripped and fell, his cocked revolver going off accidentally. This at long last alerted the Germans who began firing machine guns out to sea, whilst the commandos were forming up on the beach to re-embark.

This was in itself a perilous operation — the launches could not get near enough because of the rocks, so men and weapons had to be ferried out in a tiny dinghy until such time as it was dashed on the rocks and sank. From then on everyone had to swim for it. Somehow they managed to reach the launches where the crews pulled them to safety. They were much later than anticipated and fully expected the destroyers to have set sail for home, as per the plan. However, the captain of HMS *Scimitar* had decided to make one last sweep, fortunately saw torch signals from the launches and came to their rescue. They reached England safely, all that is except for four soldiers, who had either been dumped in the water when the dinghy had sunk or who were non-swimmers so hadn't been able to swim out from the beach (what an admission for a commando!) — they were Commandos Drain, Dumper [3], McGoldrick and Ross. They evaded capture for some days, waiting to be picked up — there had been a reserve plan to send a boat in on the following night to pick up any stragglers, but unbeknown to them it was cancelled in order to prevent further losses. Eventually they were arrested whilst walking down the road to the aerodrome in broad daylight and finished up being sent to Stalag VIIIB at Lamsdorf in Upper Silesia.

This still left Martel and Mulholland on the loose, so another Guernseyman in England, Stanley Ferbrache, volunteered to go to Guernsey and rescue them. This was agreed and he was taken over by MTB, landing at Le Jaonnet on 3 August. He went first to see his uncle, Albert Callighan, then his mother, Mrs Le Mesurier. She broke the news that the two officers had surrendered the previous week. Ferbrache then collected all the information he could gather — he is even reputed to have walked around the airfield perimeter! He was safely taken off on the night of 6 August.

Churchill was far from happy at the failure of Operation 'Ambassador'. He sent a scathing missive to the HQ Combined Forces, which included the words: 'Let there be no more silly fiascos like those perpetrated at Guernsey.' It was vital that the next operation was a success.

THE SMALL SCALE RAIDING FORCE (SSRF)

Future raids on the Channel Islands would be performed by a newly-formed Special Service Unit, which was initially designed to assist the Special Operations Executive (SOE) to carry out some of its more hazardous tasks — SOE being the organisation which had the responsibility of recruiting and training secret agents. SSRF members were a mixture of regular and reservist volunteers, plus personnel recruited by the SOE, including a number of foreigners from occupied Europe. Initially, this force was known as 'Maid Honor Force' after the Brixham trawler which they crewed in operations in 1941 in West Africa. In March 1942, they arrived back in the UK to establish the SSRF, initially at their original base (the Antelope Hotel in Poole, Dorset), then at Anderson Manor, Winterborne Anderson, near Bere Regis. This was an ideal site for their new unit (strength of about 50+ all ranks, mainly officers), remote enough for training to be carried out in secret, yet close enough to the naval base at Portland, where their dedicated raiding boat, *MTB344*, was based. The SSRF, whose cover name was '62 Commando', would stay at 'Station/Special Training Centre 62', as Anderson Manor was officially called, until January 1943 when it was expanded considerably to include outstations at Wraxall Manor, Dorset; Scorries House, Cornwall; Lupton House, Dartmouth and Inchmery at Exbury in the New Forest.

Three of the most notable members of the SSRF in those early days were Capt (later Maj) Gus March-Phillips DSO, MBE, RA, the initial OC of the SSRF, who was killed on 12 September 1942 during Operation 'Aquatint', a raid on the French coast; Lt (later Maj) Geoffrey Appleyard DSO, RASC, who helped him set up the new force and was killed in an air crash during a reconnaissance of Sicily on 13 July 1943; and 'Apple's' greatest friend, Capt Graham Hayes MC, of the Border Regiment, who was shot by the Gestapo on the very same day. They, together with such extraordinary men as Danish-born Anders Lassen VC, MC, SAS, made up the 55 members of the SSRF stationed at Anderson Manor, where there was:

'A pistol and tommy-gun range in the rear garden and a grenade range in a pit to the north of the house. An assault course was built among the trees in the drive and across the river. The cherub that used to adorn the fountain in the courtyard was an obvious target for pistols and other weapons and suffered as a result! Poole Harbour, the Dorset coast, the hills, heaths and forests of Purbeck became the training grounds for the Commandos.' [4]

MTB344 and the Goatley

When the SSRF was set up in March 1942, they were allocated two naval motor launches, but quickly found out that they were too slow for raiding. Because of this they were given the exclusive use of Motor Torpedo Boat *MTB344*, commanded by Lt Bourne DSO, RNVR, and normally based at Portland. Although a standard MTB, the 'Little Pisser', as she was

Above: Members of the SSRF training in the Lake District during the summer of 1942. Left to right: Lord Francis Howard, Andres Desgranges, unknown, Peter O'Kelly, Graham Hayes, Anders Lassen. One of them wrote: 'We went climbing in the Lake District . . . we did Pillar Rock on Great Gable . . . and Great End Gullies . . . Our gear was on a trolley, or handcart, which we pulled from the station to spend the first night at Dacre Castle . . .'
Lt-Col C. R. Messenger via Maj P. R. Ventham

Right: Maj Gus March-Phillipps DSO, MBE, RA, who was the creator of the Small Scale Raiding Force, but was killed during Operation 'Aquatint'. *Maj P. R. Ventham*

affectionately called, had numerous modifications done to improve her performance. For example, all unnecessary fittings were stripped out, including the torpedo tubes, which reduced her weight by some four tons. She was fitted with a hotted-up engine and was capable of 33 knots, but this made her extremely difficult to manage. Armament was twin Lewis machine guns and a Bren for AA protection. One very useful modification was the fitting of an auxiliary, silent-running engine with underwater exhausts, which was used for the final run-in to shore before the commandos could transfer to their landing boats. These were initially the wooden-bottomed, canvas-sided 'Goatley Boat', which could be assembled in under two minutes, weighed only some 150kg, so could be carried cross-country (assembled) by two men, and yet could take 10 men — or more at a pinch as explained below. March-Phillipps wrote in his report after Operation 'Dryad' about the boat:

'A tribute must be paid to the Goatley which comes from all members of the SSRF. This boat, which is entirely without lines or shape and designed on the principle of a flat iron, has behaved splendidly under all conditions. It has weathered moderate seas and stood up to pounding at rocky landings in a way that entirely belies its looks and the natural reactions of any seaman when confronted with such a hull.'

Sadly, the Goatley was partly to blame for the disastrous consequences of Operation 'Aquatint', when one of the boats collapsed and sank — probably because one of the struts that kept the canvas sides upright was broken by rifle-fire. (One of those captured sent back a coded message saying: 'You may have my two razors, but beware the Goatley, it folds at the first knock.') Later the SSRF used 18ft and 22ft double-ended, double-chined surf boats.

In the year that the SSRF was at Anderson Manor, only some ten operations that resulted in actual landings on enemy-held territory in France or the Channel Islands were carried out, despite the fact that the SSRF was involved in roughly one attempted raid every week during the 'raiding season'. This was because the first four months (April–July 1942) were spent training, honing up their commando skills and seamanship, until March-Phillipps was happy that his men were well-enough trained to give a good account of themselves whatever happened. The last operation in 1942 took place in November, after which the weather was really too bad, and all the raids tried in early 1943 had to be aborted due to bad weather. In addition, as all operations were seaborne, the conditions of tide, weather, moonlight, etc had to be suitable, so this limited them to an average of just six nights every month. Ideal conditions were when there was no moon so that the operation could take place in darkness, the landing occurring as soon after low tide as possible to prevent boats being stranded on a falling tide; finally, there had to be sufficient hours of darkness to enable the raid to be carried out and for the MTB to leave the enemy coast before dawn.

Operation 'Dryad'

'Shortly before midnight on 2 September 1942, Obermaat (Chief Mate) Munte, who had once been a stoker in the German Navy, was seated in his office in the Casquets lighthouse . . . He was busy making up returns — an occupation well fitted to his rank and experience. A slight noise — it may have been the click of the door as it closed softly — caused him to turn in his chair. Leaning against the door were two men with black faces, wearing crumpled khaki uniforms, somewhat damp round the ankles. Two Colt automatics, negligently poised, were in their hands. He got slowly to his feet and passed a hand across his eyes, but, when he dropped it, the figures were still there.'

This is how the official Ministry of Information pamphlet *Combined Operations 1940-1942*, published in 1943, opens a short account of Operation 'Dryad'. Fortunately, as the Prime Minister had demanded, this operation was completely successful. It concerned the 'snatch' of the entire crew of a lighthouse — the Casquets — which was located on a dangerous chain of rocks some eight miles northwest of Alderney. The first lighthouse had been built there in 1724, heightened and improved over the years, so that by the start of the war its light was visible for some 17 miles and it also incorporated a foghorn and radio communications. This was the situation on 22 June 1940, when the Trinity House crew was evacuated, the light turned off, records removed and the door locked. When the Germans occupied the Channel Islands they decided to man two lighthouses — Les Hanois and the Casquets. Some rudimentary defensive measures were taken — including putting up barbed wire entanglements and arming the small lighthouse crew. It must have been an unenviable and boring job at the best of times, being totally dependent upon a tenuous supply line which could easily be cut in bad weather.

The seven-man crew had little to entertain them as they kept their supposedly constant visual and wireless watch, operating the light only when ordered to do so to help German convoys.

Below: Operation 'Dryad'. This is the wooden-bottomed, canvas-sided collapsible boat, known as the Goatley boat after its designer. It had a pointed stem and stern so it could be paddled in either direction, and weighed only 150kg, enabling it to be carried across country by two men. Assembly took just four minutes and it was designed to carry 10 men, but could carry more — see text of raid on the Casquets. *IWM* — H 14593 *via Maj P. R. Ventham*

The crew when Operation 'Dryad' took place had started their tour of duty — which would last for three long months — on 3 August. They were about halfway through and probably at their lowest as far as morale, enthusiasm and efficiency was concerned, because for days on end they had seen neither ship nor aircraft. The highlight of their tour to date had been the arrival on 28 August of an off-course carrier pigeon, carrying a message from an undercover agent in France and destined for his 'spymaster' in England. The message — in French, but only partly legible — contained names of French towns (such as Paris, Versailles, Granville, Boulogne and Dieppe), together with references to aircraft and hangars. It was sent on to the *Hafenkommandantur* in Cherbourg. [5]

This lighthouse then was the chosen target for Operation 'Dryad' and the force selected to carry out the operation was the SSRF, under command of Maj Gus March-Phillips DSO. It was decided that they would land on the Casquets on the night of 2/3 September 1942 with a party of 12 men, including March-Phillips, Capt Geoffrey Appleyard MC (second in command) and Capt Graham Hayes MC, their aim being to kidnap the entire lighthouse crew. The SSRF normally raided in small parties of eight to ten men with the broad aim of creating alarm and despondency by killing Germans. By October 1942, it had been decided that their role should be more selective. Although they would still normally come from the sea, their task was to take prisoners, a role aptly expressed in the phrase 'the hand of steel which plucks German sentries from their posts'. It is worth pointing out that some seven previous attempts had been made on the Casquets lighthouse, but all had had to be abandoned because of bad weather.

For Operation 'Dryad', the SSRF sailed from Portland in *MTB344* at 21.00hrs, reached the Casquets at about 22.45hrs and then managed to manoeuvre to within some 800 yards of the rock. Here the MTB was anchored and the landing party went ashore soon after midnight, rowing ashore in their Goatley assault craft. The currents were tricky and it took them some 20 minutes to reach the rock, which they did just below the engine house tower. The first obstacle they encountered, once they had scrambled ashore, was coiled dannert wire, but they managed to climb through this and also to find a way around the heavy 'knife-rest' barbed wire entanglement which blocked the gateway to the lighthouse complex. Then, in accordance with a carefully rehearsed plan, they rushed the buildings and towers. They achieved complete surprise. There was no resistance and the entire garrison of seven men was captured without a shot being fired!

'Seven prisoners, all of them Germans, including two leading telegraphists, were taken in the bedrooms and living rooms. The light tower, wireless tower and engine room were all found to be empty, although the generating plant in the engine house was running, and the watch, consisting of two men, was in the living room. The rest were in bed with the exception of two telegraphists who were just turning in. A characteristic of those in bed was the wearing of hairnets which caused the Commander of the party to mistake one of them for a woman.' [6]

The raiding party and their prisoners now had to get back down the cliffs and re-embark. Some of the prisoners were still in their pyjamas, but time was getting short, so there was no chance of changing into their uniforms. The wireless was smashed up with an axe, the buildings searched for useful documents. The light and the engine room were left untouched. It was found that as well as rifles, there was an Oerlikon cannon and two large cases of 'potato-masher' stick grenades, so the lighthouse could have been well defended if the raiding party had been spotted by a more alert garrison. The Commandos dumped all the enemy weapons and ammunition into the sea as they left the lighthouse.

Re-embarking proved quite hazardous and the report pays fulsome tribute to the Goatley, which coped magnificently with a total of 19 men on board instead of the usual maximum of 10. Complete success had been achieved with just two minor casualties (an injured leg and a sprained ankle); the prisoners, who proved to be 'very docile', were soon battened down below decks and under guard, ready for the return journey which began about 01.35hrs. Despite a rising sea, the MTB reached Portland safely at about 04.00hrs. The captured material, which was passed on to higher authorities in Portland, included the codebook for harbour defence vessels, signal books, records, W/T diary, signals procedure details, personal papers, letters, photographs, etc, plus the station log, ration log and light log.

Aftermath
The Germans did not immediately realise that the Casquets garrison had been kidnapped. This was because the regular routine message (presumably saying 'Nothing to Report'!) had been sent only minutes before the attack took place. However, after a while a boat was sent to investigate and it was found that the entire crew had disappeared. The immediate result of the raid was an order from OKW withdrawing all isolated lighthouse crews. However, this was soon rescinded as it was clear that if the sea routes were to be maintained, then the lighthouses had to be manned. The Casquets garrison was strengthened to 33 (one officer, three NCOs and 21 private soldiers from the Heer; one NCO and seven from the Kriegsmarine); more weapons were provided (including a 2.5cm Pak, five machine guns, more hand grenades — and even an anti-tank rifle!); plus more defensive arrangements were put in place, including additional barbed wire entanglements, trip wires, mines, etc. The garrison remained on the Casquets, undisturbed, for the rest of the war, until 17 May 1945, when two officers and 36 men were taken prisoner.

Operation 'Branford'
Just a few days after the successful conclusion of Operation 'Dryad', a small party of 11 commandos, again from the SSRF but this time under Capt Colin Ogden-Smith, landed on the tiny, barren island of Burhou, some three miles northwest of Alderney. Again they used *MTB344*, and landed at about 00.28hrs on 8 September. The object of the raid was to assess its military potential in support of possible landings in the Channel Islands. All that there was on the Island was a partly demolished house which the Germans used as an artillery target for the battery stationed at the Giffoine on Alderney. On the way there they had problems with one of the engines of the MTB, but the problem was solved so the raid went ahead. Again they anchored

offshore and paddled in, using a trusty Goatley. Six commandos landed, carried out a search of the Island, found nothing and left after about 70 minutes. They reached Portland safely at 04.30hrs. In his report Ogden-Smith states that they saw the new crew on the Casquets, which lay to the west, communicating with Alderney to their east, using a lamp.

Operation 'Basalt'
The next operation involved a landing on the island of Sark. Once again the party was from the SSRF under the command of Geoffrey Appleyard — now a major (the original OC SSRF, Maj Gus March-Phillips, had been killed during an operation against St Honorine in Normandy on 12 September). Appleyard knew the Island quite well from prewar visits. The aim of the raid this time was to capture prisoners and reconnoitre the German defences. The party was 12 strong, including Capt Ogden-Smith and 2-Lt Anders Lassen, who had done well on Operation 'Branford'.

They left Portland in *MTB344* shortly after 19.00hrs on 3 October and reached Sark sometime after 23.00hrs. As they approached Braeline Bay, they were asked to identify

Below: Operation 'Basalt'. One of the SSRF party on this operation was Anders Lassen, 'the fearless Dane', who was awarded a posthumous Victoria Cross just three weeks before the end of the war. *IWM* — HU 2125

themselves via a lamp message flashed from the German lookout post on Little Sark. Appleyard replied that they were a German E-Boat wanting to shelter in Dixcart Bay for the night and they were allowed to proceed and finally dropped anchor close to Point Château at about 23.30hrs. The landing party then rowed ashore, left their boat under guard and made their way up the steep cliffs. At the top they were stopped by barbed wire and had to cut their way through. Suddenly, just as they had started off again, they heard a German patrol approaching, so dived for cover. Fortunately, the patrol passed them without noticing their presence and they met no further patrols on their way inland.

Reaching the first house — a big, lonely one all on its own — they tried all the downstairs doors and windows, then finally broke in and woke up the elderly lady occupant who was asleep in bed. 'The elderly lady was wonderful,' wrote one of the patrol later. 'Although alone in the house and awakened by two men with blackened faces, she remained completely calm and was immediately aware of what it was all about.' [7] Maj Appleyard quickly explained the position and she told them all she knew about enemy gun positions, defended localities and the like. She also told them about the Dixcart Hotel which was being used as a headquarters of some kind. [8]

The raiders then pushed on to the hotel, where, after Anders had disposed of the guard, they made a noisy entrance and captured five members of an engineer detachment, most of whom were asleep in bed. Tying the Germans up with their hands behind their backs, the commandos then started to search the premises. However, they had failed to gag their prisoners who, once they recovered from their initial shock, began shouting and creating a rumpus. Maj Appleyard shouted: 'Shut the prisoners up!' and this started a fist fight, which developed into a running battle as the Germans tried to escape. One did escape without any clothes on but unharmed; another also got away but was wounded in the process, two others were shot and killed, while the fifth remained a prisoner. Taking him with them, the commandos set out for the cliffs, with the Germans in hot pursuit. Fortunately, the MTB was still waiting for them, despite the fact that they were far later than agreed, and the party rowed out from the shore, were helped on board the MTB and managed to make good their escape, leaving Sark waters at about 03.45hrs.

As one might have expected, there was an immediate reaction once news of the raid was passed to higher authority! The divisional commander, GenMaj Erich Müller, was furious and ordered that both the Island commandant (Oblt Herdt) and the orderly NCO were to be court-martialled. 'Contrary to my orders,' said Müller, Herdt 'had billeted an engineer detachment carelessly in Dixcart House, without protection and away from the Company Reserve.' There were other repercussions all the way up the chain. At Island level the Sark garrison was reinforced — including sending over three FT7 light tanks — and the potential landing sites were blocked, which involved laying more and more mines. Soldiers raided houses, the *Geheime Feldpolizei* arrived and began a series of interrogations, and for weeks the Islanders lived in fear of reprisals. On the wider stage, the German reaction was just as savage. Clearly infuriated by the ease with which the commandos had made their raid, they seized upon the fact that the prisoners had had their hands tied behind their backs and that some had been shot while tied up. Coupling this with the revelation from the recent Dieppe raid, that captured Canadian orders had said that prisoners' hands would be secured to prevent them from destroying valuable documents, the German propaganda machine stridently accused all commandos of acts of barbarism, forcing the Combined Operation HQ into taking the unusual step of publishing a brief account of the raid. In this statement the British authorities attempted to explain that the purpose behind the Sark raid was to obtain first-hand information about suspected ill-treatment of British residents on the Island. This they said had now been confirmed by the seizure of a proclamation signed by Oberst Knackfuss of FK515, which ordered all male civilians between the ages of 16 and 70, who had not been born in the Channel Islands or who were not permanent residents there, to be deported to Germany together with their families. The report went on to say that 'The total British raiding force consisted of ten officers and men and there were no casualties. Five prisoners were taken, of whom four escaped after repeated struggles and were shot whilst doing so. One was brought back to this country. He has confirmed these deportations and stated they were for forced labour.' [9]

At the very top, Adolf Hitler was beside himself with rage. He ordered that all British prisoners taken at Dieppe should be put into chains and kept that way until the British War Ministry '. . . proves that it will in future make true statements regarding the binding of German prisoners or that it has succeeded in getting its orders carried out by its troops'. This began a propaganda battle which involved the shackling of unfortunate POWs on both sides, something that threatened to get out of control until the Swiss took a hand as mediators, getting both sides to see sense and unfetter all their prisoners simultaneously. However, this was not the end of the matter as it also prompted Hitler in October 1942 to issue an order to all his commanders, giving them authority to execute any commandos who might be captured on any future raids 'in uniform or not . . . whether in battle or whilst escaping . . . destroyed to the last man.' This was perhaps a measure of how upset he was by the tiny 'fleabite' attacks of the SSRF and other commando raiders on the Islands and elsewhere.

A GERMAN REPORT

Following the raid a report was sent to HQ LXXXIV Armeekorps by HQ 319. ID and signed personally by the Divisional Commander, GenMaj Müller. It was published in full in the *CIOS (Jersey) Review* in 1979 and is repeated here, by kind permission of the author of the article, Michael Ginns:

German Report On Commando Raid On Sark 3/4 Oct 42

319. ID
Divisional HQ 6 Oct 1942
Abt.IaAz34g
SECRET
No 4311 42

Subject: **Report about the Raid on Sark**

To: **HQ LXXXIV Armeekorps**

On 23 September 1942, a Pionier detachment of the 2./Pi Btl 319 consisting of one Obergefreiter and four Schutzen was sent to Sark to repair the defence barriers in the harbour. The group was billeted in Dixcart House, approximately 500-600m in a south-westerly direction from the island's reserve troops.

During the night of 3/4 October, between 03.30 and 03.50hrs, the group was suddenly attacked in their quarters by a British assault party which must have landed near Point Château. Some of our soldiers were able to free themselves in hand-to-hand fighting. In this fight Obergefreiter Bleyer was killed, Gefreiter Esslinger was mortally wounded and Gefreiter Just slightly wounded. Senior Gefreiter Weinrich is missing, while Gefreiter Klotz succeeded in escaping unwounded in the darkness.

Investigations have revealed the following:

During the night 3/4 October, at 02.10hrs, Auxiliary Customs Assistant Marburger, who was on guard duty at the pier, heard the distant noise of an engine. By telephone he informed the Orderly Obergefreiter of the 6./IR 583, Senior Gefreiter Schubert, who did not pass on the information to his Company Commander, who is also the island Commander. Gefreiter Schubert later stated that he waited for confirmation of the report from the strongpoints. He himself did not contact the strongpoints. The interrogation of the strongpoint commanders showed that their guards did not hear any engine noises. Therefore the company commander was not informed and no alarm was given.

During the night — probably between 03.30 and 03.50hrs — the soldiers of the Pionier detachment were awakened, handcuffed and marched off. Gefreiter Klotz was able to shed his handcuffs; he knocked down the British soldier guarding him and escaped into the darkness. Seeing this, the other soldiers also tried to escape, but only Gefreiter Just, who was wounded, succeeded. Obergefreiter Bleyer and Gefreiter Esslinger were shot down and stabbed. Senior Gefreiter Weinrich remained as a prisoner of war. The enemy quickly retreated in the direction of the landing point.

This fight took place at 03.55hrs. The guard of the reserve troops was alarmed by the noise and reported to Senior Gefreiter Schubert, who in turn reported at 04.00hrs to Oblt Herdt, commander of the 6./IR 583 and Island Commandant of Sark. Oblt Herdt alerted the reserve troops and the strongpoints. Oblt Herdt and some of the reserve troops went in the direction from which cries for help had been heard coming. In the garden of a house Gefreiter Klotz was found completely naked. He reported what had happened. Oblt Balga was ordered to advance with a detachment to attack the enemy before they could leave the Island. The enemy succeeded in escaping without losses as they followed a path that was unknown and could not be found in the dark.

As engine noises could be heard in the meantime, at 04.25hrs Oblt Herdt ordered a customs boat with a crew of five and armed with a light machine gun to put to sea and search Derrible and Dixcart Bays. The boat put to sea at 05.15hrs.

From the Company Command Post Oblt Herdt reported to HQ IR 583 at 04.50hrs. At 04.52hrs the report was passed on to 319. ID.

Having done this, Oblt Herdt joined the troops commanded by Oblt Balga whom he found at the steep slope to the south of La Jaspellerie. He ordered Dixcart Bay to be blocked and another detachment to advance towards Derrible Bay. The enemy, however, could not be found. At 05.00hrs it was clear that the operation had ended.

Oblt Herdt used the tracks left by the enemy to reconstruct the route of the retreat and followed it. It is very difficult and the last part leads over a piece of rock going down almost vertically. The following weapons and pieces of equipment were found on the way:

Enemy: 2 daggers, 1 sub machine-gun magazine, 1 pistol magazine, 1 pair of wire cutters, I handspike, 3 torches, 1 woollen cap, 1 muffler, several pieces of rope.
Own: 1 carbine.

Statement of the 319. ID:

1. It is known to Divisional HQ that enemy landings are possible anywhere on the island of Sark. Minefields have been laid in an attempt to impede these landings; additional minefields are planned.

2. On 12 September 1942, I inspected the situation on Sark and gave orders to deploy the troops according to the attached survey.

3. Contrary to my orders, Oblt Herdt, the former Company Commander of the 6./IR 583 — he has been relieved of his command in the meantime — had billeted an Engineer detachment (consisting of one Obergefreiter and four other ranks) which had been sent to Sark to carry out repairs to the harbour defence barriers, carelessly in Dixcart House, without protection and away

from the Company reserve. Because of his failure to comply with orders Oblt Herdt will be court-martialled. Until now his confidential report has been good. [10]

4. Senior Gefreiter Schubert, Orderly Corporal of the Company during the night of 3/4 October 1942, did not pass on the report from the guard at the pier, concerning engine noise, to his company commander. It was his duty to contact the strongpoints concerning the report of engine noises, and not wait for them to contact him. Senior Gefreiter Schubert will also be court-martialled.

5. Obgefreiter Bleyer, Senior Gefreiter Weinrich and Gefreiter Esslinger, Just and Klotz, attempted to escape despite the fact that they were handcuffed. Their behaviour meets the standard expected of a German soldier.

6. The enemy assault party succeeded in escaping without losses as it took a path which was difficult to follow.

7. It must be assumed — possibly as a result of information given by the Island inhabitants — that the enemy knew that Dixcart House was used as a billet from time to time.

(Signed) Müller
GenLt
Commanding 319. ID

Above: Operation 'Huckaback'. A photograph of Col Pat Porteous as a young captain. He commanded 'Huckaback', after being awarded the Victoria Cross on 2 October 1942 for his bravery during the Dieppe raid. He survived the war. *IWM* — HU 2018

Operations in St Peter Port

During the night of 8/9 January 1943, after three previous attempts had been aborted, another attempt was made to mine shipping in St Peter Port harbour, Guernsey, using Cockle canoes (also called the 'Folbot' these were two-man collapsible sports canoes made by the Folbot Company). Lts Ian Warren and Anders Lassen, each with an NCO, transferred from *MTB344* into their canoes for the run-in. They were hoping to attach limpet mines onto shipping in the harbour, but had to abort as the weather was so appalling.

Operation 'Huckaback'

The next commando operation would take place on the night of 27/28 February 1943, codenamed Operation 'Huckaback' and targeting the tiny island of Herm. It was to be a reconnaissance, designed to see if Herm would be a suitable location for supporting artillery to be landed in the event of a full-scale assault on Guernsey.

The Island had been completely evacuated in 1940, apart from a single caretaker (Mr M. Le Page). The Germans used it for target practice for the light artillery batteries around St Peter Port. The small commando force comprised 10 men from No 4 Commando, under the command of Capt P. A. Porteous VC, who had been awarded the Victoria Cross for his bravery during the Dieppe operation, with Lt Thompson as his second in command.

The party left from Portland, as always in the ubiquitous *MTB344*, reached Herm without incident and rowed ashore in a dory to a rocky beach on the south side of the island at about 23.00hrs. They spent three hours on the Island, examining the cottages, Belvoir House, the Château, the quay, etc and, apart from a noticeboard in the backyard of the Château which appeared to place the Château and its surrounds out of bounds to all troops, they found no visible signs of the Occupation forces. The commandos withdrew at about 02.00hrs, leaving propaganda leaflets in conspicuous places and chalking the letter 'c' on various walls. They reached Portland safely some three hours later.

Operation 'Pussyfoot'

Another visit to Herm was planned for the night of 3/4 April 1943, to be attempted by 10 members of the SSRF, with the aim of reconnoitring the western side of the Island which the Porteous raid had been unable to do. They also hoped to capture a prisoner. However, once again the weather intervened and thick fog prevented the landing so the raid had to be called off.

Operation 'Hardtack 28'

Having carried out operations on Guernsey, the Casquets, Burhou, Sark and Herm, Jersey was the obvious choice for the next raid. [11] It was to be a reconnaissance and was scheduled to take place on 25/26 December 1943. The commandos taking part were from the 2nd Special Boat Section, under the command of Capt Philip Ayton. His party comprised nine men, including a French officer and three French commandos, and they were taken to Jersey in a Motor Gun Boat (MGB) [12], arriving off the north coast and landing at about 22.45hrs at Petit Port, a quiet little bay near Belle Hougue Point (not to be confused with another Petit Port on the southwest coast of the Island, just north of Corbière Point). They made their way inland from the cove until they reached a wire fence which had notices attached saying '*MINEN*' and 'STOP — MINES'. However, to their alarm, they immediately realised that the notices were facing away from them — in other words, they were inside the minefield and had walked through it! Nevertheless, they pressed on inland and reached the small hamlet of Egypt which was deserted, some of its houses appearing to have been damaged by shell-fire. The reason for this soon became apparent when they discovered more notices which read: 'MILITARY ZONE — CIVILIANS STRICTLY FORBIDDEN'. Leaving the hamlet they next made their way to a well-camouflaged concrete strongpoint, which comprised an observation post and a pillbox facing seawards, plus a number of dilapidated trenches. The steel entry door to the pillbox was locked and it was apparent that the position was no longer in use.

Capt Ayton then decided to call at a nearby farm to try to get some information. As one can imagine, the occupant — a woman on her own — was not keen to open her door at that late hour and it took them some time to persuade her to do so. When eventually they managed to speak with her she said she could not help them, but advised Ayton to try another farmhouse nearby, which he did. [13]

The occupants here were initially equally worried, but eventually did open up and invited the raiding party inside. Some did so, whilst the rest remained on guard outside. The occupants were able to pass on some useful information about the area, which included details of the German garrison at the nearby strongpoint of Les Platons, where there were both German soldiers and Russian 'prisoners' who were required to work for the Germans (as these 'prisoners' were armed it is more likely that they were ex-Red Army soldiers who were now members of the Ostbataillonen as mentioned in Chapter 3). They estimated the Island garrison at about 1,000; explained that the Germans used mainly horse transport due to the acute shortage of petrol; confirmed that there were numerous minefields in the local area and that the beach at Petit Port was mined; that the nightly winter curfew was 21.00 to 07.00hrs and that the Germans were not actively patrolling in their area. They also said that there was no resistance movement on the Island and that the population generally tried to get on peaceably with the occupying forces, as they were afraid of reprisals. However, attitudes were hardening after

Above: Operation 'Hardtack'. This is one type of sign used by the Germans to warn of their minefields. Capt Philip Ayton's party found themselves 'on the wrong side' and realised they had walked through the minefield! *Alderney Museum via Mrs Pantcheff*

the Germans had been touring the farms for food (in particular the Russian troops who were treated badly by the Germans) and had also taken a large proportion of the Island's medical supplies for their own use.

The two farmers (John and Hedley Le Breton) then offered to guide the commandos to the German strongpoint at Les Platons, which they did, then said goodbye as they approached the eastern perimeter, leaving the raiding party to carry on with their reconnaissance. The commandos could not find the strongpoint entrance, nor any sign of a sentry to take prisoner and as time was now running short — they had just 45 minutes left to get back to the cove — Ayton decided to abandon the recce and head for the shore. They reached Petit Port safely, but the dory wasn't there, so they began moving northwards along the cliff signalling with a torch to get the dory to come in and pick them up, but got no reply. Then disaster struck. Ayton, who was leading, crawled under a fence and was some five yards in front of the rest of the party when he trod on a mine which exploded, seriously wounding him. The rest of the patrol managed to find him on the cliffside, entangled in brambles, which had probably saved

him from falling any further down the cliff. Fortunately, they then saw the MGB some 400 yards from the shore, signalled to it by torch and managed to get Capt Ayton down the cliff and into the dory. This all took some time, but the explosion did not alert the Germans and the commandos were able to re-embark at about 05.20hrs. Sadly, although they got back to Portland without further incident and Capt Ayton was taken to hospital, he died of his wounds the following day.

Operation 'Hardtack 7'

The last of the commando raids onto the Channel Islands was also called 'Hardtack' (as were a number of raids of pre-D-Day raids on the French coast) but it was numbered out of sequence as it was timed to coincide with Operation 'Hardtack 28'. The target this time was Sark. The raiding party, under Lt McGonigal, was taken by MGB to Derrible Point on the southeast side of the main island. The run-in was by dory and the party landed on the most southerly part of the Point just before midnight on Christmas Day. Unfortunately, it soon became clear that between the Point and the mainland there was a ridge with sheer drops on both sides, which proved insurmountable, so the first attempt had to be aborted. The party returned to the dory at about 01.00hrs, then proceeded westwards around to Derrible Bay, where the patrol commander and his sergeant (Sgt Boccador) made a careful reconnaissance of the beach and cliff area to confirm whether or not there were any mines. They found none. However, by then it was 04.00hrs, so they returned to the dory and rejoined the MGB at 04.25hrs.

The same raiding party returned to Derrible Bay two nights later with the object of taking a prisoner, climbing up the very steep cliffs and managing to reach a path along the top (in fact they followed a very similar route to the Operation 'Basalt' raiders of 3/4 October 1942; this was foolish as they should have appreciated that the Germans would have increased their minefields in the area — which proved to be the case). After going some distance in extended order, with the patrol commander in front feeling for mines, two mines exploded at the rear of the party, killing one man and severely wounding another. Then, as the rest of the patrol was endeavouring to carry the two casualties out of the minefield into which they had obviously strayed, two more mines went off — one in front of McGonigal and one to his side. These wounded him and killed another of the patrol, leaving Sgt Boccador as the only member of the patrol unwounded. In view of this disastrous situation, McGonigal decided to abort the mission and they began to retrace their steps. More mines exploded around them and they may have come under heavy machine gun fire in the bargain, although this was never properly confirmed and they actually saw no signs of the enemy throughout the operation. They managed to retrace their steps without further incident, but had to leave behind both a wireless set (which they had hidden under a rock on the way in but now could not find) and the rope they used to get down the last 20 feet of sheer cliff. They got back to the MGB without further incident and reached Portland safely.

The bodies of the two dead commandos (both Frenchmen) were found by the Germans the next morning and buried in the small military section of the graveyard opposite St Peter's Church. However, after the war one of them, Pte André Dignac was exhumed. The body of the other commando, Cpl R Bellamy remains there, the inscription on his cross reading: 'BELLAMY R — *Mort pour La France*, 28.12.43.' This was to be the last of the commando raids on the Channel Islands.

Chapter 11
Surrender

Would they fight?

As has been mentioned, SHAEF had quite early on started to amass a fairly good knowledge of the German defences on the Islands. What was still unknown, however, was how well the garrison would defend the territory. The men of 319. ID and all the rest of the units had undergone the 'Hunger Winter', seen little action, but were still well equipped and manning formidable defences. Therefore HQ Southern Command, who had been given the responsibility of planning and conducting the operation to retake the Islands, had to assume the worst — namely that the troops involved would have to fight. Thus those who would be involved were given a period of tough, realistic training in and around the Brixham area of Devon, which was considered to resemble closely the Channel Islands terrain. They also were trained in street fighting in the bombed areas of Plymouth.

However, it was at the same time hoped that the landings would be achieved peacefully, so, rather in the way the Germans had proceeded when they had arrived in 1940, a 'softly softly' approach was planned (given the codeword Operation 'Omlet') with small advance parties preceding the main body to 'test the water' and see if the coastal batteries would or would not engage. All hoped that the great events that were unfolding as the 'Thousand Year Reich' disintegrated would obviate the need for combat so that the surrender would proceed without any fighting taking place. Nevertheless, there would still be the need for a suitable force to disarm the German servicemen, clear minefields and other dangerous explosives, etc — wherever possible using the garrison troops to assist so as to make full use of their expertise and local knowledge.

After this had been successfully completed then there was the considerable task of arranging for the hordes of prisoners to be escorted to POW camps in the UK and elsewhere. The military force to be formed for the complete operation — now called Operation 'Nestegg' — was to be known as Task Force 135 (TF135), to be commanded by a Brig A. E. Snow OBE. He would be in charge of all aspects of the operation, having been commanding 115th Infantry Brigade in July 1944, when his Brigade HQ became the planning staff for the re-occupation of the Channel Islands.

Brig Alfred Ernest Snow was a tough, experienced soldier, born in 1898 and commissioned into the Somerset Light Infantry. He had served during the latter stages of World War 1, then in India (on the NW Frontier) and Burma between the wars, being employed with the Burma Military Police 1934–36. He was awarded the OBE in 1940. His force was to comprise an infantry brigade plus supporting services, which included a large number of Royal Artillery personnel — a Composite Coastal Unit and 127

HAA Regiment (396 and 411 HAA Btys) and 504 and 505 LAA Batteries. The force was at first held at seven days' notice to move, but as the weeks went by this was changed to 14, then 28. As the final year of the war began, it became clearly crazy for the army to have a well-trained infantry brigade standing idle in the UK, when every man was needed to take the fight into the German heartlands, so 115 Inf Bde was removed from Force 135 and sent to fight in 21 Army Group in Germany. Whilst there was a severe shortage of infantry, the need for coastal artillery to defend the UK was long past, so three artillery regiments (614, 618 and 620) were regrouped as an 'infantry brigade', given a hasty infantry training course and joined TF135 as its main 'infantry' element.

No 20 Civil Affairs Unit

There was also a great need to take with TF135 sufficient supplies of everything that would be needed to get the Islands back on their feet, so to assist him, Brig Snow was allocated No 20 Civil Affairs Unit. In the run-up to the surrender, this unit liaised with the various departments in Whitehall, to collect all manner of things for distribution to the Islanders.

Food and clothing were given top priority and the first 200 tons of essential supplies were to be preloaded onto suitable transport, so that the vehicles could leave the landing craft which had carried them over from the UK, then drive straight up the beaches and onto the Islands' roads. A further 300 tons would go into the first transport ships which would hopefully be able to use the docks, provided they hadn't been sabotaged by the defeated Germans. The food supplies to be taken were calculated as to be sufficient to raise the diet of each Islander to 2,750 calories a day [1] for a period of three months, from when normal supply routes would take over. The clothing, equivalent of 15 months' UK clothing ration, comprised the first emergency clothing instalment, to be followed shortly by a second 15 months-worth of clothing ration. The food and clothing would be sold through the shops, and price lists, showing current UK prices, were included, so that people would know what the cost of further supplies would be. The British Government, in a 'gesture of goodwill', also sent a free gift of cigarettes, tobacco and chocolate. They also stockpiled a large range of household items, pots and pans, clothes and shoe mending items and, as Charles Cruickshanks comments:

'The Home Office and other officials working with the Civil Affairs Unit did their best to make certain that nothing that mattered was overlooked. Showing a humanity not usually associated with civil servants, they even proposed that a consignment of cosmetics should be included to help rebuild the morale of the women.' [2]

Left:
Brig A. E. Snow OBE, reading out the proclamation from the steps of Elizabeth College, Guernsey.
IWM — HU 25970

Channel Islands Historian, Michael Ginns, also gives an example of the lengths to which the planners went to ensure nothing was forgotten '... going right down to the necessary 1,110,000 sheets of toilet paper!'

By early May 1945, as it became increasingly obvious that Germany was collapsing, the need to assemble TF135 and its civilian affairs unit became more and more pressing. Telegrams went out to assemble the Task Force and all the landing craft and other vessels needed, at Plymouth, by 7 May 1945.

Countdown to surrender

'When Churchill broadcast that the war was over, he said to our people in the Channel Islands, "Help is on the way".' That is how Ernest 'Bev' Bevins of the Royal Engineers began his recollections of Operation 'Nestegg.' Before going on with his eyewitness account, however, it is necessary to detail the steps which preceded the start of the operation. SHAEF had alerted HQ Southern Command on 3 May and two days later gave the go-ahead for negotiations to begin by saying: 'Subject to your being satisfied as to the intention of German Commander, Channel Islands, you should complete mounting and launch "Nestegg" earliest practical date.' As soon as this was received, a wireless message was sent to

Below: Front page of the Guernsey Star, 8 May 1945. *Guernsey Museum*

Right: Propaganda leaflet dropped by the Allies on 5 May 1945. *via Gilbert Van Grieken*

the German garrison commander that the GOC-in-C Southern Command, was authorised to receive their unconditional surrender. The following day a typically uncompromising reply was sent back, to the effect that the German commander — Vizeadmiral Friedrich Hüffmeier — would take orders only from his own government! However, in the early hours of the morning of the 7th came news that the unconditional surrender of all German forces had been signed at Rheims and that all hostilities would cease at midnight on 8 May. This news was followed by a further signal to Hüffmeier, proposing that his representatives rendezvous four miles south of the Les Hanois light to sign the surrender document. This proposal was agreed and the time set for the RV was noon on Tuesday, 8 May.

Accordingly, two destroyers, HMS *Bulldog* and HMS *Beagle*, left Plymouth at 10.00hrs, each carrying a landing party of two officers and 20 other ranks, for Guernsey and Jersey respectively. Brig Snow was also on HMS *Bulldog*. They reached the RV without incident, where they were met by a German trawler which was carrying Hüffmeier's representative Kapitänleutnant Armin Zimmermann. [3] Once on board HMS *Bulldog* he stated that he was authorised to do no more than discuss an armistice, but was told in no uncertain terms that he must return and prepare for an unconditional surrender. Zimmermann retorted that as the general cease-fire did not come into operation until 00.01hrs on 9 May, the two destroyers should withdraw from the RV or risk being shelled by the powerful coastal batteries! The Naval Force Commander, Rear-Admiral C. G. Stuart, had been told to avoid confrontation at all costs, so he decided to withdraw out of range. A signal was then received to say that, GenMaj Siegfried Heine, Hüffmeier's deputy and Commandant of Guernsey, would arrive at the RV at midnight which he did, accompanied by Zimmermann. [4] He signed eight copies of the surrender at 01.14hrs, Wednesday, 9 May 1945, on a rum cask on the quarterdeck of HMS *Bulldog*..

The destroyer then moved to St Peter Port and the Guernsey landing party went ashore under the command of Lt-Col E. G. Stoneman and accompanied by Lt-Col H. R. Power OBE, who was head of the Civil Affairs Unit. Meanwhile, Brig Snow had transferred to the other destroyer and set sail for St Aubyn's Bay, Jersey, anchoring off St Helier and sending for GenMaj Wulf to sign the surrender of Jersey. The Bailiff, Alexander Coutanche, was asked to accompany him, which he did, together with the Island's Attorney General and Solicitor General. They all met at 12.00hrs at the Kriegsmarine HQ at the Pomme D'Or Hotel, then boarded a German naval pinnace. On arrival, Wulf was 'somewhat arrogant and aggressive', but after Brig Snow had expressed his severe displeasure, he was almost reduced to tears and meekly signed the surrender document! Once this had been completed the landing party moved in, led by Lt-Col William Robinson MC of 620 Regt RA, and accompanied by Capt Hugh Le Brocq, who had left Jersey in 1940, with the Royal Jersey Militia. They made their HQ at the Pomme D'Or Hotel, where Col Robinson addressed the crowd from the balcony.

The first large naval vessel entered St Helier on the 11th and it was the same on Guernsey, but of course in both cases they had been preceded by the 'Omlet' groups. 'Bev' Bevins was part of the advance group which landed on Guernsey and said in his reminiscences that the Germans had been sent to the other side of the Island so as to avoid any clashes with our troops. He continues:

'Two of our lads had been and knocked a wall down so that we could get off and put steel wire on the sand. [5] They sent me off first. I was the first lorry off the boat. They said, "Bevins, you go first. You've got 35 tons, so if you blow up they'll know we've arrived." I had got sandbags around me, I could just move my feet and hands. And then our job was clearing mines that had been missed and God knows what.

'The people were near starvation, eating seaweed. I was able to visit some of the Island boys' families (these were Guernsey-born soldiers with whom he had trained at Barnstaple). I enjoyed several months with them. One lady and my wife wrote to each other every Christmas until, sadly, they both passed away. They cooked me some seaweed — "most horrible!" When we first landed it was hugs and kisses from the ladies; the men shook hands, patted our backs and asked if we had any cigs. We gave the children sweets; they thought it was Christmas.

'The Germans had used slave labour over there. Many died and the Russian prisoners, we had to de-louse and feed them. Then they were sent to the mainland for hospitalisation. They looked like pictures of the concentration camps and their staring eyes said, "Thank you". The Germans were all made to work clearing the mines etc. They had still left some booby traps for us.

'One thing sticks in my mind. I was standing by my lorry, the lads were clearing a Jerry store, making sure there were no booby traps, when an old lady came to me with tears in her eyes and she said, "There you are, I said that an English soldier would have the first strawberry and you are he." And I had to stand there and eat it, and I cried with her.' [6]

What's the drill for inspecting an enemy guard of honour? [7]

Another member of TF135 was ex-WO1 Bill Neely, now an In-Pensioner at the Royal Hospital, Chelsea. He was Camp Sergeant-Major, Jersey, and recalled:

'When we arrived at St Helier, the commander of our party (I think it was Col Robinson), looked at the quayside and called: "Sergeant Major". I doubled across to him and he said: "Sa'Major, how are you on the Manual of Ceremonial?" I replied that I was a regular infantry NCO and that for years I had known every word of it. He then asked: "What's the drill for inspecting an enemy guard of honour?"

'The only thing which came into my head was: "Don't inspect arms, Sir!" We disembarked and as we did, I received my first operation order from the Colonel — "Get a car and capture the airport, your clerk can take over Navy Headquarters at the

Pomme D'Or." I collected my clerk, Private Gulliman, my box of confidential documents and a machine pistol from the nearest German and, after slinging it and my sniper's rifle over my shoulder, and carrying the box between Gulliman and myself, headed for the nearest German officer and asked in my broken German for a car. He said there were none on the quay and we would have to go out of the harbour area. There were German sentries at the gates to the docks, still on duty to keep members of the public away. As we passed the gates I had a bunch of flowers stuck in my left hand, and then we had to push our way through the crowd. We were helpless, I've never been kissed by so many hairy old men in my life!

'We made our way to the rank of parked cars and were helped into one that had been requisitioned by the Germans. It must have been left at the docks in 1940, for instead of an ignition key, the German driver had a nail to start the car. Probably the key was in a drawer somewhere in England. After my clerk had been dropped at the Pomme D'Or I was driven to the airport, where the officer in charge was an Oberstleutnant in the Luftwaffe. The guard was called out by him and I was given a "Present Arms" by them. The Oberstleutnant apologised for the fact that very few of the planes flew, and those that did were short range and couldn't take part in any attempt to repulse the invasion. [8] Many of them had no guns either . . . As we talked, a German aircraftsman doubled over and saluted and said, "Herr Churchill kommt on radio" — even my faulty German understood that. I was conducted to the Officers' Mess, introduced as Offizierstellvertreter (Acting Officer) Neely, and automatically complied with British Mess rules — I took off my full webbing equipment, hung my weapons on a coat hanger and accepted the invitation to have a brandy. As I listened to Churchill saying, "Our dear Channel Islands have been liberated," I gazed idly around. It was only then that I realised my "prisoners" were still armed with Lugers, Mausers and Berettas, whilst I was unarmed. However, along came another brandy from a bottle marked "Reserviert für die Wehrmacht" which helped calm my fears. Fortunately, I was not left in this situation for long — within a couple of hours a platoon of gunners arrived (they were a platoon, not the usual gun teams; the "gunfantry" being organised on infantry lines). I was despatched to the Pomme D'Or as Garrison Sergeant Major, Transport Officer, Rations Officer, Cipher Officer and general factotum; except for these duties, the rest of my time was free — about half an hour a day!'

Bill met his wife-to-be that Sunday: she had been a nurse from Nottingham who had not managed to get away from the Island when it was occupied. He recalled that he had 'kissed her for the first time on the 19th, proposed on the 21st and left for Alderney on the 22nd to dig up decomposed Russians for the War Crimes Commission — not a pleasant job, I can assure you'. He got back to Guernsey on 11 July and they were married the following day. After honeymooning, they returned to Guernsey and Bill set up an Education Centre in Woolworth's!

He makes the point that the total casualties sustained during Operation 'Nestegg' was just one sprained wrist — a gunner had tripped over a cable and fallen on his wrist. He closed his reminiscences with an anecdote about his job as Rations Officer:

'One thing I forgot to say: we were on active service rationing and had about 300 Germans working for us every morning and another 300 every afternoon — and received roughly three-quarters of a ration for each prisoner. The result was that our ration store was overflowing, and when King George VI and Queen Elizabeth came, I was asked to supply food — so I provided 300 tins of steak and kidney pie, ie 2,100 rations, tinned fruit for 200, plus lots of chocolate bars; the only thing I couldn't get was Earl Grey tea. We also provided 40 tins of cigarettes, so the meal was a success and my 30-man protection platoon didn't go short. We even provided a large supply of booze, for, when I asked the German Quartermaster if he had any, his reply shook me. He said casually, "about 10,000 cases. We still have most of what we took from pubs and clubs when we arrived." Completely illegally, after our third week there without a drink, we sold cases of 12 mixed bottles for a pound. Our only guarantee was that, in every case, there would be a bottle of whisky and a bottle of brandy!'

Meanwhile, the Occupation forces get ready to leave

Werner Wagenknecht heard one of the last shots fired in anger just before the Armistice:

'A plane flew over us and suddenly a shot was fired from the Flak position opposite our quarters. Crying people materialised everywhere, but then they were all gone. The Treaty in Guernsey was signed just one day later.

'A British officer escorted by soldiers came to our quarters a few days after the capitulation. He wanted to see all the ambulances, medical equipment and our quarters. I had to give my last order for a roll-call. Whilst calling my comrades to attention, our little house-dog, a spaniel, who had lived with us in good times and bad, came to me in the front of the unit, then "begged" in our direction and ran off — we were not ashamed to shed a few tears. (Years later, during my first visit to Guernsey, I met our good friend the spaniel in a farmhouse opposite our former quarters — he wagged his tail!) I had to hand over all our belongings, burn our iron rations and pass over all the documents and service papers (except for our Red Cross Certificates). Then I drove with the officer in his jeep to our confiscated garages to hand over the ambulances and equipment. I stood in the jeep and called: "Drive Left! Drive Left!" to show the population that the German traffic regulations were annulled . . . The next day I reported to Elizabeth Hospital to be told that I would be supervising the embarkation of all the sick and wounded soldiers on 14 May onto a landing-craft at St Sampson harbour — it was then that I saw how half-starved these men really were.

'My service in the German Army was now finished, but my friendship with Guernsey folks is still strong — we have happy relations with them, pay visits and speak to each other every month on the telephone. I hope that your book will help to lead to a better understanding between our nations.'

Below: German POW waiting on the beach to board waiting LSTs. The beach was between West Park and First Tower, St Aubin's Bay, Jersey, 19 May 1945. *IWM* — HU 5193

The Official report

After Operation 'Nestegg' had been successfully concluded, the Office of the Naval Officer in Charge, Channel Islands, wrote a 'narrative of events', which is set out below. It is taken from *CIOS (Jersey) Review* May 1989 and appears here with their kind permission and that of D. Small, who had originally submitted the narrative.

Office of Naval Officer in Charge
Channel Islands
19th May 1945
No 0301/177

Sir,

Operation 'Nestegg' — reoccupation of the Channel Islands. Narrative

I have the honour to forward the following narrative of events in connection with Operation 'Nestegg'.

Preliminary minesweeping operations to establish searched route to Guernsey and Jersey and inter-islands, and to search anchorages were carried out, by the M/S (Minesweeping) Force detailed, on 9, 10, 11 and 12 May in accordance with Plan 'B', Appendix 'D' to the Naval Plan for Operation Nestegg. No mines were found. The M/S Force, with the exception of 3 MMS, required for clearance of the British laid minefield QZX 967, returned to Plymouth on completion. A further report regarding clearance of QZX 967 will be made in due course.

From information supplied by German Naval Authorities, as required by the surrender terms and from the general impression of their truthfulness on questioning, I feel satisfied that no German mines were laid at sea in the area of the Channel Islands Sub-command with the exception of the controlled minefields off the entrances to the harbours of St Peter's Port [9] and St Sampson's in Guernsey and St Helier in Jersey. These controlled minefields will be dealt with by exploding them at an early date after due warning and precautions.

The main body of Force 135 embarked at Plymouth under command of Brig A. E. Snow OBE. The Jersey Force (Group 11) with Commander C. A. Fremantle DSO (Captain RN retired) acting as Vice-Commodore of the Convoy in *Royal Ulsterman* sailed first, passing the gate at 15.45 on Friday, 11 May. Group 1, carrying the Guernsey Force, with Captain C. G. Stuart DSO, DSC (Rear Admiral retired) acting as Commodore in *LCH167*, passed the boom at 18.00, 11 May. The passage was made in fine, clear weather with a slight sea and Group 1, slightly ahead of time, anchored in St Peter's Port at 07.15 on 12 May; Group 11 anchored off St Helier at 08.00, 12 May.

Landing of troops in LCAs from LS is commenced, simultaneously in both islands, at 08.30/12th at jetties inside the Harbours and continued even more rapidly than had been anticipated until completed. No opposition whatsoever

except for the mobbing of the soldiers by an hilariously enthusiastic population was met with and all Orders issued to the Germans supplementary to the surrender terms, appeared to have been strictly complied with.

Guernsey

What follows refers, as regards operations in Guernsey only, a narrative of operations in Jersey is being prepared by RNO Jersey and will be forwarded when received, but it may be said here that operations in Jersey progressed according to plan and more rapidly than anticipated.

Beaching and Unloading of LSTs

(a) Arrival of ships coincided approximately with HW Springs and weather was perfect. Opportunity was taken to beach (US) *LST516* in the Old Harbour, St Peter's Port at 09.00 and her vehicles were driven off and stores unloaded as soon as tide served, a very thrilling sight for the enthusiastic crowd on the quayside.

(b) Reconnaissance proved that St Sampson's Harbour was unsuitable for beaching and unloading LSTs and that obstructions had been removed from Lancresse Bay.

(c) LSTs *59*, *137* and *324* were sailed to anchorage at Lancresse Bay, beached at 11.00/13th unloaded, unbeached and returned to St Peter's Port before dark the same night.

(d) *LST516* unbeached at 18.00/12th and berthed alongside west side of the centre pier to complete unloading of stores. *LST295* then beached on same berth, and, after unbeaching as tide served about 09.00/13th, was followed by *LST139*.

This completed the beaching and unloading of all LSTs and they returned to anchorage to await embarkation of POW.

The Force Commander landed at White Rock at 10.45, accompanied by myself. He was received by a Guard of Honour provided by the Military Advance Party, Guernsey. The German Commander of the Channel Island, Vizeadmiral Hüffemeier, had been brought to this place under guard and surrendered, personally, to the Force Commander, he explained that he had destroyed his sword in accordance with orders received from his higher authorities. He was turned over, as a prisoner, to the Commanding Officer HMS *Falknor* and taken on board, the ship then sailed to Jersey where the German Island Commander, GenMaj Woolf was embarked, after which HMS *Falknor* sailed for Plymouth.

Brigadier Snow and I attended by several Staff Officers, then marched to the Court House, through streets bedecked with flags and lined with a wildly cheering throng of people, and called on the Bailiff of Guernsey, Mr Victor Carey, who introduced us to the members of the States. Champagne which had been hidden for years was produced and the arrival of the Force and the Liberation of the Island suitably toasted.

I returned on board *LCH167* at 12.30 to attend to certain details of ships movements, landed again at 13.30 accompanied by my secretary and two seamen armed guard, and drove by car to Elizabeth College.

At 14.00 the ceremony of the reading of the Proclamation by Brigadier Snow, vesting in him by order in Council, full powers as officer commanding the military forces, took place. The reading of the Proclamation was followed by the reading of His Majesty's letter to the people of the Channel Islands. The ceremony was attended by the Bailiff and members of the States of Guernsey, standing on the steps of the entrance to Elizabeth College and in the presence of a large and enthusiastic audience of the civil population, it concluded with the singing of 'God Save the King'.

Brigadier Snow and I then marched back to the harbour, through streets still lined with cheering and jubilant people, embarked in HMS *Beagle* at 15.00 and left for Jersey. Meanwhile, the movements of units of the force to their locations and headquarters had proceeded as planned with everything going smoothly.

We landed at St Helier in Jersey at about 17.00, were received by the Island Commander and inspected Island Headquarters and Naval Headquarters, here we learnt that the landing of the force in Jersey had proceeded as planned without a hitch. We then marched to the Royal Courts, amidst wildly enthusiastic crowds, where we were received by the Bailiff of Jersey and introduced to members of the States.

The Proclamation and His Majesty's letter were read by Brigadier Snow from a raised platform in the Royal Square with a similar ceremony as in Guernsey, and in the presence of a similar jubilant and cheering crowd. Brigadier Snow remained in Jersey for the night and returned to Guernsey in HMS *Beagle* arriving at about noon on Sunday 13 May. I returned the same night in ML 910, arrived alongside *LCH167* at about 22.30 and remained on board her for the night.

I landed the following forenoon (13 May), inspected Naval billeting accommodation, offices, stores, workshops and the setting up of Naval Headquarters at the Crown Hotel.

The wireless communication between *LCH167* and Commander-in-Chief Plymouth had not been good ever since our arrival due to local adverse conditions, interference from other ships and stations and partly to inexperience of W/T operators and coding staff. Many messages were so mutilated as to be unintelligible and my Operations Staff had

considerable difficulties to contend with during the early period. However, owing to a good knowledge of intentions and the exercise of common sense, they competed very creditably with the many problems that arose and the programme of arrivals and departures, berthing and unloading of LSTs and Coasters continued with a rapidity in advance of that anticipated.

Reoccupation of Sark and Alderney

The reoccupation of Sark was carried out on Thursday, 17 May, by troops of Force 135 carried in *LCI(L)300* and landed by *LCM379*. 274 German POW were brought to Guernsey.

The reoccupation of Alderney was carried out on 16 May, by troops of Force 135 carried in *LCI(L)16* and *LCI123*. Stores being transported in WD Coaster *Beal*. On 20 May, five LSTs evacuated 2,332 POW including 170 sick from Alderney to UK. They have constructed a most useful adjunct to Braye Harbour facilities in an extremely well built 300ft extension to the pier jutting out from Little Craby Harbour in a direction parallel to the west breakwater. The four US LSTs went alongside this pier thus greatly simplifying the embarkment of POW which was completed within five hours. *LST324* (medically equipped) embarked the sick at anchor by means of DUKWs[10] which swam off which from the ramp at the shore end of the West Breakwater. The whole evolution of the embarkation of POW and the sailing of the LSTs by 17.00/12th reflects great credit on the Commanding Officers of the LSTs and their efficient handling and on the Military POW processing who had only arrived in Alderney by LCI at about 11.00.

Vehicles for the Alderney Force, including Naval W/T van were disembarked form an LCT at the West Breakwater Slipway and RNO Alderney established.

Evacuation of POW from the Channel Islands [11]

The following numbers of German POW have been evacuated from the Islands to Southampton in LSI and LST:

Guernsey	9,754
Jersey	9,838
Alderney	2,332
Sark	274
TOTAL	22,198

There remain for essential clearing up work:

Guernsey	1,500
Jersey	1,300
Alderney	500

Visit of Trinity House Officers

Capt Glasson, Elder brother of Trinity House and two other officials arrived at Guernsey in HMS *Leith* on 17 May. They visited Les Hanois Lighthouse of West Coast of Guernsey, the Casquets, and the lighthouses on Sark and Alderney. I understand that the lights' machinery were found to be in good condition and that arrangements are being made for the lights to be put into full operation at an early date. For their visit to the Casquets a military guard and RE section were embarked. German landmines were cleared and two Officers and 30 German OR taken off and landed at Guernsey as POW; six Germans being left at the Lighthouse for maintenance.

Minesweeping of QZX 967 at Little Russel

Clearance work on the above minefield has been carried out by three ships of the 142nd MMS Flotilla. A full report is being forwarded separately.

Port Clearance St Peter's Port and
St Sampson's Harbours

Work has continued steadily. No demolitions of port facilities were carried out by the Germans and they have been very co-operative in pointing out all explosive charges laid in breakwaters and jetties. These have been rendered safe as required by surrender terms and are being removed and disposed of with creditable rapidity. A fuller report on this will be forwarded in due course.

Controlled Minefields, St Peter's Port and
St Sampson's

These have been put to 'safe' by the Germans and firing arrangements have been fully explained by them. It has not yet been decided whether they will be disposed of by lifting or blowing up but I do not regard this as of immediate importance, and they will be dealt with in slow time after completion of more urgent work. A fuller report on this will be forwarded in due course.

Unloading of Coasters with Force and CA Supplies

Excellent progress has been made. 11 ships have so far been unloaded at St Peter's Port and St Sampson's, and 6,000 tons of Force and Civil Affairs supplies disembarked to date. At Jersey 11 ships discharged 4,157tons.

Establishment of Naval HQ Channel Islands at Guernsey

A Naval HQ has been established at the Crown Hotel, which is conveniently situated overlooking St Peter's Port and Anchorage, with a Signal Station on the top storey and roof; this latter is not quite as suitably situated as I would like for full efficiency, but the setting up of a fully staffed and equipped Minor War Signal Station on Castle Cornet or St Martin's Port would involve additional work, material and V/S personnel which I consider unnecessary in the circumstances and the present arrangement is, in my opinion, sufficiently good.

A German Base Engineers Workshop has been taken over on Albert Quay. This is very well equipped with suitable machines and practically any sort of minor repair and maintenance work can be undertaken. Suitable premises for Naval and Victualling Stores have been requisitioned and stocked, the Supply Staff having worked very hard and very efficiently.

Officers are billeted comfortably at the Royal Hotel; Chief and Petty Officers are billeted in comfortable conditions in a house adjacent to seven other houses in Saumarez Street where ratings are billeted. The conditions of the billets on entry was not all that could be desired as they had just been vacated by German troops. However, by dint of much cleaning they have been made habitable and everything possible is being done to improve comfort, conveniences and amenities.

The messing and cooking arrangements, at first on Army Compo rations [12] but since 24 May on Naval Victualling, have proven quite satisfactory. Hard work for long hours has been accepted by all Officers and ratings in a spirit of the utmost cheerfulness and I have heard of no single complaint from any cause.

In Conclusion

I consider that the whole operation of the re-occupation of the Channel Islands has been carried out most efficiently in every respect. The co-operation between the three Services has been perfect at all times, in the planning and the execution. I, and my staff, have invariably received from Brigadier Snow and his Staff the utmost help in all problems and difficulties and consider myself fortunate and highly honoured to have served under Brigadier Snow in the carrying out of this operation.

A list of Officers and ratings whose services have been, in my opinion, worthy of particular recognition, will be forwarded within a few days.

I have the honour to be, Sir,
Your obedient servant

CAPTAIN, RN

Left:
Victory at long last! Mrs Elsie Jory of Candie, St Peter Port, Guernsey, had painted her 'Welcome' sign under the very noses of the Germans in her husband's workshops, whilst he had planted out 150 red and 150 white tulips the previous October, so they were in full bloom on Liberation Day!
IWM — HU 25935

Left:
Men of Force 135 were
greeted by crowds of
happy locals — this
NCO gives sweets to the
children. *La Valette
Underground Museum*

Right:
Operation 'Nestegg'.
This LST came right
up onto the beach to
discharge its load in
Guernsey. *La Valette
Underground Museum*

V

ST. PETER
PORT

GUERNSEY

Liberation
MAY 8TH 1945

Bert Hill
1945

What is left to see?

A word of warning on 'Bunker Hunting'

Most of the bunkers, gun pits and defences are on private property. If you want to have a look, obtain permission from the owner. Do not enter without a strong torch or lamp. There are different designs of defences that from the outside look the same, but once inside, passages may descend without warning. Also, wellington boots may be needed as 50-plus years of dirt and dust will have blocked up the drains. We would warn you that bunkers on the coast will also have been used as unofficial toilets — so beware! Young persons should not enter without an adult, as many bunkers have awkward steps and hidden ducts that can trip the unwary. Bunkers and tunnels have been blocked up for this reason and no other; those of you who would like to find an Aladdin's Cave of war relics have been beaten to it by the scrap drive of 1947–48.

(This very sensible warning has appeared in most copies of the yearly *CIOS Review* and really does mean what it says!)

Although World War 2 ended over half a century ago, the interest in what happened during what was undoubtedly the most important event of the century still remains as strong as ever. The Channel Islands were in a unique position during this traumatic part of our history for a number of reasons, first and foremost because they were the *only* part of the British Isles to be occupied by the enemy. The Islands were then turned into a German fortress as part of Adolf Hitler's much vaunted 'Atlantic Wall', but these defences were never tested and the Islands were never devastated by war as was so much of mainland Europe, or badly bombed like so many areas of Great Britain. Consequently, although some of these fortifications were destroyed postwar and much of their weaponry cast into the sea, a significant number still remain. It could be argued that such relics should all be destroyed as they are merely reminders of an age which is best forgotten, but that is unfair to the historians and others for whom such artefacts are of abiding interest. The study of World War 2 is not diminishing, but has taken its place alongside the study of such great conflicts as the Great War and the Peninsular War. It is a part of our history which deserves to be studied for all the best motives, so it is therefore only right and proper that the Atlantic Wall defences be considered to be just as much a part of the Channel Islands heritage as are the castles and Martello Towers which also abound on the Islands. Therefore, I unashamedly applaud those who do so in the right way, which is certainly not to glorify any part of the Wehrmacht or of Nazi Germany, but rather to try to understand why they came to the Islands, what they did there, why they did it and what they have left behind them.

The leading lights in the study of the years of German Occupation are undoubtedly the Channel Islands Occupation Society, whose work has been constantly mentioned throughout this book. Therefore, before dealing in detail with what is left for visitors to see on the Islands, a word or two about this Society is necessary, especially for anyone who wants to study any aspect of the Occupation in any detail.

The main objectives of the Society are:

- To study and investigate the German Occupation of the Channel Islands.
- To further interest in the Occupation by recording, safeguarding and preserving relics and monuments of the period.

There are two branches — one in Guernsey and one in Jersey and it goes without saying that both have similar objectives, which also include extending the fullest co-operation between the said branches.

Every year since 1973, the two CIOS Branches have taken it in turns to publish a *Review* (Guernsey in the even years, Jersey in the odd years). This *Review* covers not only details of the CIOS's work during the previous year, but is also packed with interesting and authoritative articles and photographs on a wide range of relevant subjects such as fortifications, tunnels, wartime living — both civilian and military, return visits by German Servicemen, weaponry, shipping, aircraft etc, etc. The 100-page A5-size *Reviews* are sent to all society members each year and back numbers are available. In addition to producing the *Review* and other pamphlets on relevant subjects, the CIOS organises tours, excursions and talks throughout the Islands and in France. It also continues to build up an extensive sound, documentary and photographic archive, the depth of which can be judged from the excellent photographs which constantly appear in the *Review*. Any serious would-be researcher is strongly advised to join the CIOS and should write for more details to one of the two secretaries, who at this time are:

Guernsey
Maj (Retd) E. Ozanne
Les Jehans Farm
Torteval
GUERNSEY GY8 0RE
Tel: 01481 64625

Jersey
W. M. Ginns MBE
'Les Geonnais de Bas'
St Ouen
JERSEY JE3 2BS
Tel: 01534 482089

Another essential preliminary is to explain the work which has been/is being done to promote what is left to see by the tourist boards on the two main islands of Guernsey and Jersey. The great mass of tourists who come to the Channel Islands come for the beautiful scenery, the lovely beaches and all the rest of what goes towards making the Islands ideal all-year-round holiday destinations. However, as an ex-museum director myself, I am fully aware that even the most dedicated sun/sea/sand/countryside worshipper does require alternative attractions and will visit interesting museums and similar attractions, including military museums. My Tank Museum in deepest Dorset, for example, got over a quarter of a million visitors every year in the mid-1980s, while the appeal of other Service museums in places like Portsmouth and Yeovilton is equally apparent. Logically, therefore, the same applies to military sites on the Channel Islands. However, there is clearly a need for them to be marketed sensibly. Two of the most striking examples of how successful this can be are the Fortress Guernsey project on Guernsey and the German Underground Hospital on Jersey.

WHAT IS LEFT TO SEE?

Clearly the best way to tackle this complex subject is island by island and to break down the locations under the general headings of:

- Museums

- Fortifications & Tunnels

- Miscellaneous, including Graveyards and Memorial Plaques

A fair number of German and other war dead (eg foreign workers) were removed from their Island resting places in 1961 by the *Volksbund Deutsche Kriegsgräberfürsorge* and reburied in the German War Cemetery at Mont des Huisnes, in Normandy near Mont St Michel. However, it has to be said that in a number of cases the locations can clearly be classified under more than one category, so use of the index at the end of the book may also be necessary. I am deliberately not including detailed, changeable information such as hours of opening, ticket prices, etc as this is not a guidebook!

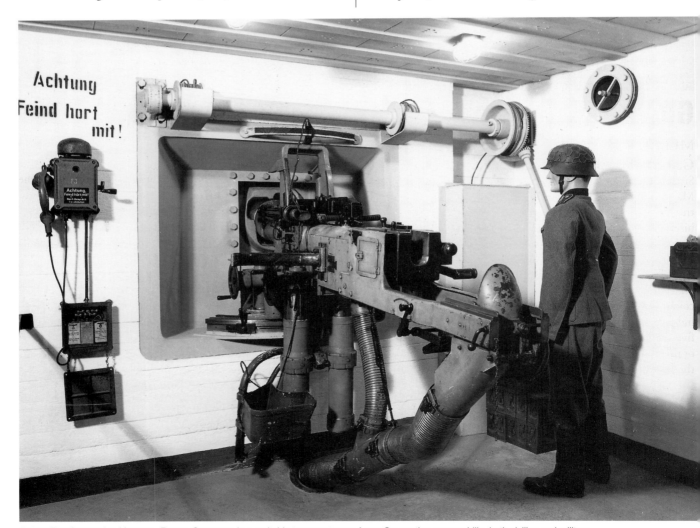

Below: The Occupation Museum, Forest, Guernsey, is a veritable treasure trove of rare Occupation memorabilia, both civilian and military, like this highly realistic gun display. *Occupation Museum*

Guernsey

MUSEUMS

German Occupation Museum

Situated behind the Forest Church, near the airport. Opened in May 1966, Richard Heaume's remarkable museum is a veritable treasure trove of rare Occupation memorabilia and the 'living history' displays are among the best and most authentic of the period. There are military rooms with displays of uniforms, equipment and weapons, civilian rooms re-creating the day-to-day life of the Islanders, a transport corridor, an Occupation Street and much, much more. Unique film footage includes colour film of the Liberation taken by a local doctor who had hidden a cine camera and film under his surgery floorboards for five years waiting for just that day! Authenticity is the hallmark of this museum — you can even drink genuine parsnip coffee in the tearoom if you ask!

La Valette Underground Military Museum, St Peter Port

Proprietors Paul and Peter Balshaw's underground museum took two years in the making and is housed within one of the 15 completed tunnels out of the 41 tunnel sites which the Germans planned to dig in Guernsey. It was established between 1987 and 1988, but only after a thorough examination had taken place, with the assistance of the States Engineers, to ensure that the tunnel was structurally safe. The whole oil storage complex then had to be rewired; air conditioning installed; smoke detectors,

emergency lights, fire alarms and burglar alarms fitted; the interior spray-painted; finally, the remaining fuel tank had to be made safe. Only then could work on the museum itself begin, but by the last days of August 1988 all had been completed. There are many fascinating exhibits on show as well as items from the Occupation, including a unique collection of uniforms and artefacts which trace the history of the Guernsey Militia. More modern uniforms include that of Brig Alfred Snow OBE, who commanded the Operation 'Nestegg' force which liberated the Islands in May 1945.

Guernsey Museums & Galleries

These incorporate the Guernsey Museum and Art Gallery, Castle Cornet and Fort Grey, which are all administered by the States of Guernsey Heritage Committee. As they cover the entire history of Guernsey, only a portion of their exhibition space is devoted to the German Occupation. Nevertheless they do deal with the subject in an innovative manner. For example, they have devoted one section in the 'Story of Castle Cornet' to that period, with a restored Flak 38 AA gun and a reconstructed corner of a gun crew mess room. In addition to their displays, they hold archive material, photographs etc, while copies of parts of *Festung Guernsey* are housed by the Royal Court Library and the Priaulx Library.

Left:
This authentic German field
kitchen now resides in the
Occupation Museum's cafe.
Author's collection

Opposite: Entrance to the remarkable La Valette
Underground Military Museum, Guernsey, which
is housed in one of Guernsey's tunnels.
La Valette Museum

Opposite below:
View inside one of the many showcases in La Valette
Underground Military Museum. *La Valette Museum*

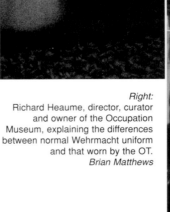

Right:
Richard Heaume, director, curator
and owner of the Occupation
Museum, explaining the differences
between normal Wehrmacht uniform
and that worn by the OT.
Brian Matthews

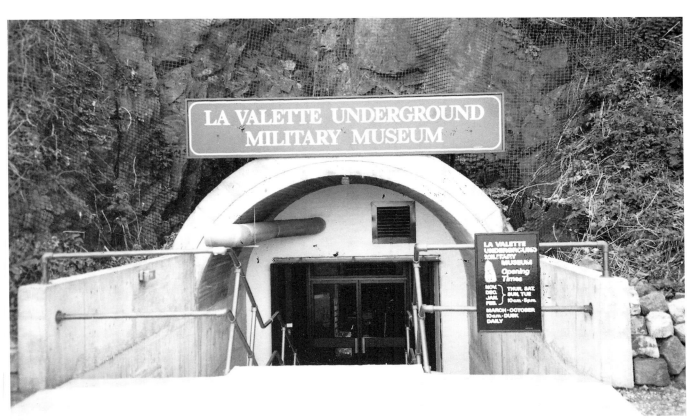

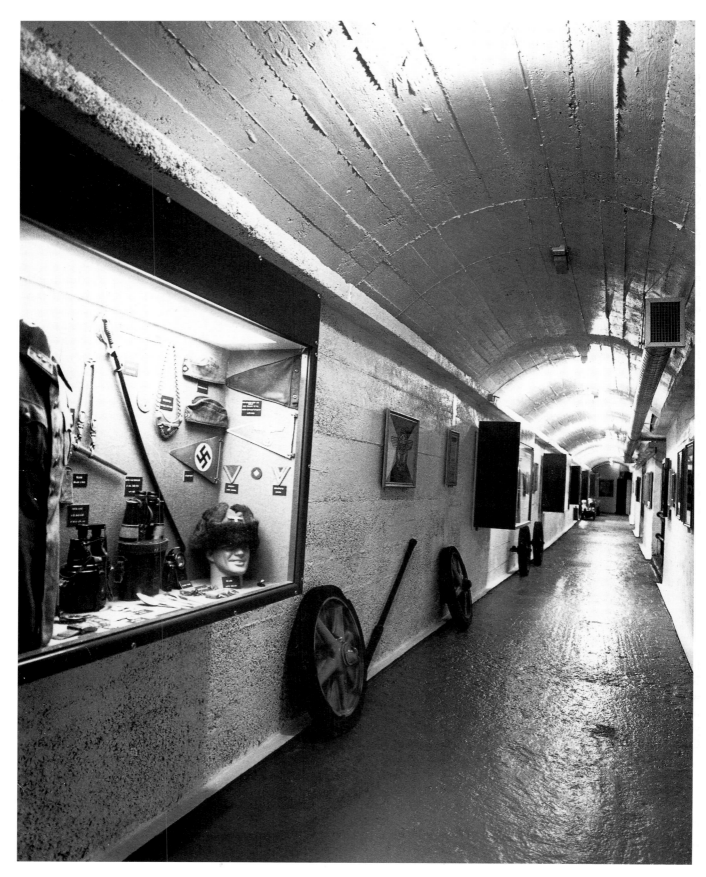

FORTIFICATIONS

Most of these sites are under the auspices of Fortress Guernsey and/or the Occupation Museum and are thus open to the public. Some, however, are on private land and visitors are requested to respect the rights and privacy of the owners. In addition to those described more fully below, other examples are: the heavy AA gun battery positions on the high ground in the middle of the golf course at L'Ancresse; a coast watching radar station, flanked by two LAA bunkers and a large command post in the rear, at La Grande Hougue; the observation tower (on private land) at Fort Saumarez, where the German engineers superimposed a coastal artillery direction tower on top of an early 19th century Martello Tower; the naval direction-finding tower at L'Angle, which originally mounted a lattice radar — its stepped profile, which is strongly reminiscent of the conning tower of a large warship, makes it probably the most impressive German defence work on the island, especially in view of its dramatic setting overlooking the precipitous cliffs of the south coast.

Finally, there are remnants of infantry strongpoints, concrete bunkers and sections of sea wall defences in such places as Vazon Bay and other coastal areas.

Fortress Guernsey

Tasked with the preservation, renovation, re-equipping and promotion of all fortifications on Guernsey, the Fortress Guernsey remit covers all structures from the Neolithic period onwards, so takes in castles, Martello Towers and all the fortifications of the German Occupation. Co-ordinated by Maj (Retd) Evan Ozanne, who was previously the Deputy Chief Executive of the Guernsey Tourist Board, their work encompasses a continuing programme of development on many sites which are explained in detail below in their relevant sections.

The restoration work is mainly undertaken by competent, volunteer enthusiasts — invariably members of the CIOS (Guernsey) — who dedicate much of their spare time to the renovation of former German sites, with the aim of bringing them back to a wartime working state, employing a high standard of accuracy and realism. From the outset, Maj Ozanne has worked with Mr Colin Partridge BA, well-known local historian, expert on the German fortifications in the Channel Islands and historical consultant to Fortress Guernsey. They were ably assisted by Mr Brian Matthews, a film producer and media consultant, whose company, Tomahawk Films, some years ago produced an excellent one-hour video on the German Occupation.

German Direction-finding Tower, Pleinmont

The Pleinmont Tower (MP3) was built in 1942 and the adjoining personnel shelter the following year (a date — 13/7/43, is scratched into the concrete of the NCOs' room windowsill). After the war all the doors and internal fittings were removed for scrap, so extensive restoration was necessary when the tower was acquired by the Occupation Museum. On the ground floor there is the entrance, a gaslock (all fortress bunkers were equipped to withstand a gas attack), an entrance defence room with an armoured embrasure covering the entrance, a cable room and a munitions room. Then there are five observation levels and finally the roof, on which there is a pit which contained a platform-mounted radar unit. The personnel shelter was for the accommodation of crew of the tower (8–10 men).

Batterie Dollmann, Pleinmont

Situated with MP3 to the west and MP4 to its east, the battery covers the four main 22cm K532(f) gun positions, command post, 150cm searchlight and 2cm Flak positions. MP4, which has not been restored and thus gives a good idea of how much hard work has been done on MP3, is one of the most impressive of all the Atlantic Wall fortifications. Currently, Guernsey Armouries, who are three enthusiastic collectors and restorers of historic arms, vehicles and fortifications, have begun a three-year project to restore one of the gun pits and its associated bunkers — see later for a description of how this project is progressing.

10.5cm Coast Defence Gun Casemate Bunker, Fort Hommet

This is one of 21 'Fortress' bunkers built in Guernsey to house 10.5cm K 331(f) guns, four of which were installed at Fort Hommet, making up Stutzpunkt Rotenstein and designed to defend against beach landings. It was built in April 1943 by OT workers and has external walls and roof of 2m-thick reinforced concrete, so was a good structure to restore. However, like so many other such casemates, it had been first stripped of all furniture and fittings soon after the war, then in the late 1940s had its gun, doors and other metal fittings taken for scrap. The bunker was then buried and landscaped over. Work began on restoration in April 1993 and it was finally opened to the public on 6 May 1995. As the photograph shows, the restoration inside is of a remarkably high standard.

Mirus Battery, St Saviour's

The heaviest of all the naval coastal artillery batteries was of course Batterie Mirus on the high ground at St Saviour's. Only two of the enormous concrete emplacements remain intact, with associated underground ammunition stores and accommodation for 72 men in each. The battery site covers a large area of open countryside and includes surviving command post, personnel shelters, radar mounting, anti-aircraft bunkers and three large reserve ammunition bunkers which stand beside the Rue du Lorier and the Rue de Clos Landais. Regrettably, the site cannot be visited at present.

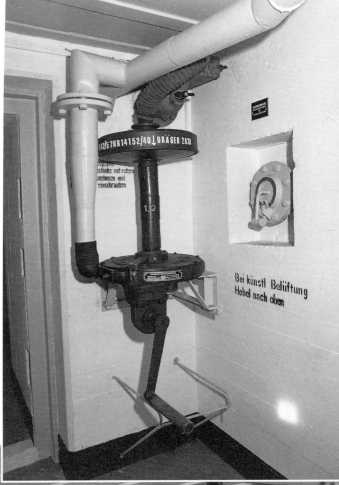

Above:
One of the most striking fortifications left in Guernsey is the naval direction and rangefinding tower (MP3) at Pleinmont. It has been authentically restored by the Occupation Museum and Fortress Guernsey.
Author's collection

Top right:
The close attention to detail can been seen in the restored ventilation equipment in the Entrance Defence Room in the Pleinmont Tower, Guernsey.
Peter Rouillard, via the Occupation Museum

Right:
Crew standby room. The casemate would normally have been manned by an NCO and four/five men, but nine bunks are provided to allow for extra crews in case of a prolonged action. Note the hatch (on the right of the stove) which is the escape shaft.
Author's collection

Sperrfeuersatz für
20 Schuß Sprengmun.

Achtun
Feind hört

Above:
10.5cm coast defence gun,
in its casemate bunker at
Fort Hommet, Guernsey.
*Fiona Adams, via the
Occupation Museum*

Right:
Seaward side view of 10.5cm
K 331(f) coast defence gun
casemate at Stutzpunkt Rotenstein,
Fort Hommet, Vazon, Guernsey,
shuttered up against the winter
weather. *Author's collection*

Above: One of the gunsites of *Batterie Dollmann,* which is currently under restoration. *Author's collection*

Above: Naval rangefinding tower (MP2) at Fort Saumerez was built on top of an old fort, with a searchlight bunker near its base. *Author's collection*

Above: Part of the restoration team at work, restoring the command bunkers at Batterie Dollmann. *Author's collection*

MISCELLANEOUS

German Naval Signal Headquarters, St Jacques

This ambitious project encompassed the restoration of two bunkers connected by a short tunnel in the grounds of La Collinette Hotel, which housed the powerful radio transmitters that provided the only communications with Berlin when the Islands were isolated after September 1944. It was the naval signal headquarters of SEEKO-KI (the German Naval Commander, Channel Islands) and the erstwhile Naval Signals Officer, Oberleutnant Willi Hagedorn, who ran the signals HQ in the war, was most helpful in providing a wealth of information for the restorers, who were members of the CIOS (Guernsey), working under Phil Martin and in co-operation with and funding from the Heritage Committee. Many of the original fittings have survived, including the ventilation pumps, the heating boiler and toilets, whilst the rooms were refitted and equipped during 1996–97 to as near original condition as possible. It was to have been opened by Willi Hagedorn, but sadly he died before the date of the actual opening.

German Military Underground Hospital, St Andrew's

Another remarkable feature of the German defence network on Guernsey was the construction of tunnels for a variety of deep shelter requirements. The underground hospital was linked to a second complex for ammunition storage and was the largest single project of its type undertaken by the Germans. It has been open to the public since 1954.

Below: Fort George Military Cemetery, Guernsey, contains the graves of both British and German military from World War 2. This view is from the bottom of the cemetery, looking towards the gate. *Author's collection*

Channel Islands Occupied Video

Made by Tomahawk Films, this 50-minute video was filmed in Guernsey and Alderney, using rare captured wartime newsreels including such sights as a German infantry unit marching up the High Street in St Peter Port, and the moving of the massive gun barrels of *Batterie Mirus* along the island's twisting, narrow roads, using a team of large half-tracks. Other footage includes interviews with survivors of the Occupation, plus views inside Richard Heaume's Occupation Museum, of his superb collection of uniforms, equipment, weaponry, medals and other rare items, left behind in 1945.

Graveyards and Plaques

One of the most evocative cemeteries on the islands is the Fort George Military Cemetery, St Peter Port, which contains the graves of both British and German servicemen from two world wars, lying side by side. The majority of the British graves are from World War 1, there being just two from World War 2 (one RAF and one RCAF), whilst there are 111 German (19 sailors, 88 soldiers and 4 merchant seamen) from World War 2. Other graveyards in Guernsey do contain a number of both World War 1 and 2 graves; for example, the RN casualties from the sinking of HMS *Charybdis* are buried in the St Peter Port (Foulon) Cemetery. On St Julian's Pier, St Peter Port, there is a plaque which records the names of the 34 civilians who lost their lives in the air- aid on 28 June 1940. On 17 January 1999, in the presence of Ambassadors and Ministers from Algeria, China, France and Russia, a Service of Dedication was held and a plaque unveiled to the memory of all the foreign workers who died during the Occupation — 112 of them from 11 different countries (Algeria, Belgium, China, France, Germany, Italy, the Netherlands, Poland, Portugal, Russia and Spain).

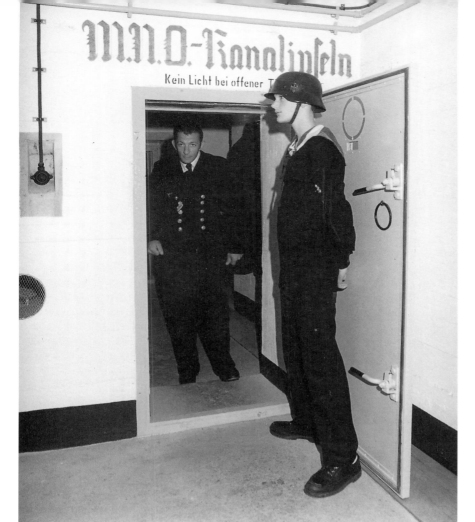

Opposite:
Dedication ceremony of the plaque to the memory of all foreign workers who lost their lives on Guernsey during the Occupation, which was unveiled by the Bailiff, Sir Graham Dorey, on 17 January 1999 in the presence of four representatives from London Embassies. That day was chosen as it was the 57th anniversary of the RAF raid on the harbour — an attempt to destroy the Batterie Mirus guns which were arriving that day. 14 foreign workers were killed in the raid. Left to right: HE The Algerian Ambassador, HE The Lieutenant-Governor of Guernsey, HE The Russian Ambassador, The Chinese Minister Counsellor and the French Defence Attaché.
Brian Green via Fortress Guernsey

Opposite below:
Close-up of the foreign workers memorial plaque, unveiled on 7 January 1999.
Brian Green via Fortress Guernsey

Left:
Entrance to the German Naval Signal Headquarters at St Jacques, Guernsey, has been faithfully restored as this photograph off the front of their new leaflet shows.
Fortress Guernsey

Left:
Entrance gate to Fort George Military Cemetery.
Author's collection

Below:
Inscription at the side of the entrance gate to Fort George Military Cemetery. *Author's collection*

IN MEMORY OF ALL FOREIGN WORKERS WHO LOST THEIR LIVES ON GUERNSEY UNDER THE GERMAN OCCUPYING POWER, 1940-1945

The Following Deaths Are Recorded

ALGERIA

Name	Age	Date of Death
MOHAMED BEN ABDULAH	26	23/03/42
MOHAMED ABES	51	16/06/42
MEDSOUK AMAR	35	27/03/44
ACHMED BENALI	25	17/01/42
HACENE MOHAMED BENMADANI	38	22/08/42
ALI BOUALAME	45	17/07/42
LARBI BOUDEKAH	32	05/02/42
MOHAMED CHIKNI	24	17/01/42
MOHAMED FEHIK	35	17/01/42
AMEDEE GRUPPI	49	23/04/42
MOHAMED HADDADI	34	28/04/42
ARAN MAMMUL HADY	47	26/04/42
HAMMICHE HAMMAS	40	15/05/43
BILL BEN ABDALLAH BEN HAMOU	35	20/03/42
RABA KEDACHE	51	21/03/41
CHINAR MEBROUK	36	10/10/42
BOUFIOI MOHAMED	36	21/11/42
MECHOUICHE MOHAMED	30	06/12/43
OUAD MOUAZ	48	18/08/42
MOHAMED SANANI	45	05/02/43
SAID TOMOMET	31	17/01/42

BELGIUM

Name	Age	Date of Death
HEINDRICK ALBERT		07/04/43
NICHOLAS BAUDUIN	31	13/10/42
ARTHUR BOUCHEZ	35	11/10/42
OSKAR de BOUCK	52	10/10/42
CYRILLE CLAEYS	41	23/08/42
CHARLES DESEREYR	17	04/06/42
MAURICE GELDORF		17/01/42
PETER GONZALES		27/05/42
RAYMOND HUYS		17/01/42
JAKOBE JOHANNES	53	26/08/42
JOSEPH MATHI	68	30/03/43
HONVRE MORELS	49	25/03/42
PETRUS ROSSAERT	51	17/03/42
ALBERT VENSTACHEM	17	10/11/42
JOSEF VERSTRACTE	22	27/06/42
LEON WYFFELS	19	17/01/42

CHINA

Name	Age	Date of Death
KEI LIANG TIEN	41	24/08/42

FRANCE

Name	Age	Date of Death
RENE ALMEDA	20	10/09/42
PAUL BAQUET	21	26/06/42
MARCEL BERLOT	59	05/10/42
JEAN BEZAND	17	06/09/42
RENE BOESSEAU	56	17/01/42
ROGER BONAY	30	02/02/43
ALBERT CAILLY	37	05/06/42
JOSEF CAVANNE	57	29/03/42
FERDINAND DAJEN	43	22/08/42
PIERRE DEBOVE	20	28/02/42
CAMILLE DUPONT	24	16/01/44
JACQUES GARANCHE	21	26/07/42
MAURICE GUICHARD	36	07/09/42
GUSTAV GULAY	40	09/04/43
MAURICE GUMINET		13/10/42
MARCEL MAUGEL	21	11/12/42
CAMILLE JACQUART	30	09/09/42
ALEXANDRE JOLY	18	30/08/42
CASPER LACOMBE	33	27/11/42
CHARLES LADRETTE	42	19/07/43
EUGENE LAGAIZE	35	02/08/43
MARCEL LANCON	46	08/06/42
JULIAN LAURET	50	17/01/42
AIME LEGRAND	32	26/12/42
HENRI LEPES	40	14/02/42
FRANCOIS LOMBARDE	37	29/03/42
HUBERTUS MENNENS	27	05/12/42
GUSTAV MEOT	18	21/09/42
THEOPHILE MIALET	49	18/10/42
FRANCINE MURRIEL	22	18/09/43
MAURICE PAGE	52	18/06/42
PIERRE PAZIN	50	14/11/42
RENE PERCHEC	22	22/04/42
JEAN PETIT	20	25/01/43
RENE PREVOST	21	27/09/42
LOUIS SABOUREAU	44	08/10/42
SCHEIBE SALLAH	28	05/07/44
JEAN-BAPTISTE SIMON	30	11/10/42
LUCIN SINAIS	41	17/01/42
HENRI STEFAN	47	19/02/44
MARCEL STERNBERGER	16	25/04/42

POLAND

Name	Age	Date of Death
FRANZ PRZYMUZINSKI	31	25/08/42
ALBERT ZALEWSKI	59	25/05/43

GERMANY

Name	Age	Date of Death
FRANZ BERGANSKI	32	20/02/43
FRANZ BUCHMANN	35	17/09/42
JOHANN KAMINIAREK	50	17/05/43
HEINRICH KOCK	43	10/04/43
MICHAEL KRIEGEL	57	11/06/42
HEINRICH JURGENS	58	09/05/43
WALTER RECHLER	45	05/04/44
ALFRED RICHTER	33	06/07/42
BERNHARD SHADOWSKI	57	06/11/42
VINCENC TOMANEC	49	16/08/42

ITALY

Name	Age	Date of Death
VINCENZO CHIARO	37	17/01/42

NETHERLANDS

Name	Age	Date of Death
JAN ARDEMA	23	12/12/41
ERNST DUPONT	50	06/12/42
ROGER FLAMEZ	15	17/01/42
DIRK IDSINGA	19	04/06/42
EDMOND PUYSCHEYR	22	17/01/42
JOCHEM SANDERS	25	13/03/42
BUI VAN TUEN	21	27/08/42
CHARLES VERHELLE		22/02/42
ANDRE VERMERSCH	23	17/01/42
KLAUS de VREIS	19	16/09/42

PORTUGAL

Name	Age	Date of Death
LADISLAV GONCALVES	49	25/05/43

RUSSIA

Name	Age	Date of Death
H M. BONOCATAH		00/00/45
BORIS GUERASIMOFF	44	22/03/43
FEDOR HEZEON		06/11/42

SPAIN

Name	Age	Date of Death
LUIS BLANCO	30	08/01/43
PEDRO ESPINOSA	32	28/10/42
VICENTE SANCHEZ PEREZ	40	30/10/42
VICTOR POBEDA	51	04/02/43
JOSE ARANDA TERUEL	18	05/03/43
MARIANO VIZCAINO	55	20/11/41

Above: Entrance to the German Underground Hospital, Jersey. Despite the prominent Red Cross, both entrances were covered with camouflage nets, to hide them from hostile aircraft. *Direct Input Ltd*

Jersey

MUSEUMS

Operating under the direction of the Jersey Museum Service, the following museums all have sections devoted to the German Occupation: The Jersey Museum, St Helier; Elizabeth Castle, St Helier and the La Hougue Bie Museum, St Saviour. The Jersey Museum has occupied the same premises since 1817, but has of course been enlarged. The collection covers many aspects of the Island's history and rural development, including the period of Occupation. The last of this threesome is explained in more detail below. Working in step with the Jersey Museum Service is the Société Jersiaise, which was founded in 1873 for the study of Jersey archaeology, history and natural history. They hold a significant photographic archive.

The German Underground Hospital Museum (GUH), St Lawrence

This is probably the 'star' attraction of its kind in Jersey, being the largest museum of its type on the Island, with several tonnes of wartime artefacts on display. Jack Higgins once described the hospital as being 'a time capsule of the Occupation'. Additionally, as in Guernsey, the enthusiasts of the CIOS (Jersey) have authentically restored the numerous fortifications that are dotted about the island and are described in more detail later. The States of Jersey Tourism Committee recently provided a grant of £30,000 towards the development of Noirmont Point.

'A chill is apparent within moments of entering the echoing entrance tunnel. This is no fabrication, no late 20th century theme park fantasy. This is the real thing.' That short quote from the Visitor Centre brief on the underground hospital sets the scene on this remarkable structure, built by large numbers of forced labourers, augmented by Russian prisoners of war, who '. . . toiled for twelve hours a day, like ants in an underground hell'. Fittingly there is a plaque to their memory situated very close to the entrance, set onto a section of bare, splintered rock face which reads, 'Under these conditions men of many nations laboured to construct this hospital. Those who survived will never forget; those who did not will never be forgotten.' The complex of kilometre-long tunnels and galleries was originally planned as a bomb-proof artillery barracks and ammunition store, but was then converted into a hospital in the weeks leading up to D-Day. The tunnels were blasted out of the shale using gunpowder, then hand-excavated with picks and shovels. Finally they had to be clad in 6,000 tonnes of concrete. The excavations were made deliberately on a slope so that the complex would drain naturally through a system of pipes and culverts, which still today keep the tunnels amazingly dry. When it became a hospital, all unfinished tunnels were sealed off and air-conditioning and central heating systems installed, behind massive gas-proof doors.

Below: A dramatic view of one of the connecting galleries in the German Underground Hospital, Jersey, which has undergone extensive refurbishment. *Direct Input Ltd*

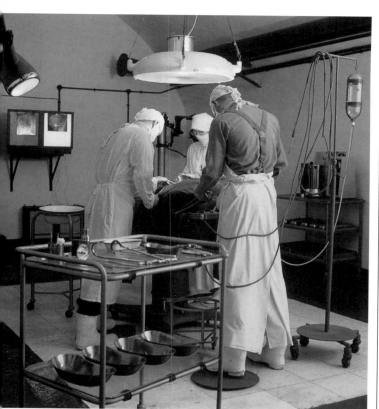

Since the 1960s, the complex has been carefully restored, so that there are now many areas of the hospital 'fully functioning' as the photographs show, such as the operating theatre, doctors' and nurses' quarters, wards, offices, stores, etc, bringing everything to life. Inevitably, perhaps, the paintwork is presently a little too pristine and new, but this will soften in time to become more in keeping with the sombre purposes of the GUH. In addition to these displays there is a large selection of Occupation memorabilia, plus rare wartime archive film and a special exhibition entitled 'A Year in the Life', which commemorates the 50th anniversary of the Island's liberation in 1995. There is also the unique Joe Miere collection of memorabilia and ephemera — an ex-curator of the museum, Joe Miere was a teenager during the Occupation, and was imprisoned by the Germans.

Finally, adjacent to the hospital there is an area of untouched habitat which is now open to walkers and which covers an area that was heavily fortified with AA gun positions, crawl trenches, barbed wire entanglements, personnel shelters, etc — fascinating for enthusiasts provided they keep to the well-defined footpaths — obligatory because of the concealed barbed wire, trenches, etc!

Left: An operation in progress. One of the realistic scenes in the German Underground Hospital. *Direct Input Ltd*

Below: A 'ministering angel'. A Red Cross nurse helps one of the patients in the Underground Hospital to use his crutches. *Brian Matthews*

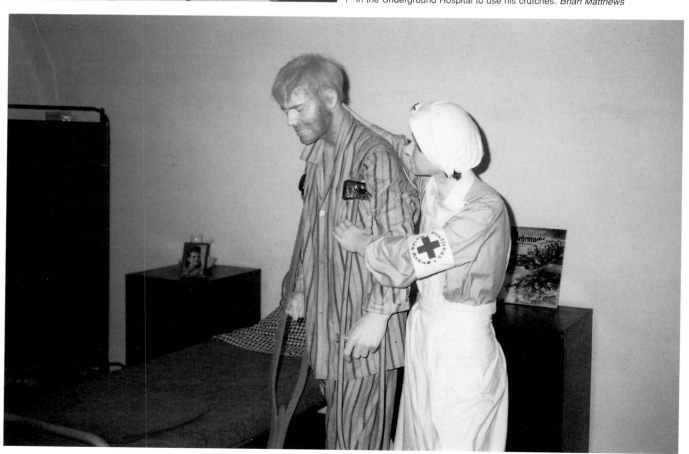

Above: Fully centrally-heated and air-conditioned like all the rest of the hospital were the doctors' living quarters, 100ft down in the solid rock! *Direct Input Ltd*

Above: One of the realistic displays in the St Peter's Bunker Museum. *Damien Horn*

Below: A selection of mines and booby traps on show at the St Peter's Bunker Museum, Jersey. *Damien Horn*

Above: The Channel Islands Military Museum, Jersey, has both German and Allied uniforms on display — and an Enigma coding machine.
CI Military Museum

The Channel Islands Military Museum, St Ouen

Housed in a carefully restored 10.5cm coastal casemate bunker is a large collection of original wartime military and civilian artefacts. The museum has over 5,000 exhibits to chose from, so is constantly able to change its displays. These include a working collection of military motorcycles, both British and German, including BSA, Royal Enfield, Norton, DKW, NSU and Zundapp models. Another rare exhibit is an Enigma code machine. A 45-minute taped commentary recounts Occupation events and German marching songs.

St Peter's Bunker Museum, St Peter

The museum is housed in an underground German bunker which was built in 1942 and was formerly the headquarters of MG Btl 16, with sleeping accommodation for 33 soldiers and an MG loophole covering the crossroads leading to the west of the Island and the airport. The complex has been restored to its original condition with an exhibition of German equipment and Occupation relics, with one room re-created as it may well have been during the war, with soldiers in their bunks, coffee on the stove and the sounds of *Lili Marleen* on the radio. Among the many exhibits is another example of the Enigma code machine, on loan from its 'sister' museum at St Ouen.

La Hougue Bie Museum, St Saviour

On 10 March 1942 the Germans began to construct a battalion command bunker for the eastern sector of Jersey. It was built on the western side of a Neolithic mound and over the next few years some 70 trenches were dug in the grounds of La Hougue Bie. The bunker was made as a single-pour reinforced concrete structure, moulded by wooden shuttering. In the winter of 1947–8, it was turned into a museum and is now used to display World War 2 equipment from around the Island, whilst several of the rooms have been set up as reconstructions of their original appearance. It is run by the Jersey Museums Service.

The Island Fortress Occupation Museum

9 Esplanade, St Helier. Housed in a converted warehouse, the museum contains numerous World War 2 relics and has a miniature cinema showing Occupation films.

FORTIFICATIONS

The following eight fortifications are in the care of CIOS (Jersey); they have all been authentically restored and are open to the public. Full details of all these sites are contained in a leaflet issued free of charge at tourism information centres, etc. As already mentioned, the Noirmont Point location is being developed as a 'package' with as many bunkers as possible being excavated and restored and interpretative plaques erected.

Underground Command Bunker, Noirmont Point, St Brelade

This impressive bunker was the Command Post for a coastal artillery battery and extends into the ground to a depth of 40ft on two floors.

Coastal Artillery Observation Tower, Noirmont Point

This massive structure is most spectacular and undoubtedly enhanced by its 'brooding cliff-top presence'.

10.5cm Coastal Defence Gun Casemate, La Corbière, St Brelade

The only bunker in the St Ouen's Bay area that still has its original 10.5cm gun and numerous other original fixtures and fittings.

'M19' Fortress Mortar Bunker with Tunnel System, La Corbière

This bunker once housed a rare type of automatic mortar and is joined to another bunker via a tunnel.

Coastal Defence Gun and Anti-Tank Gun Casemates, La Carrière, St Ouen's Bay

This twin bunker complex houses some of the larger wartime artefacts — such as a tank turret, a searchlight and a railway truck.

Heavy Machine Gun Turret Bunker, Val de la Mare, St Ouen

This is one of the few surviving examples of these bunkers that once proliferated along the Atlantic Wall.

Gun Emplacements and Underground Bunkers, Les Landes, St Ouen

The passage-linked gun emplacements and bunkers of this site have been carefully restored to a high standard, which includes coastal defence guns recovered from the foot of nearby cliffs where they were dumped soon after the war ended. These include a 22cm gun barrel on display at Batterie Moltke.

Anti-Tank Gun Casemate, Millbrook, St Lawrence

This bunker has been restored to pristine condition and contains a rare 4.7cm Czech anti-tank gun, together with a wealth of original fixtures and fittings.

MISCELLANEOUS
The Occupation Tapestry Gallery, New North Quay, St Helier

To celebrate the 50th anniversary of the liberation of Jersey, the Occupation Tapestry was created by the people of Jersey. Its 12 panels tell the story of the Occupation years from the outbreak

of war, restrictions, everyday life, social life, civil government, deportations, escapes, liberation and so on. It is run by the Jersey Museums Service.

Cemeteries and plaques

The largest number of World War 2 graves are at the St Helier War Cemetery in Howard Davis Park, which contains some 40 British and Allied servicemen — in fact 52 were originally buried there, but 11 American and one Belgian were moved in June 1946. This portion of the park was dedicated on 26 November 1943 as the place to bury British and Allied war casualties. Graves include a number of sailors from HMS *Charybdis*, whose bodies were washed ashore after their ship was sunk in the Channel on 23 October 1943 (all were unidentifiable so their gravestones merely say 'A Naval Rating — Known To God'), together with one World War 1 grave moved there by the Germans when they took over St Brelade's Churchyard to bury their own dead. There were originally 218 foreign burials relating to World War 2 in the St Brelade's *Heldenfriedhof* — according to the official West German War Graves Commission list in 1961 they were:

- Heer — 126 German soldiers; 2 Italian *Hilfswillinge* ('Helpers'. They were foreigners who joined the Heer); 6 OT men; 2 Russian Liberation Army; 3 NSKK (*Nationalsozialistiches Kraftfahrerkorps* — a special motorised unit that oversaw the preliminary training of recruits for motorised/armoured units)
- Kriegsmarine — 41
- Luftwaffe — 38

The Luftwaffe personnel were mainly Flak, but there were at least eight air crew from crashed planes. All the German war dead were exhumed in 1961 and moved to Mont des Huisnes in Normandy. All the foreign workers who died were buried in the Strangers Cemetery, Westmount, but they were also transferred to Mont des Huisnes in 1961. Finally, there is a large plaque at Noirmont headland dedicated to all those men and women of Jersey who perished in World War 2, 1939–45.

The German Occupation of Jersey Map

As you will have seen from its reproduction on pages 44–45, Howard B. Baker's map of the Occupation contains a mass of detailed information which makes it indispensable to any dedicated military enthusiast who wants to explore Jersey. The map also has on its back a number of smaller maps, plus a wealth of informative text, which contains a comprehensive history of the Island's war years, written by Mr Baker after considerable detailed research.

Above & right:
The Allied Military
Cemetery, Howard
Davis Park, Jersey,
and close-up of
dedication plaque.
Michael Ginns

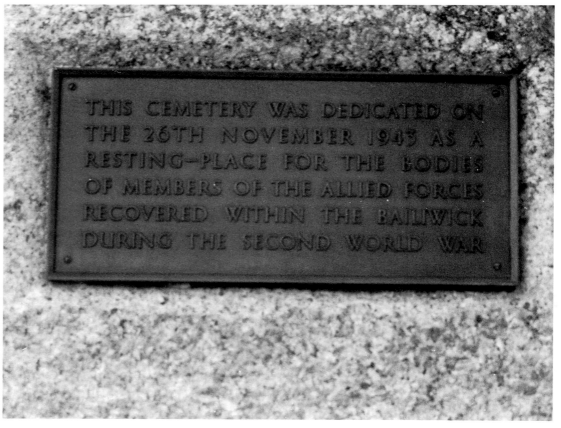

THIS CEMETERY WAS DEDICATED ON
THE 26TH NOVEMBER 1943 AS A
RESTING-PLACE FOR THE BODIES
OF MEMBERS OF THE ALLIED FORCES
RECOVERED WITHIN THE BAILIWICK
DURING THE SECOND WORLD WAR

A LA MEMOIRE
DES TRAVAILLEURS FRANCAIS
CONTRAINTS AU TRAVAIL
VICTIMES DES ALLEMANDS
1940 - 1945

IN MEMORY OF SOVIET PEOPLE
WHO LOST THEIR LIVES IN JERSEY
IN THE WAR AGAINST NAZISM
ПАМЯТИ СОВЕТСКИХ ЛЮДЕЙ
ПОГИБШИХ НА ОСТРОВЕ ДЖЕРСИ
В ПЕРИОД ВОЙНЫ ПРОТИВ
ГЕРМАНСКОГО ФАШИЗМА

A LOS
ESPANOLES
REPUBLICANOS
VICTIMAS
DEL NAZISMO
1942 - 1945

TO THE MEMORY OF THE JEWS
WHO SUFFERED
DURING THE OCCUPATION
1940 - 1945

Above & right:
The foreign workers
memorial, Westmount,
Jersey. *Michael Ginns*

THIS HEADLAND WAS ACQUIRED BY THE
STATES OF JERSEY ON BEHALF OF THE
PUBLIC IN COMMEMORATION OF THOSE
MEN AND WOMEN OF JERSEY WHO
PERISHED IN THE SECOND WORLD WAR
1939 - 1945

Left:
Plaque on Noirmont Point,
Jersey, dedicated to all those
Islanders who perished
during World War 2.
Michael Ginns

Alderney

MUSEUMS

Alderney Society Museum

Housed in the former schoolhouse, the collection illustrates the history of Alderney from prehistoric times to the present day, thus covering the period of the German Occupation. However, it has to be remembered that Alderney was almost completely evacuated during the war and that many of the German records of the Occupation were destroyed. A reference collection of photographs does exist, but originals cannot leave the museum.

FORTIFICATIONS

As yet, none of the Alderney fortifications have been properly restored; indeed, despite the vast amount of hardware that was installed in gun emplacements of various types all over the tiny island — Nazi propaganda described Alderney as being '. . . this battleship of concrete and steel anchored in front of the Atlantic Wall' — very little visual evidence remains immediately apparent today, apart of course from the larger structures, just overgrown foundations and little else. The Ordnance Survey map does show the defences in some detail, so their locations can be found and anyone interested can have a field day seeking them out. Amongst the most outwardly obvious are concrete beach defences such as the anti-tank wall at La Saline Bay, the fire control tower (MP3) which overlooks the Mannez Quarry, Les Mouriaux Water Tower, the artillery battery positions at La Giffoine and the radar pen at Le Rond.

MISCELLANEOUS

The same applies to the graveyards where the German military, OT and forced/slave labour workers were buried. All were exhumed and moved to France in 1961, so the erstwhile graveyards are no more.

Left:
Coastal bunker overlooking Clonque Bay, Alderney.
Brian Matthews

Right:
This naval direction-finding tower (MP3) at Mannez Hill is unique amongst all Atlantic Wall fortifications.
Martin Pocock

Right:
I wonder who Erika was? This lovesick German
soldier's graffiti — a timeless memorial to his
girlfriend, was scratched into the rocks on Alderney,
and is a poignant reminder of the Occupation.
Martin Pocock

Below: The Hammond Memorial, Alderney. *Martin Pocock*

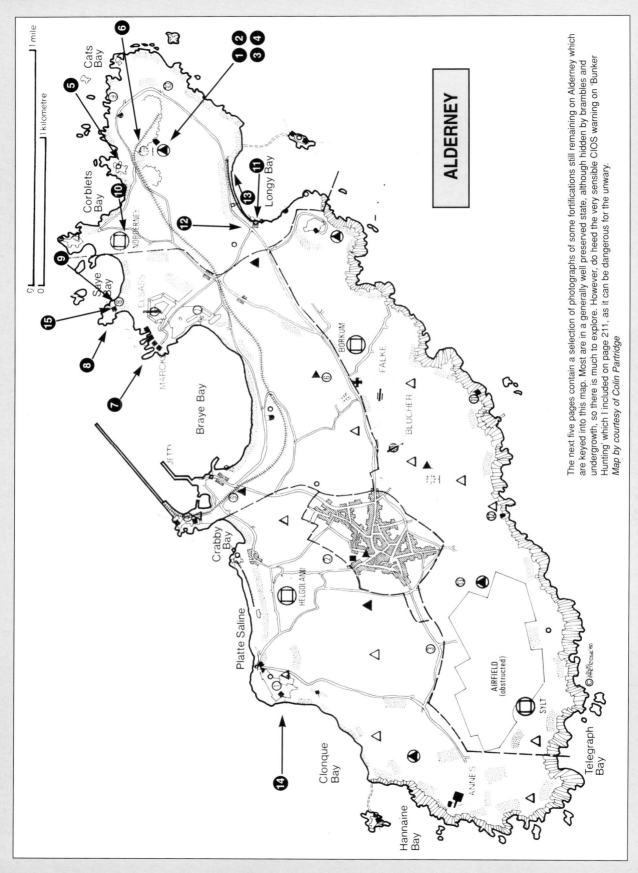

ALDERNEY

The next five pages contain a selection of photographs of some fortifications still remaining on Alderney which are keyed into this map. Most are in a generally well preserved state, although hidden by brambles and undergrowth, so there is much to explore. However, do heed the very sensible CIOS warning on 'Bunker Hunting' which I included on page 211, as it can be dangerous for the unwary.
Map by courtesy of Colin Partridge

Cats Bay

Corblets Bay

Saye Bay

Longy Bay

NORDERNEY

ELSASS

MARCKS

Braye Bay

JETTY

Crabby Bay

Platte Saline

HELGOLAND

BORKUM

FALKE

BLUCHER

AIRFIELD (obstructed)

SYLT

Clonque Bay

Hannaine Bay

ANNES

Telegraph Bay

© PARTRIDGE '80

1 mile

1 kilometre

1

Above: German Flak battery (probably 8.8cm guns) at Mannez Garenne. *Martin Pocock*

2

Above: Looking at the same battery at Mannez Garenne from above. *Martin Pocock*

3

Above: The Entrance to the same battery; note the stairs to the operational area above and entrances/exits to crew quarters bunker to the right. *Martin Pocock*

Above: A light Flak battery position at Mannez Garenne, some 50m from the last site. *Martin Pocock*

Above: The Naval-Direction-finding Tower at Mannez Garenne, near to the lighthouse. It was of a unique design seen nowhere else on the Atlantic Wall. *Martin Pocock*

Above: One of the concrete bunkers at Mannez Garenne. *Martin Pocock*

7

This page: Views of Saye Bay, with the site of Lager Norderney (OT workers) and the defence works in the background. *Martin Pocock*

8

9

Above: The view of Lager Norderney approaching from the interior. *Martin Pocock*

Above: The end of the anti-tank wall on Longey beach, with Chateau de Longy (Roman Fort) on the left. *Martin Pocock*

Above: The inland side of the bunker close by the Roman Fort. *Martin Pocock*

13

14

15

Above: The entire length of the anti-tank wall along Longy beach, viewed from the Roman Fort.
Martin Pocock

Left: Fort Tourgis at Clonque Bay, with a 10.5cm coastal defence gun casemate in the foreground.
Brian Matthews

Right: One of the many trench systems on the island, this one is on the Bibette headland. *Brian Matthews*

Sark

Even this tiny island now has its own small Occupation museum.

THE FUTURE

As well as this wealth of items, more and more is being uncovered, restored and improved by the dedicated collectors and restorers whose hobby has almost taken over their lives! I was privileged to meet a number of these enthusiasts during an all-too-brief visit to Guernsey whilst researching this book, and I have chosen one project which is presently under way as a good example of what is being done.

Batterie Dollmann: project to restore Gun Pit No 3 and the 22cm K 532(f) Gun

Dave Malledent and his two co-restorers Ian Brehaut and Tony Froome have set themselves a massive three-year project to restore one of the gun pits and its associated bunkers. They have already acquired the barrel, wheels and cradle of the gun — the barrel alone weighs 10 tonnes and had to be recovered from the bottom of 300ft cliffs at Les Landes in Jersey. Parts of the gun are still missing, such as the chassis and the carriage, which will almost certainly have to be fabricated. However, thanks to the French Ministry of Defence putting them in touch with the Centre of Archives of Armaments at Châtellerault, they have been able to obtain copies of the original blueprints for this old 22cm gun, which is now probably the only one in existence — apart from the barrel already mentioned at Batterie Moltke, Les Landes, Jersey. The gun, originally known as Canon de 220 L mle 1917 Schneider, was manufactured in World War 1 for the French Army and was captured by the Germans when they overran France. Weighing over 25 tonnes and 17.7m long, it was the second largest coastal artillery weapon on the Channel Islands after the massive guns of Batterie Mirus.

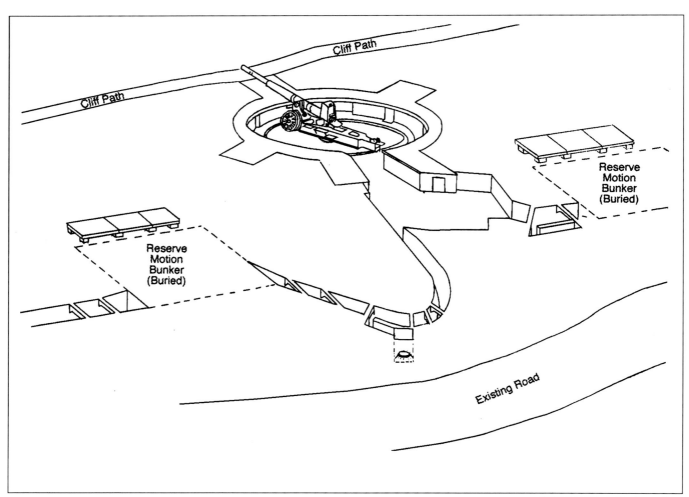

Courtesy of Guernsey Armouries

Appendix 1

Organisational Chart for 216. ID

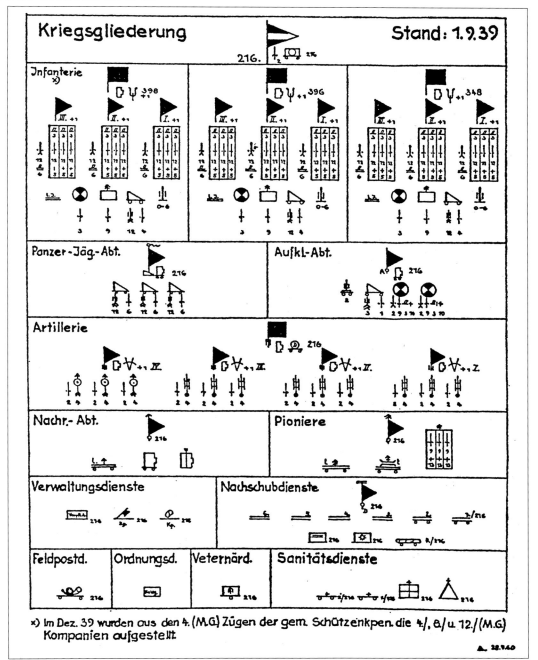

KEY			
Infanterie	Infantry	**Verwaltungsdienste**	Administrative Services
Panzer-Jäg-Abt	Anti-Tank unit	**Naschubdienste**	Supply Services
Aufklr-Abt	Recce unit	**Feldpostd**	Field Post
Artillerie	Artillery	**Ordungsd**	Provost Service
Nachr-Abt	Signals unit	**Veternard**	Veterinary Service
Pioniere	Engineers	**Sanitätsdienste**	Medical Service

243

Appendix 2

Aircraft Losses in the Channel Islands July 1940-May 1945

DATE	TYPE	DESCRIPTION AND LOCATION
?? Jul 40	German ac (Type NK)	Landing accident, western edge of Guernsey aerodrome.
29 Jul 40	He111	Engine failure, crashed in sea off Guernsey, crew rescued.
09 Aug 40	Me Bf109F-1	Collided with Flak position at Guernsey aerodrome, three gnrs killed.
13 Aug 40	Ju87R	Damaged in combat, caught fire and crashed in sea off Guernsey. Crew of two killed.
13 Aug 40	Me Bf109E-4	Take-off collision, Guernsey aerodrome, pilot unhurt.
23 Aug 40	Ju52	Forced landing at Jersey aerodrome, crew unhurt.
25 Sep 40	Do18	Shot down by Blenheim off west coast of Guernsey. Crew of four rescued.
01 Nov 40	Do17P	Engine failure. Crashed at La Pulente, Jersey. Crew of four killed.
03 Nov 40	Ju88A-1	Technical failure, crash-landed at Jersey aerodrome. Crew unhurt.
05 Nov 40	Bu131	Crashed at Rozel, Jersey, cause unknown. Pilot baled out but his parachute failed to open.
05 Nov 40	Ju88A-1	Crash-landed at Jersey aerodrome, cause unknown.
16 Nov 40	Anson	Ditched in Channel, crew of four came ashore in a dinghy at Portfiner Guernsey. 19 Nov picked up by St John's Ambulance Brigade.
19 Nov 40	He111	Possible engine failure followed by fire. Crashed between Jethou and Crevichon. Blew up and crew killed.
22 Jan 41	Ju88A-5	Crashed on landing at Jersey aerodrome, technical failure, crew unhurt.
10 Mar 41	Ju88A-5	Collided with another Ju88 whilst landing at Jersey aerodrome. Crew unhurt.
10 Mar 41	Ju88A-5	In collision with above aircraft. Crew unhurt.
14 Mar 41	Ju88A-5	Crashed in sea off Corbière, Jersey, cause unknown. Crew killed.
11 Apr 41	Hurricane	Crashed in sea, pilot baled out and landed near Lihou Island.
29 Dec 41	Me Bf109F-2	Forced landing near Jersey aerodrome, engine failure, pilot hurt.
31 Jan/1 Feb 42	British ac?	Believed shot down Flak, crew rescued off Jersey and taken to St Helier.
?? Sep 42	Spitfire	Believed shot down Flak, crash-landed at Longy, Alderney. Pilot saved.
08 Nov 42	Spitfire I	Shot down by German fighter, crashed into sea near Le Gouffre, Guernsey. Pilot baled out and was rescued.
18 Nov 42	Spitfire Vb	Believed damaged in combat, fore landed at Trinity, Jersey. Pilot unhurt.
Nov/Dec 42	Lancaster	Believed damaged by Flak over Continent, crash-landed near La Seigneurie Sark, crew reported saved.
07 Dec 42	Whirlwind	Shot down by Flak whilst attacking small convoy. Crashed in the sea, SW of Jersey. Pilot lost.
10 Apr 43	British ac	Believed damaged by Flak ditched in St Ouen's Bay, some of crew reported saved.
13 Jun 43	German seaplane	Damaged in rescue mission, N of Jersey, rescued British airman in dinghy. On 15 June, seaplane was severely damaged while attempting to take off. Two crew injured.
24 Aug 43	German ac	Shot down in error by Flak. Crashed in sea off Herm coast.
31 Dec 43	Fortress B-17F	Damaged over Continent. Shot down by Guernsey Flak and ditched in sea off Grande Havre, crew reported saved.
07 Jan 44	Unknown ac	Shot down by fighters, crashed in sea off Herm.
28 Jan 44	Lancaster	Damaged by Flak over Continent, ditched west of Alderney. Crew saved.
08 Feb 44	Mustang P-51	Crashed near Five Mile Road, Jersey, cause unknown. Pilot baled out and landed safely.
22 Feb 44	Typhoon Ib	Engine failure. Ditched 16km W of Guernsey. Pilot lost.
22 Feb 44	Typhoon Ib	Pilot deliberately baled out to help the above, but was also lost.
07 Mar 44	FW 190	Cause unknown, crashed at La Ponchez, Castel, Guernsey. Pilot killed.
19 Mar 44	He177	Shot down by a Beaufighter, crashed in sea SW of Guernsey.
?? Apr 44	Ju88	Shot down by British nightfighter. Crashed off Alderney coast.
06 Apr 44	Ju88A-4	Shot down in error by Flak. Crashed near Eden Chapel, Jersey. Crew of four killed.
22 May 44	Spitfire XIV	Shot down by Flak. Ac crashed in sea S of Guernsey. Pilot baled out but parachute failed to open.
23 May 44	German ac	Cause unknown. Ac reported washed ashore at La Rocque, Jersey.
05 Jun 44	Typhoon Ib	Shot down by Flak. Crashed in sea off Castle Cornet, Guernsey, pilot lost.
08 Jun 44	Liberator B-24	Shot down by German fighters near Jersey. Two of crew known to have been killed.
14 Jun 44	Typhoon Ib	Shot down by Flak whilst attacking convoy, crashed at Grantez, Jersey. pilot killed.
20 Jun 44	He111	Cause unknown, crashed in field at Samares, Jersey. Crew of five killed.
23 Jun 44	Thunderbolt P-47	Technical failure, crash-landed near Jubilee Hill, St Ouen's, Jersey. Pilot saved.
25 Aug 44	Marauder B-26	Shot down by Flak, crashed in sea off Guernsey.
30 Oct 44	Dakota C-47	Shot down by Flak, crashed off Bouley Bay, Jersey, one survivor.
07 Jan 45	Lightning P-38J	Shot down by Flak, crashed on headland near St Brelade's Church, Jersey. Pilot baled out and was rescued from sea.

Mr Goodwin also lists three more aircraft, viz;		
Date NK	Hellcat	Believed shot down by Flak, ditched off N coast of Herm. Remains of ac brought to Guernsey in 1970.
Ditto	Spitfire V	Cause unknown. Wreckage found by a diver near Roustel Beacon in 1970, engine now at Occupation Museum, Guernsey.
?? 44	American ac	Cause unknown, pilot rescued from sea between Guernsey and Sark.

KEY: He= Heinkel   Me=Messerschmitt   Ju=Junkers   Do=Dornier   Bu=Bucker   FW=Focke-Wulf.

Notes to Text

Prelims
1. Baron von Aufsess: *The von Aufsess Occupation Diary;* Phillimore & Co Ltd.
2. GenLt Hans Speidel: *We Defended Normandy;* Herbert Jenkins.

Notes to Introduction
1. Charles Cruickshank: *The German Occupation of the Channel Islands.*
2. Chris Ashworth: *Action Stations No 5, Military Airfields in the South West.*
3. Ships were sent to remove almost the entire population to Weymouth, Dorset. A handful made their own way to Guernsey, whilst some seven elderly couples flatly refused to go anywhere and had to be almost forcibly removed by the Guernsey St John Ambulance Brigade! Those who stayed on Alderney were Frank Oselton, a farmer, and late arrivals, George Pope and his family. Pope later became the lighthouse pilot for the Casquets Lighthouse. (See later for more on this mysterious character.)

Notes to Chapter 1
1. As quoted in *The Channel Islands War 1940-1945*, by Peter King.
2. The Heinkel He111 was one of the mainstays of the Luftwaffe World War 2. It entered service in late 1936 and some 7,000 were built in total. The major production version was the H series and those in service in the summer of 1940 had a bombload capacity of 1,800kg in external racks.
3. The Imperial War Museum Sound Archive, Accession No 0010103/2.
4. Ibid, Accession No 10715/3/1.
5. The Dornier Do17P was the photographic version of this versatile aircraft and was introduced into service in 1938. It was equipped with both continuous strip and hand-held aerial cameras.
6. The *Channel Islands Occupation Review* is published annually and in turn by the Guernsey and Jersey branches of the Channel Islands Occupation Society.
7. In German General Staff parlance 'Ic' stood for 'G Intelligence'.
8. The Royal Hotel was never used as an HQ, but rather for billeting visiting officers, whilst its restaurant became a favourite dining-out spot for senior officers. The local manager, a Mr Mentha, who was of German extraction, was kept in his post, together with some of his prewar staff, and ran the hotel for the entire war years. (See page 247 of *The War in the Channel Islands then and now*, by Winston G. Ramsey).
9. The message took the form of an ultimatum, signed by GenOb Wolfram von Richthofen, Commander of the German Air Forces in Normandy, and addressed to the Chief of the Military and Civil Authorities, Jersey (St Helier). It read:

'I intend to neutralise military establishments in Jersey by Occupation.
As evidence that the Island will surrender the military and other establishments without resistance and without destroying them, a large White Cross is to be shown as follows, from 7am, July 2nd, 1940,

a. In the centre of the airport in the East of the Island.
b. On the highest point of the fortifications of the port.
c. On the square to the north of the Inner Basin of the Harbour.

Moreover, all fortifications, buildings, establishments and houses are to show the White Flag.
If these signs of peaceful surrender are not observed by 7am July 2nd, heavy bombardment will take place,

a. Against all military objects.
b. Against all establishments and objects useful for defence.

The signs of surrender must remain up to the time of the occupation of the Island by German troops.
Representatives of the Authorities must stay at the air port until the Occupation.
All Radio traffic and other communications with Authorities outside the Island will be considered hostile actions and will be followed by bombardment.
Every hostile action against my representatives will be followed by bombardment.
In case of peaceful surrender, the lives, property, and liberty of peaceful inhabitants are solemnly guaranteed.
The Commander of the German Air Forces in Normandy.

RICHTHOFEN
Generaloberst'

10. See *The War in the Channel Islands then and now.*
11. Quoted from *Dame of Sark, an autobiography* by Sibyl Hathaway.
12. Maj Lanz's report is slightly at variance here with one written by Admiral Lindau which states that as it was not possible to land an aircraft, the Harbour Commander of Cherbourg was ordered to ferry men of the naval assault group to the island having first established that there were no British troops there.
13. See *Alderney, Fortress Island* by T. X. H. Pantcheff.

Notes to Chapter 3
1. It is not clear whether these were an ordinary infantry platoon from Regt 396, which had been equipped with bicycles, or part of the cyclist battalion which formed part of the infantry divisional reconnaissance unit (*Divisions-Aufklärungs-Abteilung*), the latter is more likely.
2. The German Wehrkreis, or military district, had special importance to the army divisions. Each had the responsibility for recruiting, drafting, inducting and training the soldiers destined for their respective divisions, both on mobilisation and thereafter for replacements.
3. Landwehr personnel were reserves of age groups 35 to 45.
4. German mobilisation had been in a series of 'Waves' (Welle) as they were called, which continued throughout most of the war. Each Wave comprised enough men to form a specific number of divisions. Wave 1 was the 39 divisions of the peacetime regular army and the next four waves were mainly called-up reservists, but thereafter they were conscripts who were moulded around a battle-experienced cadre.
5. See *The German Occupation of the Channel Islands.*
6. PzJg319 was also reinforced in its role as the mobile reserve by the arrival of tanks and SP anti-tank guns. The latter were Czech 4.7cm Pak guns mounted on Renault tank chassis — known in German parlance as the 4.7cm Pak (t) auf PzKpfw 35R (f) *ohne Turm* (without turret). Over 180 Renault 35Rs were converted to this role and saw service mainly in France, with a few on the Islands — a figure of 15 is quoted — from 1942 onwards.

Notes for Chapter 4

1. Imperial War Museum, Dept of Sound Records, Accession No 0010103/2.
2. Hitler believed that the survival of his Reich depended upon the education of youth. 'A violently active, dominating, brutal youth — that is what I am after,' he wrote 'Youth must be indifferent to pain . . . I will have no intellectual training. Knowledge is ruin to my young men.' The *Hitler Jugend* was made a state agency on 1 December 1936 and every young German was expected to belong. The equivalent for girls was the *Bund der Deutscher Mädchen*.
3. The RAD was established to overcome unemployment by placing the jobless into labour battalions. From 26 June 1936, all young Germans between the ages of 19 and 25 were required by law to work in labour camps. Hitler regarded the RAD as an important step towards rearmament. Men spent six months in the RAD, many on farmwork.
4. Imperial War Museum, Dept of Sound Archives, Accession No 01000/4.
5. The Schmeisser was the nickname given to the Maschinenpistole 40, the highly effective 9mm machine pistol, which had a magazine capacity of 32 rounds and a cyclic rate of fire of 500rpm.
6. IWM Department of Sound Records, Accession No 010006/8.
7. Ibid.
8. Ibid.
9. 'German Armour in the Channel Islands 1941-1945' Archives Book 4
10. This was the known layout in September 1944 and thereafter.

Notes to Chapter 5

1. Krancke (1893–1973) came to prominence in the planning of the conquest of Norway, after which he became known as 'Admiral Norway'. Later he took the pocket battleship *Admiral Scheer* to sea for a highly successful 'cruise' by the lone warship. From September 1942 to March 1943 he served at OKW, but was then promoted to full admiral and made Naval C-in-C West.
2. The wearing of army uniform, especially when coupled with the word marine — meaning 'sailor' in German and 'Royal Marine' in British parlance — gave rise to some confusion that these sailors were the Kriegsmarine equivalent of the Royal Marines. This was not the case. All land-based sailors were still sailors, no matter what job they did or what uniform they wore.
3. Fred Lucke — IWM Sound Archive Tape 17433.

Notes for Chapter 6

1. Designed by the great Willy Messerschmitt in the mid-1930s, it is ironic that both the first prototype and final production versions, which were built in Spain, were powered with Rolls-Royce engines! It entered full-scale production in 1939 as the Bf109E. The nomenclature is slightly strange. The Bf (used for 109s and 110s) indicates *Bayernfabrik*, ie that they were designed in Bavaria.
2. Based on an article by Dieter Hankel which appeared in the *Channel Islands Occupation Review No 24* and appears here with kind permission from CIOS (Guernsey).

Notes to Chapter 7

1. The Condor Legion was a German 'volunteer' formation sent to fight for Gen Franco's Nationalists in the Spanish Civil War. Although mainly Luftwaffe, it did contain a significant proportion of ground troops (including tank and anti-tank), providing the Germans with much useful battlefield experience prior to World War 2. It was withdrawn in 1939.
2. Actual numbers of slave workers and the casualties which occurred are very difficult to verify. Perhaps the most accurate were those collected on Alderney immediately after the war by Maj Theodore 'Bunny' Pantcheff (see later). Due to the fact that most of the OT records of their work on the Channel Islands were destroyed, it is impossible to say whether the numbers of deaths which, for example, John Dalmau says occurred, can be justified. The evidence that has been found and carefully examined to date tends to suggest that most casualty figures which talk about thousands of workers being killed and their bodies either buried in the foundations of the fortifications or thrown off the cliffs have been greatly exaggerated. What there is no doubt about, however, is that brutal treatment was meted out to some of the workforce by both the SS and OT, in particular to the 'Russian workers' and French colonials, and that this was standard procedure and nothing out of the ordinary.
3. *Alderney, Fortress Island* by T. X. H. Pantcheff.
4. The SS *Schutzstaffel* was a paramilitary organisation within the National Socialist Party, under Reichsführer Heinrich Himmler. Those who ran Baubrigade I were all from the Death's Head formation *(Totenkopfverband)*, the real SS and responsible for running all the concentration camps in Germany and in occupied territory.
5. Gerald Reitlinger: *The SS, Alibi of a Nation 1922-1945*.

Notes to Chapter 8

1. Details are from a cutting taken from *Kinematograph Weekly* dated 21 June 1945, which appeared in *Aspects of War — Entertainments and Pastimes* by June Money
2. Charles Cruickshank: *The German Occupation of the Channel Islands*.
3. Another soldier told me that they made tobacco out of dried strawberry, raspberry and bramble leaves, mixed with mint — but to be smoked in the fresh air only! They also even tried smoking dried seaweed!
4. Taken from an article by Georg Brefka which appeared in CIOS (Jersey) *Review No 23* of May 1995.

Notes to Chapter 9

1. Kapt z.S. Mirus had fought in World War 1, being a gunnery officer on the *Nassau* during the Battle of Jutland. His World War 2 service had included being first gunnery officer on the battleship *Schlesien*. At the time of his death he was serving with OKK as a gunnery adviser and it was on Grossadmiral Raeder's personal orders that the battery be named after him, 'to perpetuate the name of an ever cheerful person and of a helpful comrade who was favoured with great talent'. (Quote taken from a war correspondent's report which was reproduced in CIOS Review of 1974.)
2. Quoted in *Alderney, Fortress Island* by T. X.H. Pantcheff.

Notes to Chapter 10

1. It was at this time that Churchill was involved in the creation of the Commandos, the first 10 independent 'striking companies' having been raised to take part in the abortive Norway campaign (Apr-Jun 1940). The first proper operation they launched was on 23 June 1940, in the Pas de Calais area.
2. Taken from Lt-Col Durford-Slater's autobiography *Commando*.
3. Cpl Dumper left his pistol and personal possessions behind in one of the houses in which they had hidden — Walter and Ada Bourgaize's general store in Torteval. The pistol was hidden in a tin buried underneath their coal tip. They are now on show at Richard Heaume's Occupation Museum (see Postscript).
4. Taken from a leaflet produced for an exhibition held at Anderson Manor in April 1989 which showed the role of Anderson during the war and telling the history of SSRF. I am very grateful to Maj (Retd) Philip Ventham, who organised the event, for allowing me to use this and other background information.
5. See *CIOS (Guernsey) Review No 20* for full details of this intriguing item, written by Ken Tough.

6. Taken verbatim from one of the official reports on this and other SSRF operations, which were used in the exhibition held at Anderson Manor (see Note 4 above).

7. Written by Bdr Redborn, whose account of the operation appears in *The War in the Channel Islands then and now*.

8. The isolated house belonged to Mrs Frances Pittard, who was asked by the commandos if she wanted to go back to England with them. However, she could not go because of her property commitments. Later she was questioned by the Germans and, as a result of admitting that she had talked to the raiding party, was first put into Guernsey prison for some eleven weeks, then later in February 1943, deported to an internment camp near Paris.

9. *The War in the Channel Islands then and now*.

10. Michael Ginns told me that, for some inexplicable reason, Lt Herdt was never court-martialled and later he returned to Sark as Island Commander (on rotation) several times afterwards. Unlike some other Island Commanders, Herdt was familiar with farming methods and never tried to interfere with Sark farming. Consequently, he was popular with the farmers, who called him 'Little Steve'!

11. In fact, two previous raids on Jersey had been planned, codenamed Operation 'Tomato' (in September 1940) and Operation 'Condor' (July 1943), but both had been cancelled.

12. The MGB was equipped with heavier guns in place of the torpedoes of the MTB. They were designed with the specific purpose of fighting the German E-Boats which were threatening British coastal convoys.

13. The next morning she told a neighbour: 'There was some Jerries around in the night, but couldn't they speak good English!'

Notes to Chapter 11

1. By way of comparison, Great Britain was on some 3,500 calories a day and it was estimated that the Channel Islanders were surviving on 1,137.5 calories per day.

2. *The German Occupation of the Channel Islands.*

3. Zimmermann would, postwar, become the Inspector General for NATO.

4. Interestingly, the vessel which Heine and Zimmermann used to get to the RV was minesweeper M4613 *Kanalblitz* which had been used a few weeks previously for the German commando raid on the Cotentin Peninsula in mid-April 1945.

5. Presumably he is referring to special metal matting which the engineers laid on the approaches to river crossing areas/temporary airstrips/beaches, etc, so that wheeled vehicles could more easily negotiate soft surfaces.

6. The reminiscences of the late Ernest 'Bev' Bevins appear here by kind permission of the Tank Museum Library, Bovington, Devon.

7. This narrative is taken from an article which WO1 Neely wrote for the *CIOS Review* in 1986 and is reproduced here with their kind permission as he is deceased.

8. In fact, there was only one aircraft at Jersey Airport on 9 May 1945. It was an unserviceable Heinkel He111 which had been used as a target tower for practice by Flak guns.

9. The report consistently spells St Peter Port as St Peter's Port, but this has been left unchanged as it is a quotation.

10. The American DUKW — the Truck Amphibious 2½ tons 6x6 — was based upon their standard 2½ ton GMC truck, with a propeller and rudder added. On land it used normal drive. Over 21,000 were built. (D = 1942, U = amphibian, K = all wheel drive, W = dual rear axles.) Max load was 2.25tons.

11. Compare this figure with the final assessment made of the strength of the German garrison as being a total 26,849, broken down as follows: Guernsey — 11,755; Jersey — 11,611, Alderney — 3,202 and Sark — 281.

12. Compo = as the name implies the 'Composite' ration packs contained a balanced diet, in tinned rations, plus all the necessities (eg tin opener, sweets and chocolate, even loo paper and a suggested menu!).

Bibliography

Operational Reports

BRITISH

Operational Report No 5062 dated 9 September 1942 on Operation 'Dryad' by Maj G. March-Phillipps, SSRF.

Combined Operations HQ Report SR 1186/42 of 19 November 1942 on Operation 'Basalt' by Maj J. G. Appleyard, SSRF.

Combined Operations Report SR 1272/43 dated 4 March 1943 on Operation 'Huckaback'.

Office of Naval Officer in Charge, Channel Islands, Operation 'Nestegg' — Reoccupation of the Channel Islands No 0301/17 of 19 May 1945.

GERMAN

319. ID report on Commando Raid on Sark 3/4 October 1942. Abt.IaAz34g No 431142 of 6 October 1942.

Books and Magazines

Ashworth, Chris: *Action Stations No 5, Military Airfields of the South-West*; PSL, 1982.

Aufsess, Baron Von: *The Von Aufsess Occupation Diary*; Phillimore & Co Ltd, 1985.

CIOS Archive Books: *No 4 — German Armour in the Channel Islands 1941-45*; CIOS Jersey Branch.

CIOS Archive Books: *No 5 — Merchant Shipping 1940-45*; CIOS Jersey Branch.

CIOS Archive Books: *No 8 — The Organization Todt and the Fortress Engineers*; CIOS Jersey Branch.

CIOS (Guernsey) and CIOS (Jersey) *Annual Reviews* 1973–97

Combined Operations Command: *Combined Operations 1940-1942*; HMSO 1943.

Cruickshank, Charles: *The German Occupation of the Channel Islands*; Sutton Publishing, 1990.

Dalmau, John: *Slave Worker*; Privately published, 1946.

Durnford-Slater, Brig John, DSO & Bar: *Commando*; William Kimber & Co Ltd, 1953.

Gavey, Ernie H. N. C.: *A guide to German Fortifications in Guernsey*; Guernsey Armouries, 1997.

Grieken, Gilbert Van: *Destination 'Gustav'*; The Guernsey Press Co Ltd, 1992.   Hathaway, Sibyl: *Dame of Sark, an autobiography*; William Heinemann Ltd, 1961.

Hathaway, Sibyl: *Dame of Sark*; Heinemann; 1961.

King, Peter: *The Channel Islands War 1940-1945*; Robert Hale, 1991.

Longmate, Norman: *If Britain had Fallen;* British Broadcasting Corporation, 1972.

Mollet, Ralph: *Jersey under the Swastika*; Hyperion Press, 1945

Money, June: *Aspects of War — Entertainment and Pastimes*; The Education development Centre, Guernsey, 1993.

Pantcheff, T. X.H.: *Alderney, Fortress Island*; Phillimore & Co Ltd, 1981.

Ramsey, Winston G.: *The War in the Channel Islands then and now*; After the Battle, 1981.

Reitlinger, Gerald: *The SS, Alibi of a Nation 1922-1945*; Arms & Armour Press, 1981.

Speidel, *Generalleutnant* Hans: *We Defended Normandy*; Herbert Jenkins, 1951.

Wallbridge, Captain John H.: *German M-Class Minesweepers of the Channel Islands 1940-45*; CIOS (Jersey).

Wailimont, Walter: *Inside Hitler's Headquarters*; Weinenfeld & Nicholson, 1964.

Whitley, M. J.: *German Coastal Forces of World War Two*; Arms & Armour, 1992.

Index

Aircraft:
British:
Bristol Blenheim 31
Hawker Hurricane 20
German:
Dornier Do17P 31, 109
Dornier Do217 115
Fieseler Storch 109, 115
Heinkel He111 . . . . .27, 28
Henschel Hs126 109
Junkers Ju52 . . . . .30, 31, 33, 34
Junkers Ju87 29
Messerschmit Bf109 . . . . .109, 113, 114
Messerschmit Bf110 109
Table of types 110
Aircraft losses (all types, both Allied and German) 111
Airfields:
Guernsey 20, 109
Jersey .20, 110, 112, 202
Anderson Manor . . . . .188 et seq
Appleyard, Maj G. 188, 192-3
Artillery:
AA . . . . .75, 94, 111 et seq,
. . . . .114 et seq, 119, 120, 121, 173
Anti-tank 74, 75, 80, 81, 172
Batterie Elefant 14, 86, 91, 86-91
Batterie Mirus . . . . .158, 164 et seq, 217
Coastal (Army) . . . . .15, 76 et seq, 85,
. . . . .86 et seq, 170
(also) Batterie Dollmann 242
Field 74, 83
General .55, 76 et seq
Infantry Support 74
Naval . . . . .92 et seq
Aufsess, Baron von 13, 49, 126
Ayton, Capt P. . . . . .196 et seq

Baker, Howard B. . . . . .44-5 (map), 231
Bevins, E. . . . . .200 et seq
Bicycle troops 73
Boccador, Sgt 197
Böttcher, Gen Lt H. 35, 46
Brauchitsch, Gen Ob W. von 17, 38
Brefka, G. . . . . .68 et seq, 147 et seq,
. . . . .168 et seq
British Commandos/Commando raids . . . .182 et seq, 188
Brocq, Capt H. le 201
Brothels 146

Candie Gardens 142, 151
Carey, Victor (Bailiff Guernsey) 17, 31, 33
Casquets Lighthouse . . . . .102, 190 et seq
Cemeteries and Memorials 108, 122, 127, 156,
. . . . .197, 212, 221, 222,
. . . . .223, 231, 232, 233, 235

Chevallerie, Gen Lt K. von 49
Church and Church-going 69, 141
Cinemas 141, 149, 150
Coutanche, Alexander (Bailiff Jersey) 17, 33, 35, 201
Crespigny, Capt V. de 184, 185
Croix, E. J de Ste 27, 63

Dalmau, J. . . . . .124 et seq, 129 et seq,
. . . . .161, 168
Dollmann, Gen Ob F. 39
Durnford-Slater, Lt Col J. . . . . .183 et seq

Evacuees . . . . .22 et seq

Falla, R 64, 136, 138
Festung Jersey and Guernsey 13, 14, 15, 158
Feld Kommandantur (FK 515) 42, 48, 54,
. . . . .136, 158
Fortifications:
Alderney . . . . .234 et seq
General . . . . .157 et seq, 217 et seq
Guernsey . . . . .217 et seq
Jersey . . . . .230 et seq
Fraternisation 147, 154
Freemantle, Cdr C.A. 204
French North Africans 126, 129, 168

Gerhaher, J. H. . . . . .118, 139 et seq
Ginns, M. 52, 76, 124,
. . . . .193, 200, 211
Gleden, Ob Lt 50
Göring, Herman 17, 41, 109
Gotenhafen (Kriegsmarineabteilung) 29, 32, 37, 47
Grieken, G van . . . . .129 et seq, 133
Grubba, E. A. .64, 65, 66
Grüne Pfeil . . . . .see Operation Green Arrow
Gusseck, Hptm .37, 43, 48

Hagedorn, Ob Lt W. 101, 105
Hankel, D. . . . . .114 et seq, 118
Harrison, Maj Gen J. M. R. Lt Gov Jersey 17, 19,
. . . . .20, 22
Hathaway, Dame Sibyl 34, 37, 63, 138, 184
Hayes, Capt G. 188
Herdt, Ob Lt 193
Heaume, R 213, 214
Heider, Maj I. V. 48
Heldorf, Ob Graf von 105
Herm . . . . .195 et seq, 4
Hessel, Maj .31, 32, 35, 37
Himer, Gen K. 46
Hitler, Adolf 16, 17, 38, 39, 42,
. . . . .53, 129, 132, 157, 193
Hobbies 146
Hoffmann, Hptm K. 50

Hoogh, Dr H. . . . . .97 et seq, 147
Hüffmeier, V Adm F. 41, 49, 51, 92, 104,
. . . . .105, 136, 204, 210
Hunger Winter 42, 51, 64, 104,
. . . . .147 et seq, 198

Infantry Divs (German):
83 . . . . .42, 49, 50, 55
216 . . . . .29, 35, 42, 49,
. . . . .50, 64 et seq, 243
319 . . . . .13, 42, 48, 51, 53
. . . . .et seq, 194 et seq
327 53

Jodl, Gen A. 38, 53

Keitel, FM W. 17
Kern, Lt R. 33, 35, 37
King, HM George VI 22, 205
Knackfuss, Ob F. 48, 54
Koch, Kpt Lt 19, 37
Krancke, Adm T. 41, 92
Kreckler, D 103

Lanz, Maj Dr A. 19, 26, 32, 33,
. . . . .35, 37, 42, 43, 48
Lassen, Anders VC 188, 192, 195
Liebe-Pieteritz, Hptm 31
Lindau, V Adm E. 29, 32, 33, 35, 47
Lucke, H. . . . . .102 et seq
Luftflotte 29, 41

Maas, Maj 26, 33, 37
Maltzahn, Lt . . . . .105 et seq
March-Philips, Maj G. 188, 189, 191, 192
Marcks, Gen Lt E. 39, 103, 132
Martel, 2nd Lt P. .184, 188
Matthews, B. 221, 227
McGonigal, Lt 197
Money, June 142
Motorcycle Troops 73
Mulholland, 2nd Lt D. 184, 188
Müller, Gen E . . . . .48, 51, 193 et seq
Müller, Lt 26
Museums:
Alderney:
Alderney Museum .234
Guernsey:
Occupation Museum . . . . .212, 213 et seq
La Valette Underground Military Museum 163,
. . . . .213, 215, 216
Guernsey Museum and Gallery 213
German Naval Signal HQ, St Jacques 221, 222
German Military Underground Hospital, St Andrews . .
. 221
Jersey:
German Military Underground Hospital, St Lawrence .
. . . . .224, 225, 226, 227
St Peters Bunker Museum 228, 230
Channel Islands Military Museum 230

Island Fortress Occupation Museum 230
Sark:
Sark Museum 242

Neely, WOI W. . . . . .201 et seq
Nicolle, 2nd Lt H. .182 et seq
Nostig, Kapt Freiherr von .92

Obernitz, Hptm von 31, 33, 37 47
Observation Towers . . . . .158 et seq, 218, 220
Ogden-Smith Capt C. 192
Operations:
British:
'Ambassador' . . . . .182 et seq
'Anger' . . . . .182 et seq
'Aquatint' . . . . .188 et seq
'Basalt' 192
'Branford' 192
'Dryad' . . . . .190 et seq
'Hardtack 7' 197
'Hardtack 28' 196
'Huckaback' 195
'Nest Egg' . . . . .198 et seq, 204 et seq, 208
'Pussyfoot' .195 et seq
German:
'Cotentin' . . . . .104 et seq
'Granville' 104
'Grüne Pfeil' . . . . .29 et seq
Organization Todt (OT) . . . . .50, 123 et seq, 125,
. . . . .134, 135, 155, 158
Ozanne, Maj E. 211, 217

Page, M. Le 109
Pantcheff, Maj T. X. F. . . . . .128 et seq, 168, 195
Partridge, C. . . . . .43, 46 (maps), 217
Porteous, Capt P. A. VC 195,
. 202
Power, Col H. H. 202
Prigent, G. . . . . .130 et seq

Radar 21, 177, 178
Raeder, Adm E. .17, 39, 92
Rang, W 67
Red Cross parcels 156
Resistance points . . . . .168 et seq, 169
Restoration Project (Batterie Dollmann) 242
Rettighaus, Oblt 33
Robinson, Lt Col W. 201
Roll Bomb 181
Rommel, FM E. 13, 38 40, 41, 51
Rundstedt, FM Gerd von 38, 40, 49
Russians 53, 61, 127, 168, 196

Sandmann, G. 65, 141
Sark 37, 56, 184,
. . . . .187, 193, 205
Schmettow, Gen Lt Graf von 13, 48, 49, 51,
. . . . .54, 99, 136, 158
Schmetzer, Gen R. 50, 158
Schulpher, Insp W. R. 31, 32, 35
Schumacher, Ob F. 48, 136

Schuster, Adm Karlgorg 29
Searchlights 175, 176
Sherwill, A. 33, 49, 136
Ships:
  British:
    Crash Launches (RAF) 186
    Goatley ....188 et seq, 190
    HMS Beagle ....201 et seq
    HMS Bulldog ....201 et seq
    HMS Falknor ....204 et seq
    HMS Saladin ....184 et seq
    HMS Scimitar ....184 et seq
    MGB (Motor Gun Boat) ....196 et seq
    MTB 344 ....188, 191, 192, 195
    MTBs 186, 191, 192, 195
  German:
    Artillerieträger ....99 et seq, 100
    E boats ....95, 97 et seq, 103, 147
    Merchant 98, 106, 107, 108
    Minesweepers 98
    Submarines 98
    Trawlers 95
Ships losses (all types, Allied and German) 99
Smale, St J. 185
Small Scale Raiding Force (SSRF) ....188 et seq,
.................................195 et seq
Snow, Brig A. E. ....198 et seq, 202,
.........................204 et seq, 209, 213
Soldatenheime (Soldiers Homes) 62, 69,
..............................130, 146, 153
Soldatenkufhäuser (Soldiers Shops) 146
Speer, Dr A. 132
Speidel, Gen Lt H. 13, 39, 51
Sperle, FM H. 41, 92
Sport ....142 et seq
SS and SS Concentration Camp 56, 127,
.................................131 et seq
Steinbach, Kapt J 41, 109

Stuart, Rear Adm C. G. 201, 202, 204
Sueur, R. W. le 29, 124
Swayne, Sir Richard 187

Tanks 16, 55, 60,
..........................75 et seq, 82
Tapestry, St Helier Occupation 230, 231
Telfer-Smollet, Maj Gen Lt Gov Guernsey 17, 19,
.................................20, 22
Todd, Maj 184
Todt, Dr F. 50, 123, 132
Tomahawk Films 221
Tunnels ....161 et seq
Uniforms:
  Airforce ....111 et seq
  Army ....69 et seq
  Navy ....101 et seq
Wagenknecht, W. 49, 67, 77, 140, 142,
.........................144, 147, 149, 203
Warlimont, Gen W. 157
Warren, Lt I. 195
Weapons (German) (See also under Artillery and Tanks):
  Alternative 74
  Flamethrowers 75
  Heavy ....74 et seq, 80 et seq
  LMG MG 34 ....5, 168, 174
  Mines 75, 196
  Mortars 71, 76
  Small Arms 70, 71, 72, 74, 102
  Table of types 52
Westoff, B. ....104 et seq
Wülf, Gen R. 51, 201, 204, 210

Young, 2nd Lt P. 185

Zimmermann, Kapt Lt A. ....201 et seq